The Classics of Marxism

Volume Two

Marx, Engels, Lenin and Trotsky

London

Wage Labour and Capital

Karl Marx
with an introduction by
Frederick Engels

Value Price and Profit

Karl Marx

"Left-Wing" Communism: An Infantile Disorder

V I Lenin

In Defence of October

Leon Trotsky

Stalinism and Bolshevism

Leon Trotsky

The Classics of Marxism: Volume Two
Published by Wellred Books December 2015

Contains:

Wage Labour and Capital by Karl Marx
First published in 1847
Introduction by Frederick Engels published in 1891

Value, Price and Profit by Karl Marx
First published in 1865

Left Wing Communism: An Infantile Disorder by V I Lenin
First published in 1920

In Defence of October by Leon Trotsky
First published in 1932

Stalinism and Bolshevism by Leon Trotsky
First published in 1937

Texts sourced from Marxists Internet Archive (www.marxists.org)
and proofread by Sion Reynolds, Julianna Grant and Philip Sharpe.

Introduction by Alan Woods

Cover design by Mark Rahman
Typeset and layout by Wellred Books

Printed by Lightning Source, London, United Kingdom.

British Library cataloguing in Publication Data
A catalogue record for this book is available from the British Library.

ISBN: 978 1 900 007 61 0

United Kingdom Distribution:

Wellred Books
PO Box 50525
London
E14 6WG

Email: books@wellredbooks.net

Wellred UK online Sales:
www.wellredbooks.net

United States Distribution:

Wellred Books
PO Box 1575
New York
NY 10013

Email: sales@wellredusa.com

Wellred U.S.A. online sales:
www.marxistbooks.com

Contents

Introduction

Alan Woods

Following the great success of the first volume of the *Classics of Marxism*, a second volume is now published containing five more important titles: Marx's pioneering works on economics, *Wage Labour and Capital* and *Value, Price and Profit*; Lenin's *Left-Wing Communism: An Infantile Disorder* and *In Defence of October* and *Stalinism and Bolshevism* by Trotsky.

Broadly speaking, Marxism can be split into three distinct yet interconnected parts – what Lenin called the three sources and three component parts of Marxism. These generally go under the headings of Marxist economics, dialectical materialism and historical materialism. Each of these stands in a dialectical relation to the others and they cannot be understood in isolation from one another.

The present work opens with two of Karl Marx's best-known works on economics. *Wage Labour and Capital* is based on lectures delivered by Marx at the German Workingmen's Club of Brussels in 1847, that is, before the *Communist Manifesto* and at a time when Marx had not yet fully developed his theories of political economy. Engels later explained that if Marx had had the opportunity to have revised this text he "would unquestionably have brought the old work, dating from 1849, into harmony with his new point of view."

Engels nevertheless decided to publish it unchanged – with one important exception. When he gave these lectures, Marx said that what the worker "sold" to the capitalist was his or her labour (that was the accepted theory of the time as put forward by classical bourgeois economists like Ricardo). But in reality what the worker sells is not labour, but labour-power, as Marx explains in *Capital* and Engels points out in his introduction to *Wage Labour and Capital*:

> "My alterations centre about one point. According to the original reading, the worker sells his labour for wages, which he receives from the capitalist; according to the present text, he sells his labour-power. And for this change,

I must render an explanation: to the workers, in order that they may understand that we are not quibbling or word-juggling, but are dealing here with one of the most important points in the whole range of political economy; to the bourgeois, in order that they may convince themselves how greatly the uneducated workers, who can be easily made to grasp the most difficult economic analyses, excel our supercilious "cultured" folk, for whom such ticklish problems remain insoluble their whole life long.

"Classical political economy borrowed from the industrial practice the current notion of the manufacturer that he buys and pays for the labour of his employees. This conception had been quite serviceable for the business purposes of the manufacturer, his book-keeping and price calculation. But naively carried over into political economy, it there produced truly wonderful errors and confusions."

Although it is an early work, *Wage Labour and Capital* contains the outline of the Labour Theory of Value and many important insights into the workings of the capitalist system and the way in which workers are exploited. It is well worth reading. *Value, Price and Profit*, however, was produced at a time when the labour theory of value had already matured in Marx's brain. *It was first delivered as a* speech delivered by Marx to the International Working Men's Association (The First International) in June 1865, while he was working on the first volume of *Capital* that was published two years later. Marx writes in *Capital*:

"In order to be able to extract value from the consumption of a commodity, our friend Money Bags must be so lucky as to find in the market a commodity whose use-value possesses the peculiar property of being a source of value, and consequently a creation of value. This special commodity is labour-power and other as seller of the commodity labour-power. This is the difference between wage labour and other forms of exploitation. In slavery it appears as if the owner of the slave gets the entire value of the labour of the slave (of course this is not so). Under serfdom, the relation between serfs and lords, and the division of labour of the serfs, was clear." (*Capital Volume I*, Chapter 6)

When the worker accepts employment he or she arrives at a "voluntary" contract whereby the worker advances the use-value of labour-power to the capitalist. The workers give their labour-power to the capitalists, but only receive payment after it is used, in the form of a monthly or weekly salary. Thus, the workers extend free credit to the bosses. Moreover, the value of labour-power (wages) has nothing to do with the real value of labour. Once the worker has agreed to sell labour-power, the boss can use it for as long as he wants.

The value of labour-power is determined by the labour-time necessary for production and reproduction of the labourer. It is the value of the means of subsistence necessary for the maintenance of the labourer in his normal state. The value of labour-power, however, differs from that of other commodities insofar as it has a moral and historical element. As Marx explains:

> "It is the product of historical development and depends therefore, to a great extent, on the degree of civilisation of a country." (Ibid)

What was an acceptable level of sustenance to a worker in Victorian England is not the same as what it is today. What may be an acceptable level of sustenance to an agricultural labourer in India today will not be for a farm worker in the USA. However, in a given country, in a given period, at different times, the average quantity of the means of subsistence necessary for the labourer, in practice, is known.

Through the consumption of labour-power the capitalists produce commodities, but also surplus value, which is nothing more than the unpaid labour of the working class. The aim of the capitalist is to produce the maximum surplus value from the labour-power of the workers. This he achieves by a number of means: lengthening the working day, intensifying the labour process, productivity incentives, etc.

The process of the extraction of surplus value takes place in the field of production – within the four walls of the workplace. The value of labour-power (wages) is what the worker receives, but the product of the workers' labour is the property of the capitalist, not the worker. However, in order to convert the commodities produced by the workers into actual profit, the capitalist must find a market for them. New contradictions arise as soon as the commodity leaves the factory and enters the anarchy of the market. The greed of the capitalists for surplus value knows no limits. But the power of capitalist society to absorb the mass of commodities produced is limited by the poverty of the masses. Moreover, the individual capitalist has to compete with many other capitalists for a share of the market. In the end the inevitable result is periodic crises of overproduction.

The class struggle under capitalism is the struggle for the division of the surplus value created by the labour of the working class. As long as the capitalists are extracting surplus value in sufficient quantities, they can buy social peace. But that is not the case now. The present crisis has an unprecedented character. Even the most modest demands of the workers are met with stubborn resistance. This is a finished recipe for an intensification of the class struggle. Sooner or later the workers will come to understand that the only solution is a complete transformation of society – a revolution.

Until recently the accepted wisdom was that the market, if left to itself, was capable of solving all the problems. According to the bourgeois economists, crises of overproduction were not supposed to happen. The university professors were convinced that that the free market forces of supply and demand would automatically arrive at equilibrium (the "efficient market hypothesis"). The bourgeois economists never tire of repeating that Marx's economic theories were outdated "ideas of the 19th century". But the economic collapse of 2008 completely demolished the smug assertions of the alleged superiority of market economics. Nothing that has happened since then gives us any reason to doubt it. As I write these lines China, which was one of the main motor forces of the world economy, is facing a serious crisis of overproduction that can very easily turn into a deep slump that will drag down the whole world.

For further reading on economics, go to the first volume of *Capital*. My friend and comrade Ted Grant used to say that you could then go straight to *Volume III*. I would also recommend *The Living Thoughts of Karl Marx*, a condensed version of *Capital Volume I* with a brilliant introduction by Trotsky (an extract of which is available in the economics section of Wellred Books' *What Is Marxism?*). Normally I would not recommend selections, but the Penguin *Marx on Economics* is very well done. We hope that by reading these works, the reader will be encouraged to study Marx's writings themselves. After all, nobody has ever expounded Marx's ideas better than Marx himself.

Lenin's *"Left-Wing" Communism*

The International Marxist Tendency has been formed in a constant struggle against sectarian or opportunist tendencies. In this we continue in the footsteps of Marx, Engels, Lenin and Trotsky. Ever since it was born, Marxism has had to wage a continual war to free itself of ultraleftism and opportunism. Marx and Engels waged a stubborn struggle against the ultraleft Bakunin. And the whole history of Bolshevism was a history of sharp ideological battles. Lenin was obliged more than once to combat ultraleft tendencies within the ranks of Bolshevism – for example after the defeat of the 1905 Revolution, when he found himself in a minority in the leadership on the question of the need to participate in elections to a rigged tsarist parliament and work in the trade unions and other legal and semi-legal organizations.

Lenin and Trotsky explained many times that a revolutionary must be patient. They also emphasized that every Party member must be obliged to join the trade unions. They stressed the need for the revolutionaries to establish closer links to the mass organizations, above all the unions. However, not everyone who called themselves Marxists (and even Leninists) understood this. In the difficult years of the First World War, when Lenin once again found himself isolated in exile, he wrote many articles condemning the Social Democracy, demanding a break with opportunism and social chauvinism. He saw that the Second International was dead as an organization for carrying out the socialist revolution, and he was absolutely correct in this. But it is one thing for the Marxists to understand this, and quite another thing how the politically uneducated masses see the mass reformist organizations.

This distinction has never been understood by the ultraleft sectarians. For them, the independence of the revolutionary party is a principle – whether it be a party of ten or ten million. This sectarianism was answered by Trotsky when he wrote:

> "But Lenin had in mind a break with reformists as the inevitable consequence of a struggle against them, and not an act of salvation regardless of time and place. He required a split with the social patriots not in order to save his own soul but in order to tear the masses away from social patriotism."
> (Trotsky, *Writings 1935-36*, p156)

The Leninist tactic of the united front was a concrete policy for establishing links between the advanced Communist workers and the masses who were still under the influence of the reformist leaders. The flexible, dialectical method of Lenin presents a stark contrast with the sterile formalism of the sects, who imagine that in order to create a revolutionary party all that they have to do is call upon the working class to join them. Unfortunately all history shows that the masses do not understand small organizations, even if their programme is 100 percent correct. In order to win the masses it is necessary to combine theoretical firmness with tactical and organizational flexibility. That was always Lenin's way and in *Left-Wing Communism* we have a splendid example of this:

"If you want to help the 'masses' and win the sympathy and support of the 'masses', you should not fear difficulties or pin-pricks, chicanery, insults and persecution from the 'leaders' (who, being opportunists and social-chauvinists, are in most cases directly or indirectly connected with the bourgeoisie and the police), but must absolutely work wherever the masses are to be found. You must be capable of any sacrifice, of overcoming the greatest obstacles, in order to carry on agitation and propaganda systematically, perseveringly, persistently and patiently in those institutions, societies and associations - even the most reactionary - in which proletarian or semi-proletarian masses are to be found." (Lenin, *Collected Works*, Vol 31, p53)

The period through which we are now passing is one of great turbulence. Since 2008 the bourgeoisie has been struggling to restore the old equilibrium. But every attempt to restore the economic equilibrium only serves to destroy the social and political equilibrium. Seven years later, they have not succeeded in restoring anything remotely resembling economic equilibrium, but everywhere there is a social and political crisis of an unprecedented character.

The crisis of capitalism is also the crisis of reformism. The reformists have the illusion that it is possible to go back to the situation that existed before. But this is ruled out. The right reformist leaders imagine that it was their "clever" and "realistic" policies that enabled them to win elections. In reality, wherever they have won elections it has been in spite of their policies, not because of them. They were helped by the boom of capitalism and the lack of an alternative to their left. But now here is a deep crisis, their policies stand exposed as bankrupt.

Everywhere the masses are looking for a way out of the crisis. They are testing parties, leaders and programmes one by one, and they are learning many lessons. Parties that appeared to be stable and fixed for all time have been plunged into crisis, split or destroyed. The fate of PASOK in Greece is just one example of this. There are clear signs of sudden changes in consciousness in Greece, in Spain, in Ireland, in Scotland and lately also in the rest of Britain.

In the heat of great events the old right wing leaders will be vomited out and replaced by others, standing further to the left, who reflect the discontent of the masses, in however a confused, partial or inconsistent way. This is an inevitable stage. The Marxist tendency, following Lenin's advice, will be part of this movement, actively encouraging it, pushing it to go further and criticising the hesitancy, vacillations and inconsistency of its leaders. Only in this way can we build a solid bridge that will unite the proletarian advanced guard with the mass of leftward-moving workers.

In Defence of October

Trotsky's work *In Defence of October* is the title of a speech delivered to a meeting of Social Democratic students in Copenhagen, Denmark in November 1932. At that time Trotsky was living in exile on the tiny island of Prinkipo in Turkey where he was like a caged tiger. He applied to various countries for a visa, but one after another the "democratic" countries of Europe refused to grant asylum to the revolutionary, who they still regarded as a threat.

Isolated from the mainstream of world politics, he continued to influence the course of the class struggle through the building of the International Left Opposition. Under these difficult conditions, Trotsky eagerly seized an invitation he had received to come to Denmark, and used every opportunity to speak to the press and activists in the Danish labour movement.

But Trotsky's hope that his stay in Denmark might lead to the granting of asylum were soon dashed. The Stalinist leaders of the Danish Communist Party organised demonstrations against him in a kind of united front with the Danish Royal Family, who protested against the decision to permit the visit, accusing Trotsky as being responsible for the death of the Russian Tsar and his family, who were their relatives.

After the meeting, in Copenhagen just as before it, Trotsky found himself a prisoner of the Planet without a visa. Nevertheless, it has left us with one priceless asset – the text of his speech, which we reproduce here. It is possibly the best concise work one can read on the subject. For Marxists, the October Revolution of 1917 was the greatest single event in human history. If we exclude the brief but glorious episode of the Paris Commune, for the first time the working class succeeded in overthrowing its oppressors and at least began the task of the socialist transformation of society.

Trotsky later pointed out in *The Revolution Betrayed* that the October Revolution demonstrated for the viability of socialism the first time, not in the language of dialectics, but in the language of steel, coal, electricity and cement. The nationalised planned economy established by the October Revolution succeeded in a remarkably short time in transforming an economy as backward as Pakistan today into the second most powerful nation on earth.

The Bolshevik Revolution has therefore been completely justified by history. However, the Revolution took place not in an advanced capitalist country as Marx had expected but in semi-feudal tsarist Russia, on the basis of the most frightful backwardness. To give an approximate idea of the conditions that confronted the Bolsheviks, it is sufficient to point out that in just one year, 1920, six million people starved to death in Soviet Russia.

The possibility of real socialism depends on the development of the means of production to a level far in excess of even the most developed capitalist societies, like the USA, Germany or Japan. This was explained by Marx even before he wrote the *Communist Manifesto*. In the *German Ideology* he wrote that "where want is generalised all the old crap revives." And by "all the old crap" he meant class oppression, inequality and exploitation. The reason why the October Revolution degenerated into Stalinism was that it remained isolated in a backward country where the material conditions for building socialism were absent.

The low level of the productive forces and culture in Russia were the objective reasons for the bureaucratic degeneration of the Revolution, which finally ended with Stalin's totalitarian dictatorship – the very antithesis of the democratic workers' state established by Lenin and Trotsky. The productive forces in the USSR had developed to a tremendous extent thanks to the nationalised planned economy, but came up against the obstacle of bureaucratic control, which inevitably led to colossal mismanagement, waste, corruption and inefficiency.

In the end the bureaucratic overlords preferred to return to capitalism rather than hand power back to the working class. Trotsky had already warned that the bureaucrats would not be satisfied with their enormous privileges, luxurious cars, dachas and servants. Because all this was based upon state property, they could not pass these things on to their children. Sooner or later, therefore, they would seek to transform state property into private property. And that was just what occurred.

Contrary to the predictions of the bourgeoisie and its hired agents in the universities and the media, the fall of Stalinism was neither the end of socialism nor the end of history. What failed in the USSR was not socialism in any sense that would be recognised by Marx or Lenin, but a bureaucratic and totalitarian caricature of socialism. That certainly failed and it was bound to fail for reasons that Trotsky explained decades in advance.

Now history has taken its revenge on the advocates of the "free market economy", which has plunged the whole world into a bottomless abyss. Twenty five years ago the bourgeois economists predicted a world of peace and prosperity after the fall of "Communism". But instead of peace there is war after war. Instead of prosperity there is economic collapse, mass unemployment, huge and unsustainable levels of debt, mass unemployment and growing misery alongside the most obscene wealth and luxury.

The collapse of Stalinism was undoubtedly a historical drama of the first magnitude. But it will be seen by future historians as merely the prelude to a far greater drama: the downfall of capitalism. The present socio-economic system is displaying all the symptoms of senile decay. The old order has outlived its usefulness and exhausted any progressive potential it may once have possessed. It is rotten-ripe for overthrow.

Let the pessimists and sceptics tremble for the future. Let them weep and wail about the present state of the world. What we are witnessing are the symptoms of the death agony of an outmoded, reactionary and barbarous system. Its overthrow is the prior condition for the preservation of civilization, culture and the human race itself. We Marxists look forward to that day, we welcome it with enthusiasm and we will do everything in our power to hasten it, to put an end to the nightmare into which it has plunged our world and to open a new and glorious page in the history of humanity.

London, 23rd September 2015

Wage Labour and Capital

Karl Marx
with an introduction by
Frederick Engels

Introduction to Karl Marx's *Wage Labour and Capital*

Frederick Engels

This pamphlet first appeared in the form of a series of leading articles in the *Neue Rheinische Zeitung*, beginning on 4th April, 1849. The text is made up of lectures delivered by Marx before the German Workingmen's Club of Brussels in 1847. The series was never completed. The promise "to be continued," at the end of the editorial in Number 269 of the newspaper, remained unfulfilled in consequence of the precipitous events of that time: the invasion of Hungary by the Russians [Tsarist troops invaded Hungary in 1849 to keep the Austrian Hapsburg dynasty in power], and the uprisings in Dresden, Iserlohn, Elberfeld, the Palatinate, and in Baden [Spontaneous uprisings in Germany in May-July 1849, supporting the Imperial Constitution which were crushed in mid-July], which led to the suppression of the paper on 19th May, 1849. And among the papers left by Marx no manuscript of any continuation of these articles has been found.

Wage-Labour and Capital has appeared as an independent publication in several editions, the last of which was issued by the Swiss Co-operative Printing Association, in Hottingen-Zurich, in 1884. Hitherto, the several editions have contained the exact wording of the original articles. But since at least 10,000 copies of the present edition are to be circulated as a propaganda tract, the question necessarily forced itself upon me, would Marx himself, under these circumstance, have approved of an unaltered literal reproduction of the original?

Marx, in the '40s, had not yet completed his criticism of political economy. This was not done until toward the end of the fifties. Consequently, such of his writings as were published before the first instalment of his *Critique of Political Economy* was finished, deviate in some points from those written after 1859, and contain expressions and whole sentences which, viewed from the standpoint of his later writings, appear inexact, and even incorrect. Now, it goes without saying that in ordinary editions, intended for the public in general, this earlier standpoint, as a part of the intellectual development of the author, has its place; that the author as well as the public, has an indisputable right to an unaltered reprint of these older writings. In such a case, I would not have dreamed of changing a single word in it. But it is otherwise when the edition is destined almost exclusively for the purpose of propaganda. In such a case, Marx himself would unquestionably have brought the old work, dating from 1849, into harmony with his new point of view, and I feel sure that I am acting in his spirit when I insert in this edition the few changes and additions which are necessary in order to attain this object in all essential point.

Therefore, I say to the reader at once: this pamphlet is not as Marx wrote it in 1849, but approximately as Marx would have written it in 1891. Moreover, so many copies of the original text are in circulation, that these will suffice until I can publish it again unaltered in a complete edition of Marx's works, to appear at some future time.

My alterations centre about one point. According to the original reading, the worker sells his *labour* for wages, which he receives from the capitalist; according to the present text, he sells his *labour-power*. And for this change, I must render an explanation: to the workers, in order that they may understand that we are not quibbling or word-juggling, but are dealing here with one of the most important points in the whole range of political economy; to the bourgeois, in order that they may convince themselves how greatly the uneducated workers, who can be easily made to grasp the most difficult economic analyses, excel our supercilious "cultured" folk, for whom such ticklish problems remain insoluble their whole life long.

Classical political economy[1] borrowed from the industrial practice the current notion of the manufacturer, that he buys and pays for the labour of his employees. This conception had been quite serviceable for the business purposes of the manufacturer, his bookkeeping and price calculation. But naively carried over into political economy, it there produced truly wonderful errors and confusions.

Political economy finds it an established fact that the prices of all commodities, among them the price of the commodity which it calls "labour," continually change; that they rise and fall in consequence of the most diverse circumstances, which often have no connection whatsoever with the production of the commodities themselves, so that prices appear to be determined, as a rule, by pure chance. As soon, therefore, as political economy stepped forth as a science, it was one of its first tasks to search for the law that hid itself behind this chance, which apparently determined the prices of commodities, and which in reality controlled this very chance. Among the prices of commodities, fluctuating and oscillating, now upward, now downward, the fixed central point was searched for around which these fluctuations and oscillations were taking place. In short, starting from the price of commodities, political economy sought for the value of commodities as the regulating law, by means of which all price fluctuations could be explained, and to which they could all be reduced in the last resort.

And so, classical political economy found that the value of a commodity was determined by the labour incorporated in it and requisite to its production. With this explanation, it was satisfied. And we, too, may, for the present, stop at this point. But, to avoid misconceptions, I will remind the reader that today this explanation has become wholly inadequate. Marx was the first to investigate thoroughly into the value-forming quality of labour and to discover that not all labour which is apparently, or even really, necessary to the production of a commodity, imparts under all circumstances to this commodity a magnitude of value corresponding to the quantity of labour used up. If, therefore, we say today in short, with economists like Ricardo, that the value of a commodity is determined by the labour necessary to its production, we always imply the reservations and restrictions made by Marx. Thus much for our present purpose; further information can be found in Marx's *Critique of Political Economy*, which appeared in 1859, and in the first volume of *Capital*.

But, as soon as the economists applied this determination of value by labour to the commodity "labour", they fell from one contradiction into another. How is the value of "labour" determined? By the necessary labour embodied in it. But how much labour is embodied in the labour of a labourer of a day a week, a month, a year. If labour is the measure of all values, we can express the "value of labour" only in labour. But we know absolutely nothing about the value of an hour's labour, if all that we know about it is that it is equal to one hour's labour. So, thereby, we have not advanced one hair's breadth nearer our goal; we are constantly turning about in a circle.

Classical economics, therefore, essayed another turn. It said: the value of a commodity is equal to its cost of production. But, what is the cost of production of "labour"? In order to answer this question, the economists are forced to strain logic just a little. Instead of investigating the cost of production of labour itself, which, unfortunately, cannot be ascertained, they now investigate the cost of production of *the labourer*. And this latter can be ascertained. It changes according to time and circumstances, but for a given condition of society, in a given locality, and in a given branch of production, it, too, is given, at least within quite narrow limits. We live today under the regime of capitalist production, under which a large and steadily growing class of the population can live only on the condition that it works for the owners of the means of production – tools, machines, raw materials, and means of subsistence – in return for wages. On the basis of this mode of production, the labourer's cost of production consists of the sum of the means of subsistence (or their price in money) which on the average are requisite to enable him to work, to maintain in him this capacity for work, and to replace him at his departure, by reason of age, sickness, or death, with another labourer – that is to say, to propagate the working class in required numbers.

Let us assume that the money price of these means of subsistence averages 3 shillings a day. Our labourer gets, therefore, a daily wage of 3 shillings from his employer. For this, the capitalist lets him work, say, 12 hours a day. Our capitalist, moreover, calculates somewhat in the following fashion· Let us assume that our labourer (a machinist) has to make a part of a machine which he finishes in one day. The raw material (iron and brass in the necessary prepared form) costs 20 shillings. The consumption of coal by the steam-engine, the wear-and-tear of this engine itself, of the turning-lathe, and of the other tools with which our labourer works, represent, for one day and one labourer, a value of 1 shilling. The wages for one day are, according to our assumption, 3 shillings. This makes a total of 24 shillings for our piece of a machine.

But, the capitalist calculates that, on an average, he will receive for it a price of 27 shillings from his customers, or 3 shillings over and above his outlay.

Whence do the 3 shillings pocketed by the capitalist come? According to the assertion of classical political economy, commodities are in the long run sold at their values, that is, they are sold at prices which correspond to the necessary quantities of labour contained in them. The average price of our part of a machine – 27 shillings – would therefore equal its value, i.e., equal the amount of labour embodied in it. But, of these 27 shillings, 21 shillings were values were values already existing before the machinist began to work; 20 shillings were contained in the raw material, 1 shilling in the fuel consumed during the work and in the machines and tools used in the process and reduced in their efficiency to the value of this amount. There remains 6 shillings, which have been added to the value of the raw material. But, according to the supposition of our economists, themselves, these 6 shillings can arise only from the labour added to the raw material by the labourer. His 12 hours' labour has created, according to this, a new value of 6 shillings. Therefore, the value of his 12 hours' labour would be equivalent to 6 shillings. So we have at last discovered what the "value of labour" is.

"Hold on there!" cries our machinist. "Six shillings? But I have received only 3 shillings! My capitalist swears high and day that the value of my 12 hours' labour is no more than 3 shillings, and if I were to demand 6, he'd laugh at me. What kind of a story is that?"

If before this we got with our value of labour into a vicious circle, we now surely have driven straight into an insoluble contradiction. We searched for the value of labour, and we found more than we can use. For the labourer, the value of the 12 hours' labour is 3 shillings; for the capitalist, it is 6 shillings, of which he pays the workingman 3 shillings as wages, and pockets the remaining 3 shilling himself. According to this, labour has not one but two values, and, moreover, two very different values!

As soon as we reduce the values, now expressed in money, to labour-time, the contradiction becomes even more absurd. By the 12 hours' labour, a new value of 6 shillings is created. Therefore, in 6 hours, the new value created equals 3 shillings – the amount which the labourer receives for 12 hours' labour. For 12 hours' labour, the workingman receives, as an equivalent, the product of 6 hours' labour. We are, thus, forced to one of two conclusions: either labour has two values, one of which is twice as large as the other, or 12 equals 6! In both cases, we get pure absurdities. Turn and twist as we may, we will not get out of this contradiction as long as we speak of the buying and selling of "labour" and of the "value of labour." And just so it happened to the political economists. The last offshoot of classical political economy –

the Ricardian school – was largely wrecked on the insolubility of this contradiction. Classical political economy had run itself into a blind alley. The man who discovered the way out of this blind alley was Karl Marx.

What the economists had considered as the cost of production of "labour" was really the cost of production, not of "labour," but of the living labourer himself. And what this labourer sold to the capitalist was not his labour.

> "So soon as his labour really begins," says Marx, "it ceases to belong to him, and therefore can no longer be sold by him."

At the most, he could sell his *future* labour – i.e., assume the obligation of executing a certain piece of work in a certain time. But, in this way, he does not sell labour (which would first have to be performed), but not for a stipulated payment he places his labour-power at the disposal of the capitalist for a certain time (in case of time-wages), or for the performance of a certain task (in case of piece-wages). He hires out or sells his *labour-power*. But this labour-power has grown up with his person and is inseparable from it. Its cost of production, therefore, coincides with his own cost of production; what the economist called the cost of production of labour is really the cost of production of the labourer, and therewith of his labour-power. And, thus, we can also go back from the cost of production of labour-power to the value of labour-power, and determine the quantity of social labour that is required for the production of a labour-power of a given quantity, as Marx has done in the chapter on *The Buying and Selling of Labour Power*. [*Capital, Vol. I*]

Now what takes place after the worker has sold his labour-power, i.e., after he has placed his labour-power at the disposal of the capitalist for stipulated-wages – whether time-wages or piece-wages? The capitalist takes the labourer into his workshop or factory, where all the articles required for the work can be found – raw materials, auxiliary materials (coal, dyestuffs, etc.), tools, and machines. Here, the worker begins to work. His daily wages are, as above, 3 shillings, and it makes no difference whether he earns them as day-wages or piece-wages. We again assume that in 12 hours the worker adds by his labour a new value of 6 shillings to the value of the raw materials consumed, which new value the capitalist realizes by the sale of the finished piece of work. Out of this new value, he pays the worker his 3 shillings, and the remaining

3 shillings he keeps for himself. If, now, the labourer creates in 12 hours a value of 6 shillings, in 6 hours he creates a value of 3 shillings. Consequently, after working 6 hours for the capitalist, the labourer has returned to him the equivalent of the 3 shillings received as wages. After 6 hours' work, both are quits, neither one owing a penny to the other.

"Hold on there!" now cries out the capitalist. "I have hired the labourer for a whole day, for 12 hours. But 6 hours are only half-a-day. So work along lively there until the other 6 hours are at an end – only then will we be even." And, in fact, the labourer has to submit to the conditions of the contract upon which he entered of "his own free will", and according to which he bound himself to work 12 whole hours for a product of labour which cost only 6 hours' labour.

Similarly, with piece-wages. Let us suppose that in 12 hours our worker makes 12 commodities. Each of these costs a shilling in raw materials and wear-and-tear, and is sold for 2.5 shillings. On our former assumption, the capitalist gives the labourer .25 of a shilling for each piece, which makes a total of 3 shillings for 12 pieces. To earn this, the worker requires 12 hours. The capitalist receives 30 shillings for the 12 pieces; deducting 24 shillings for raw materials and wear-and-tear, there remains 6 shillings, of which he pays 3 shillings in wages and pockets the remaining 3. Just as before! Here, also, the worker labours 6 hours for himself – i.e., to replace his wages (half-an-hour in each of the 12 hours), and 6 hours for the capitalist.

The rock upon which the best economists were stranded, as long as they started out from the value of labour, vanishes as soon as we make our starting-point the value of *labour-power*. Labour-power is, in our present-day capitalist society, a commodity like every other commodity, but yet a very peculiar commodity. It has, namely, the peculiarity of being a value-creating force, the source of value, and, moreover, when properly treated, the source of more value than it possesses itself. In the present state of production, human labour-power not only produces in a day a greater value than it itself possesses and costs; but with each new scientific discovery, with each new technical invention, there also rises the surplus of its daily production over its daily cost, while as a consequence there diminishes that part of the working-day in which the labourer produces the equivalent of his day's wages, and, on the other hand, lengthens that part of the working-day in which he must present labour gratis to the capitalist.

And this is the economic constitution of our entire modern society: the working class alone produces all values. For value is only another expression for labour, that expression, namely, by which is designated, in our capitalist society of today, the amount of socially necessary labour embodied in a particular commodity. But, these values produced by the workers do not belong to the workers. They belong to the owners of the raw materials, machines, tools, and money, which enable them to buy the labour-power of the working class. Hence, the working class gets back only a part of the entire mass of products produced by it. And, as we have just seen, the other portion, which the capitalist class retains, and which it has to share, at most, only with the landlord class, is increasing with every new discovery and invention, while the share which falls to the working class (per capita) rises but little and very slowly, or not at all, and under certain conditions it may even fall.

But, these discoveries and inventions which supplant one another with ever-increasing speed, this productiveness of human labour which increases from day to day to unheard-of proportions, at last gives rise to a conflict, in which present capitalistic economy must go to ruin. On the one hand, immeasurable wealth and a superfluidity of products with which the buyers cannot cope. On the other hand, the great mass of society proletarianised, transformed into wage-labourers, and thereby disabled from appropriating to themselves that superfluidity of products. The splitting up of society into a small class, immoderately rich, and a large class of wage-labourers devoid of all property, brings it about that this society smothers in its own superfluidity, while the great majority of its members are scarcely, or not at all, protected from extreme want.

This condition becomes every day more absurd and more unnecessary. It *must* be gotten rid of; it can be gotten rid of. A new social order is possible, in which the class differences of today will have disappeared, and in which – perhaps after a short transition period, which, though somewhat deficient in other respects, will in any case be very useful morally – there will be the means of life, of the enjoyment of life, and of the development and activity of all bodily and mental faculties, through the systematic use and further development of the enormous productive powers of society, which exists with us even now, with equal obligation upon all to work. And that the workers are growing ever more determined to achieve this new social order will be proven on both sides of the ocean on this dawning May Day, and on Sunday, 3ʳᵈ May. [Engels is referring to the May Day celebrations of 1891]

FREDERICK ENGELS
London, 30ᵗʰ April, 1891.

Footnotes

[1] "By classical political economy, I understand that economy which, since the time of W. Petty, has investigated the real relations of production in bourgeois society, in contradistinction to vulgar economy, which deals with appearances only, ruminates without ceasing on the materials long since provided by scientific economy, and there seeks plausible explanations of the most obtrusive phenomena for bourgeois daily use, but for the rest confines itself to systematizing in a pedantic way, and proclaiming for everlasting truths, trite ideas held by the self-complacent bourgeoisie with regard to their own world, to them the best of all possible worlds."

Preliminary

From various quarters we have been reproached for neglecting to portray the economic conditions which form the material basis of the present struggles between classes and nations. With set purpose we have hitherto touched upon these conditions only when they forced themselves upon the surface of the political conflicts.

It was necessary, beyond everything else, to follow the development of the class struggle in the history of our own day, and to prove empirically, by the actual and daily newly created historical material, that with the subjugation of the working class, accomplished in the days of February and March, 1848, the opponents of that class – the bourgeois republicans in France, and the bourgeois and peasant classes who were fighting feudal absolutism throughout the whole continent of Europe – were simultaneously conquered; that the victory of the "moderate republic" in France sounded at the same time the fall of the nations which had responded to the February revolution with heroic wars of independence; and finally that, by the victory over the revolutionary workingmen, Europe fell back into its old double slavery, into the English-Russian slavery. The June conflict in Paris, the fall of Vienna, the tragi-comedy in Berlin in November 1848, the desperate efforts of Poland, Italy, and Hungary, the starvation of Ireland into submission – these were the chief events in which the European class struggle between the bourgeoisie and the working class was summed up, and from which we proved that every revolutionary uprising, however remote from the class struggle its object might appear, must of necessity fail until the revolutionary working class shall have conquered; – that every social reform must remain a Utopia until the proletarian revolution and the feudalistic counter-revolution have been pitted against each other in a world-wide war. In our presentation, as in reality, Belgium and Switzerland were tragicomic caricaturish genre pictures in the great historic tableau; the one the model State of the bourgeois monarchy, the other the model State of the bourgeois republic; both of them, States that flatter themselves to be just as free from the class struggle as from the European revolution.

But now, after our readers have seen the class struggle of the year 1848 develop into colossal political proportions, it is time to examine more closely the economic conditions themselves upon which is founded the existence of the capitalist class and its class rule, as well as the slavery of the workers.

We shall present the subject in three great divisions:

1. The Relation of Wage-labour to Capital, the Slavery of the Worker, the Rule of the Capitalist.

2. The Inevitable Ruin of the Middle Classes [petty-bourgeois] and the so-called Commons [peasants] under the present system.

3. The Commercial Subjugation and Exploitation of the Bourgeois classes of the various European nations by the Despot of the World Market – England.

We shall seek to portray this as simply and popularly as possible, and shall not presuppose a knowledge of even the most elementary notions of political economy. We wish to be understood by the workers. And, moreover, there prevails in Germany the most remarkable ignorance and confusion of ideas in regard to the simplest economic relations, from the patented defenders of existing conditions, down to the socialist wonder-workers and the unrecognized political geniuses, in which divided Germany is even richer than in duodecimo princelings. We therefore proceed to the consideration of the first problem.

I

What Are Wages?
How Are They Determined?

I f several workmen were to be asked: "How much wages do you get?", one would reply, "I get two shillings a day", and so on. According to the different branches of industry in which they are employed, they would mention different sums of money that they receive from their respective employers for the completion of a certain task; for example, for weaving a yard of linen, or for setting a page of type. Despite the variety of their statements, they would all agree upon one point: that wages are the amount of money which the capitalist pays for a certain period of work or for a certain amount of work.

Consequently, it appears that the capitalist buys their labour with money, and that for money they sell him their labour. But this is merely an illusion. What they actually sell to the capitalist for money is their labour-power. This labour-power the capitalist buys for a day, a week, a month, etc. And after he has bought it, he uses it up by letting the worker labour during the stipulated time. With the same amount of money with which the capitalist has bought their labour-power (for example, with two shillings) he could have bought a certain amount of sugar or of any other commodity. The two shillings with which he bought 20 pounds of sugar is the price of the 20 pounds of sugar. The two shillings with which he bought 12 hours' use of labour-power, is the price of 12 hours' labour. Labour-power, then, is a commodity, no more, no less so than is the sugar. The first is measured by the clock, the other by the scales.

Their commodity, labour-power, the workers exchange for the commodity of the capitalist, for money, and, moreover, this exchange takes place at a certain ratio. So much money for so long a use of labour-power. For 12 hours' weaving, two shillings. And these two shillings, do they not represent all the other commodities which I can buy for two shillings? Therefore, actually, the worker has exchanged his commodity, labour-power, for commodities of all kinds, and, moreover, at a certain ratio. By giving him two shillings, the capitalist has given him so much meat, so much clothing, so much wood, light, etc., in exchange for his day's work. The two shillings therefore express the relation in which labour-power is exchanged for other commodities, the exchange-value of labour-power.

The exchange value of a commodity estimated in money is called its price. Wages therefore are only a special name for the price of labour-power, and are usually called the price of labour; it is the special name for the price of this peculiar commodity, which has no other repository than human flesh and blood.

Let us take any worker; for example, a weaver. The capitalist supplies him with the loom and yarn. The weaver applies himself to work, and the yarn is turned into cloth. The capitalist takes possession of the cloth and sells it for 20 shillings, for example. Now are the wages of the weaver a share of the cloth, of the 20 shillings, of the product of the work? By no means. Long before the cloth is sold, perhaps long before it is fully woven, the weaver has received his wages. The capitalist, then, does not pay his wages out of the money which he will obtain from the cloth, but out of money already on hand. Just as little as loom and yarn are the product of the weaver to whom they are supplied by the employer, just so little are the commodities which he receives in exchange for his commodity – labour-power – his product. It is possible that the employer found no purchasers at all for the cloth. It is possible that he did not get even the amount of the wages by its sale. It is possible that he sells it very profitably in proportion to the weaver's wages. But all that does not concern the weaver. With a part of his existing wealth, of his capital, the capitalist buys the labour-power of the weaver in exactly the same manner as, with another part of his wealth, he has bought the raw material – the yarn – and the instrument of labour – the loom. After he has made these purchases, and among them belongs the labour-power necessary to the production of the cloth he produces only with raw materials and instruments of labour belonging to him. For our good weaver, too, is one of the instruments of labour, and being in this respect on a par with the loom, he has no more share in the product (the cloth), or in the price of the product, than the loom itself has.

Wages, therefore, are not a share of the worker in the commodities produced by himself. Wages are that part of already existing commodities with which the capitalist buys a certain amount of productive labour-power.

Consequently, labour-power is a commodity which its possessor, the wage-worker, sells to the capitalist. Why does he sell it? It is in order to live.

But the putting of labour-power into action – i.e., the work – is the active expression of the labourer's own life. And this life activity he sells to another person in order to secure the necessary means of life. His life-activity, therefore, is but a means of securing his own existence. He works that he may keep alive. He does not count the labour itself as a part of his life; it is rather a sacrifice of his life. It is a commodity that he has auctioned off to another. The product of his activity, therefore, is not the aim of his activity. What he produces for himself is not the silk that he weaves, not the gold that he draws up the mining shaft, not the palace that he builds. What he produces for himself is wages; and the silk, the gold, and the palace are resolved for him into a certain quantity of necessaries of life, perhaps into a cotton jacket, into copper coins, and into a basement dwelling. And the labourer who for 12 hours long, weaves, spins, bores, turns, builds, shovels, breaks stone, carries hods, and so on – is this 12 hours' weaving, spinning, boring, turning, building, shovelling, stone-breaking, regarded by him as a manifestation of life, as life? Quite the contrary. Life for him begins where this activity ceases, at the table, at the tavern, in bed. The 12 hours' work, on the other hand, has no meaning for him as weaving, spinning, boring, and so on, but only as earnings, which enable him to sit down at a table, to take his seat in the tavern, and to lie down in a bed. If the silk-worm's object in spinning were to prolong its existence as caterpillar, it would be a perfect example of a wage-worker.

Labour-power was not always a commodity (merchandise). Labour was not always wage-labour, i.e., free labour. The slave did not sell his labour-power to the slave-owner, any more than the ox sells his labour to the farmer. The slave, together with his labour-power, was sold to his owner once for all. He is a commodity that can pass from the hand of one owner to that of another. He himself is a commodity, but his labour-power is not his commodity. The serf sells only a portion of his labour-power. It is not he who receives wages from the owner of the land; it is rather the owner of the land who receives a tribute from him. The serf belongs to the soil, and to the lord of the soil he brings its fruit. The free labourer, on the other hand, sells his very self, and that by fractions. He auctions off eight, 10, 12, 15 hours of his life, one day like the next, to the highest bidder, to the owner of raw materials, tools, and the means of life – i.e., to the capitalist. The labourer belongs neither to an owner nor to the soil, but eight, 10, 12, 15 hours of his daily life belong to whomsoever buys them. The worker leaves the capitalist, to whom he has sold himself, as often as he chooses, and the capitalist discharges him as often as he sees fit, as soon as he no longer gets any use, or not the required use, out of him. But the worker, whose only source of income is the sale of his labour-power, cannot leave the whole class of buyers, i.e., the capitalist class, unless he gives up his own existence. He does not belong to this or that capitalist, but to the capitalist class; and it is for him to find his man – i.e., to find a buyer in this capitalist class.

Before entering more closely upon the relation of capital to wage-labour, we shall present briefly the most general conditions which come into consideration in the determination of wages.

Wages, as we have seen, are the price of a certain commodity, labour-power. Wages, therefore, are determined by the same laws that determine the price of every other commodity. The question then is, How is the price of a commodity determined?

II

By What Is the Price of a Commodity Determined?

By the competition between buyers and sellers, by the relation of the demand to the supply, of the call to the offer. The competition by which the price of a commodity is determined is threefold.

The same commodity is offered for sale by various sellers. Whoever sells commodities of the same quality most cheaply, is sure to drive the other sellers from the field and to secure the greatest market for himself. The sellers therefore fight among themselves for the sales, for the market. Each one of them wishes to sell, and to sell as much as possible, and if possible to sell alone, to the exclusion of all other sellers. Each one sells cheaper than the other. Thus there takes place a competition among the sellers which forces down the price of the commodities offered by them.

But there is also a competition among the buyers; this upon its side causes the price of the proffered commodities to rise.

Finally, there is competition between the buyers and the sellers: these wish to purchase as cheaply as possible, those to sell as dearly as possible. The result of this competition between buyers and sellers will depend upon the relations between the two above-mentioned camps of competitors – i.e., upon whether the competition in the army of sellers is stronger. Industry leads two great armies into the field against each other, and each of these again is engaged in a battle among its own troops in its own ranks. The army among whose troops there is less fighting, carries off the victory over the opposing host.

Let us suppose that there are 100 bales of cotton in the market and at the same time purchasers for 1,000 bales of cotton. In this case, the demand is 10 times greater than the supply. Competition among the buyers, then, will be very strong; each of them tries to get hold of one bale, if possible, of the whole 100 bales. This example is no arbitrary supposition. In the history of commerce we have experienced periods of scarcity of cotton, when some capitalists united together and sought to buy up not 100 bales, but the whole cotton supply of the world.

In the given case, then, one buyer seeks to drive the others from the field by offering a relatively higher price for the bales of cotton. The cotton sellers, who perceive the troops of the enemy in the most violent contention among themselves, and who therefore are fully assured of the sale of their whole 100 bales, will beware of pulling one another's hair in order to force down the price of cotton at the very moment in which their opponents race with one another to screw it up high. So, all of a sudden, peace reigns in the army of sellers. They stand opposed to the buyers like one man, fold their arms in philosophic contentment and their claims would find no limit did not the offers of even the most importunate of buyers have a very definite limit.

If, then, the supply of a commodity is less than the demand for it, competition among the sellers is very slight, or there may be none at all among them. In the same proportion in which this competition decreases, the competition among the buyers increases. Result: a more or less considerable rise in the prices of commodities.

It is well known that the opposite case, with the opposite result, happens more frequently. Great excess of supply over demand; desperate competition among the sellers, and a lack of buyers; forced sales of commodities at ridiculously low prices.

But what is a rise, and what a fall of prices? What is a high and what a low price? A grain of sand is high when examined through a microscope, and a tower is low when compared with a mountain. And if the price is determined by the relation of supply and demand, by what is the relation of supply and demand determined?

Let us turn to the first worthy citizen we meet. He will not hesitate one moment, but, like Alexander the Great, will cut this metaphysical knot with his multiplication table. He will say to us: "If the production of the commodities which I sell has cost me 100 pounds, and out of the sale of these goods I make 110 pounds – within the year, you understand – that's an honest, sound, reasonable profit. But if in the exchange I receive 120 or 130 pounds, that's a higher profit; and if I should get as much as 200 pounds, that would be an extraordinary, and enormous profit." What is it, then, that serves this citizen as the standard of his profit? The cost of the production of his commodities. If in exchange for these goods he receives a quantity of other goods whose production has cost less, he has lost. If he receives in exchange for his goods a quantity of other goods whose production has cost more, he has gained. And he reckons the falling or rising of the profit according to the degree at which the exchange value of his goods stands, whether above or below his zero – the cost of production.

We have seen how the changing relation of supply and demand causes now a rise, now a fall of prices; now high, now low prices. If the price of a commodity rises considerably owing to a failing supply or a disproportionately growing demand, then the price of some other commodity must have fallen in proportion; for of course the price of a commodity only expresses in money the proportion in which other commodities will be given in exchange for it. If, for example, the price of a yard of silk rises from two to three shillings, the price of silver has fallen in relation to the silk, and in the same way the prices of all other commodities whose prices have remained stationary have fallen in relation to the price of silk. A large quantity of them must be given in exchange in order to obtain the same amount of silk. Now, what will be the consequence of a rise in the price of a particular commodity? A mass of capital will be thrown into the prosperous branch of industry, and this immigration of capital into the provinces of the favoured industry will continue until it yields no more than the customary profits, or, rather until the price of its products, owing to overproduction, sinks below the cost of production.

Conversely: if the price of a commodity falls below its cost of production, then capital will be withdrawn from the production of this commodity. Except in the case of a branch of industry which has become obsolete and is therefore doomed to disappear, the production of such a commodity (that is, its supply), will, owing to this flight of capital, continue to decrease until it corresponds to the demand, and the price of the commodity rises again to the level of its cost of production; or, rather, until the supply has fallen below the demand and its price has risen above its cost of production, for the current price of a commodity is always either above or below its cost of production.

We see how capital continually emigrates out of the province of one industry and immigrates into that of another. The high price produces an excessive immigration, and the low price an excessive emigration.

We could show, from another point of view, how not only the supply, but also the demand, is determined by the cost of production. But this would lead us too far away from our subject.

We have just seen how the fluctuation of supply and demand always bring the price of a commodity back to its cost of production. The actual price of a commodity, indeed, stands always above or below the cost of production; but the rise and fall reciprocally balance each other, so that, within a certain period of time, if the ebbs and flows of the industry are reckoned up together, the commodities will be exchanged for one another in accordance with their cost of production. Their price is thus determined by their cost of production.

The determination of price by the cost of production is not to be understood in the sense of the bourgeois economists. The economists say that the average price of commodities equals the cost of production: that is the law. The anarchic movement, in which the rise is compensated for by a fall and the fall by a rise, they regard as an accident. We might just as well consider the fluctuations as the law, and the determination of the price by cost of production as an accident – as is, in fact, done by certain other economists. But it is precisely these fluctuations which, viewed more closely, carry the most frightful devastation in their train, and, like an earthquake, cause bourgeois society to shake to its very foundations – it is precisely these fluctuations that force the price to conform to the cost of production. In the totality of this disorderly movement is to be found its order. In the total course of this industrial anarchy, in this circular movement, competition balances, as it were, the one extravagance by the other.

We thus see that the price of a commodity is indeed determined by its cost of production, but in such a manner that the periods in which the price of these commodities rises above the costs of production are balanced by the periods in which it sinks below the cost of production, and vice versa. Of course this does not hold good for a single given product of an industry, but only for that branch of industry. So also it does not hold good for an individual manufacturer, but only for the whole class of manufacturers.

The determination of price by cost of production is tantamount to the determination of price by the labour-time requisite to the production of a commodity, for the cost of production consists, first of raw materials and wear and tear of tools, etc., i.e., of industrial products whose production has cost a certain number of work-days, which therefore represent a certain amount of labour-time, and, secondly, of direct labour, which is also measured by its duration.

III

By What Are Wages Determined?

Now, the same general laws which regulate the price of commodities in general, naturally regulate wages, or the price of labour-power. Wages will now rise, now fall, according to the relation of supply and demand, according as competition shapes itself between the buyers of labour-power, the capitalists, and the sellers of labour-power, the workers. The fluctuations of wages correspond to the fluctuation in the price of commodities in general. But within the limits of these fluctuations the price of labour-power will be determined by the cost of production, by the labour-time necessary for production of this commodity: labour-power.

What, then, is the cost of production of labour-power?

It is the cost required for the maintenance of the labourer as a labourer, and for his education and training as a labourer.

Therefore, the shorter the time required for training up to a particular sort of work, the smaller is the cost of production of the worker, the lower is the price of his labour-power, his wages. In those branches of industry in which hardly any period of apprenticeship is necessary and the mere bodily existence of the worker is sufficient, the cost of his production is limited almost exclusively to the commodities necessary for keeping him in working condition. The price of his work will therefore be determined by the price of the necessary means of subsistence.

Here, however, there enters another consideration. The manufacturer who calculates his cost of production and, in accordance with it, the price of the product, takes into account the wear and tear of the instruments of labour. If a machine costs him, for example, 1,000 shillings, and this machine is used up in 10 years, he adds 100 shillings annually to the price of the commodities, in order to be able after 10 years to replace the worn-out machine with a new one. In the same manner, the cost of production of simple labour-power must include the cost of propagation, by means of which the race of workers is enabled to multiply itself, and to replace worn-out workers with new ones. The wear and tear of the worker, therefore, is calculated in the same manner as the wear and tear of the machine.

Thus, the cost of production of simple labour-power amounts to the cost of the existence and propagation of the worker. The price of this cost of existence and propagation constitutes wages. The wages thus determined are called the minimum of wages. This minimum wage, like the determination of the price of commodities in general by cost of production, does not hold good for the single individual, but only for the race. Individual workers, indeed, millions of workers, do not receive enough to be able to exist and to propagate themselves; but the wages of the whole working class adjust themselves, within the limits of their fluctuations, to this minimum.

Now that we have come to an understanding in regard to the most general laws which govern wages, as well as the price of every other commodity, we can examine our subject more particularly.

IV

The Nature and Growth of Capital

Capital consists of raw materials, instruments of labour, and means of subsistence of all kinds, which are employed in producing new raw materials, new instruments, and new means of subsistence. All these components of capital are created by labour, products of labour, accumulated labour. Accumulated labour that serves as a means to new production is capital.

So say the economists.

What is a Negro slave? A man of the black race. The one explanation is worthy of the other.

A Negro is a Negro. Only under certain conditions does he become a slave. A cotton-spinning machine is a machine for spinning cotton. Only under certain conditions does it become capital. Torn away from these conditions, it is as little capital as gold is itself money, or sugar is the price of sugar.

In the process of production, human beings work not only upon nature, but also upon one another. They produce only by working together in a specified manner and reciprocally exchanging their activities. In order to produce, they enter into definite connections and relations to one another, and only within these social connections and relations does their influence upon nature operate – i.e., does production take place.

These social relations between the producers, and the conditions under which they exchange their activities and share in the total act of production, will naturally vary according to the character of the means of production. With the discovery of a new instrument of warfare, the firearm, the whole internal organization of the army was necessarily altered, the relations within which individuals compose an army and can work as an army were transformed, and the relation of different armies to another was likewise changed.

We thus see that the social relations within which individuals produce, the social relations of production, are altered, transformed, with the change and development of the material means of production, of the forces of production. The relations of production in their totality constitute what is called the social relations, society, and, moreover, a society at a definite stage of historical development, a society with peculiar, distinctive characteristics. Ancient society, feudal society, bourgeois (or capitalist) society, are such totalities of relations of production, each of which denotes a particular stage of development in the history of mankind.

Capital also is a social relation of production. It is a bourgeois relation of production, a relation of production of bourgeois society. The means of subsistence, the instruments of labour, the raw materials, of which capital consists – have they not been produced and accumulated under given social conditions, within definite special relations? Are they not employed for new production, under given special conditions, within definite social relations? And does not just the definite social character stamp the products which serve for new production as capital?

Capital consists not only of means of subsistence, instruments of labour, and raw materials, not only as material products; it consists just as much of exchange values. All products of which it consists are commodities. Capital, consequently, is not only a sum of material products, it is a sum of commodities, of exchange values, of social magnitudes. Capital remains the same whether we put cotton in the place of wool, rice in the place of wheat, steamships in the place of railroads, provided only that the cotton, the rice, the steamships – the body of capital – have the same exchange value, the same price, as the wool, the wheat, the railroads, in which it was previously embodied. The bodily form of capital may transform itself continually, while capital does not suffer the least alteration.

But though every capital is a sum of commodities – i.e., of exchange values – it does not follow that every sum of commodities, of exchange values, is capital.

Every sum of exchange values is an exchange value. Each particular exchange value is a sum of exchange values. For example: a house worth 1,000 pounds is an exchange value of 1,000 pounds: a piece of paper worth one penny is a sum of exchange values of 100 1/100ths of a penny. Products which are exchangeable for others are commodities. The definite proportion in which they are exchangeable forms their exchange value, or, expressed in money, their price. The quantity of these products can have no effect on their character as commodities, as representing an exchange value , as having a certain price. Whether a tree be large or small, it remains a tree. Whether we exchange iron in pennyweights or in hundredweights, for other products, does this alter its character: its being a commodity, or exchange value? According to the quantity, it is a commodity of greater or of lesser value, of higher or of lower price.

How then does a sum of commodities, of exchange values, become capital?

Thereby, that as an independent social power – i.e., as the power of a part of society – it preserves itself and multiplies by exchange with direct, living labour-power.

The existence of a class which possesses nothing but the ability to work is a necessary presupposition of capital.

It is only the dominion of past, accumulated, materialized labour over immediate living labour that stamps the accumulated labour with the character of capital.

Capital does not consist in the fact that accumulated labour serves living labour as a means for new production. It consists in the fact that living labour serves accumulated labour as the means of preserving and multiplying its exchange value.

V

Relation of Wage-Labour to Capital

What is it that takes place in the exchange between the capitalist and the wage-labourer?

The labourer receives means of subsistence in exchange for his labour-power; the capitalist receives, in exchange for his means of subsistence, labour, the productive activity of the labourer, the creative force by which the worker not only replaces what he consumes, but also gives to the accumulated labour a greater value than it previously possessed. The labourer gets from the capitalist a portion of the existing means of subsistence. For what purpose do these means of subsistence serve him? For immediate consumption. But as soon as I consume means of subsistence, they are irrevocably lost to me, unless I employ the time during which these means sustain my life in producing new means of subsistence, in creating by my labour new values in place of the values lost in consumption. But it is just this noble reproductive power that the labourer surrenders to the capitalist in exchange for means of subsistence received. Consequently, he has lost it for himself.

Let us take an example. For one shilling a labourer works all day long in the fields of a farmer, to whom he thus secures a return of two shillings. The farmer not only receives the replaced value which he has given to the day labourer, he has doubled it. Therefore, he has consumed the one shilling that he gave to the day labourer in a fruitful, productive manner. For the one shilling he has bought the labour-power of the day-labourer, which creates products of the soil of twice the value, and out of one shilling makes two. The day-labourer, on the contrary, receives in the place of his productive force, whose results he has just surrendered to the farmer, one shilling, which he exchanges for means of subsistence, which he consumes more or less quickly. The one shilling has therefore been consumed in a double manner – reproductively for the capitalist, for it has been exchanged for labour-power, which brought forth two shillings; unproductively for the worker, for it has been exchanged for means of subsistence which are lost for ever, and whose value he can obtain again only by repeating the same exchange with the farmer. Capital therefore presupposes wage-labour; wage-labour presupposes capital. They condition each other; each brings the other into existence.

Does a worker in a cotton factory produce only cotton? No. He produces capital. He produces values which serve anew to command his work and to create by means of it new values.

Capital can multiply itself only by exchanging itself for labour-power, by calling wage-labour into life. The labour-power of the wage-labourer can exchange itself for capital only by increasing capital, by strengthening that very power whose slave it is. Increase of capital, therefore, is increase of the proletariat, i.e., of the working class.

And so, the bourgeoisie and its economists maintain that the interest of the capitalist and of the labourer is the same. And in fact, so they are! The worker perishes if capital does not keep him busy. Capital perishes if it does not exploit labour-power, which, in order to exploit, it must buy. The more quickly the capital destined for production – the productive capital – increases, the more prosperous industry is, the more the bourgeoisie enriches itself, the better business gets, so many more workers does the capitalist need, so much the dearer does the worker sell himself. The fastest possible growth of productive capital is, therefore, the indispensable condition for a tolerable life to the labourer.

But what is growth of productive capital? Growth of the power of accumulated labour over living labour; growth of the rule of the bourgeoisie over the working class. When wage-labour produces the alien wealth dominating it, the power hostile to it, capital, there flow back to it its means of employment – i.e., its means of subsistence, under the condition that it again become a part of capital, that is become again the lever whereby capital is to be forced into an accelerated expansive movement.

To say that the interests of capital and the interests of the workers are identical, signifies only this: that capital and wage-labour are two sides of one and the same relation. The one conditions the other in the same way that the usurer and the borrower condition each other.

As long as the wage-labourer remains a wage-labourer, his lot is dependent upon capital. That is what the boasted community of interests between worker and capitalists amounts to.

If capital grows, the mass of wage-labour grows, the number of wage-workers increases; in a word, the sway of capital extends over a greater mass of individuals.

Let us suppose the most favourable case: if productive capital grows, the demand for labour grows. It therefore increases the price of labour-power, wages.

A house may be large or small; as long as the neighbouring houses are likewise small, it satisfies all social requirement for a residence. But let there arise next to the little house a palace, and the little house shrinks to a hut. The little house now makes it clear that its inmate has no social position at all to maintain, or but a very insignificant one; and however high it may shoot up in the course of civilization, if the neighbouring palace rises in equal or even in greater measure, the occupant of the relatively little house will always find himself more uncomfortable, more dissatisfied, more cramped within his four walls.

An appreciable rise in wages presupposes a rapid growth of productive capital. Rapid growth of productive capital calls forth just as rapid a growth of wealth, of luxury, of social needs and social pleasures. Therefore, although the pleasures of the labourer have increased, the social gratification which they afford has fallen in comparison with the increased pleasures of the capitalist, which are inaccessible to the worker, in comparison with the stage of development of society in general. Our wants and pleasures have their origin in society; we therefore measure them in relation to society; we do not measure them in relation to the objects which serve for their gratification. Since they are of a social nature, they are of a relative nature.

But wages are not at all determined merely by the sum of commodities for which they may be exchanged. Other factors enter into the problem. What the workers directly receive for their labour-power is a certain sum of money. Are wages determined merely by this money price?

In the 16th century, the gold and silver circulation in Europe increased in consequence of the discovery of richer and more easily worked mines in America. The value of gold and silver, therefore, fell in relation to other commodities. The workers received the same amount of coined silver for their labour-power as before. The money price of their work remained the same, and yet their wages had fallen, for in exchange for the same amount of silver they obtained a smaller amount of other commodities. This was one of the circumstances which furthered the growth of capital, the rise of the bourgeoisie, in the 18th century.

Let us take another case. In the winter of 1847, in consequence of bad harvest, the most indispensable means of subsistence – grains, meat, butter, cheese, etc. – rose greatly in price. Let us suppose that the workers still received the same sum of money for their labour-power as before. Did not their wages fall? To be sure. For the same money they received in exchange less bread, meat, etc. Their wages fell, not because the value of silver was less, but because the value of the means of subsistence had increased.

Finally, let us suppose that the money price of labour-power remained the same, while all agricultural and manufactured commodities had fallen in price because of the employment of new machines, of favourable seasons, etc. For the same money the workers could now buy more commodities of all kinds. Their wages have therefore risen, just because their money value has not changed.

The money price of labour-power, the nominal wages, do not therefore coincide with the actual or real wages – i.e., with the amount of commodities which are actually given in exchange for the wages. If then we speak of a rise or fall of wages, we have to keep in mind not only the money price of labour-power, the nominal wages, but also the real wages.

But neither the nominal wages – i.e., the amount of money for which the labourer sells himself to the capitalist – nor the real wages – i.e., the amount of commodities which he can buy for this money – exhausts the relations which are comprehended in the term wages.

Wages are determined above all by their relations to the gain, the profit, of the capitalist. In other words, wages are a proportionate, relative quantity.

Real wages express the price of labour-power in relation to the price of commodities; relative wages, on the other hand, express the share of immediate labour in the value newly created by it, in relation to the share of it which falls to accumulated labour, to capital.

VI

The General Law That Determines the Rise and Fall of Wages and Profits

We have said: "Wages are not a share of the worker in the commodities produced by him. Wages are that part of already existing commodities with which the capitalist buys a certain amount of productive labour-power." But the capitalist must replace these wages out of the price for which he sells the product made by the worker; he must so replace it that, as a rule, there remains to him a surplus above the cost of production expended by him, that is, he must get a profit.

The selling price of the commodities produced by the worker is divided, from the point of view of the capitalist, into three parts:

- First, the replacement of the price of the raw materials advanced by him, in addition to the replacement of the wear and tear of the tools, machines, and other instruments of labour likewise advanced by him;

- Second, the replacement of the wages advanced; and

- Third, the surplus leftover – i.e., the profit of the capitalist.

While the first part merely replaces previously existing values, it is evident that the replacement of the wages and the surplus (the profit of capital) are as a whole taken out of the new value, which is produced by the labour of the worker and added to the raw materials. And in this sense we can view wages as well as profit, for the purpose of comparing them with each other, as shares in the product of the worker.

Real wages may remain the same, they may even rise, nevertheless the relative wages may fall. Let us suppose, for instance, that all means of subsistence have fallen 2/3rds in price, while the day's wages have fallen but 1/3rd – for example, from three to two shillings. Although the worker can now get a greater amount of commodities with these two shillings than he formerly did with three shillings, yet his wages have decreased in proportion to the gain of the capitalist. The profit of the capitalist – the manufacturer's for instance – has increased one shilling, which means that for a smaller amount of exchange values, which he pays to the worker, the latter must produce a greater amount of exchange values than before. The share of capitals in proportion to the share of labour has risen. The distribution of social wealth between capital and labour has become still more unequal. The capitalist commands a greater amount of labour with the same capital. The power of the capitalist class over the working class has grown, the social position of the worker has become worse, has been forced down still another degree below that of the capitalist.

What, then, is the general law that determines the rise and fall of wages and profit in their reciprocal relation?

They stand in inverse proportion to each other. The share of (profit) increases in the same proportion in which the share of labour (wages) falls, and vice versa. Profit rises in the same degree in which wages fall; it falls in the same degree in which wages rise.

It might perhaps be argued that the capitalist class can gain by an advantageous exchange of his products with other capitalists, by a rise in the demand for his commodities, whether in consequence of the opening up of new markets, or in consequence of temporarily increased demands in the old market, and so on; that the profit of the capitalist, therefore, may be multiplied by taking advantage of other capitalists, independently of the rise and fall of wages, of the exchange value of labour-power; or that the profit of the capitalist may also rise through improvements in the instruments of labour, new applications of the forces of nature, and so on.

But in the first place it must be admitted that the result remains the same, although brought about in an opposite manner. Profit, indeed, has not risen because wages have fallen, but wages have fallen because profit has risen. With the same amount of another man's labour the capitalist has bought a larger amount of exchange values without having paid more for the labour on that account – i.e., the work is paid for less in proportion to the net gain which it yields to the capitalist.

In the second place, it must be borne in mind that, despite the fluctuations in the prices of commodities, the average price of every commodity, the proportion in which it exchanges for other commodities, is determined by its cost of production. The acts of overreaching and taking advantage of one another within the capitalist ranks necessarily equalize themselves. The improvements of machinery, the new applications of the forces of nature in the service of production, make it possible to produce in a given period of time, with the same amount of labour and capital, a larger amount of products, but in no wise a larger amount of exchange values. If by the use of the spinning-machine I can furnish twice as much yarn in an hour as before its invention – for instance, 100 pounds instead of 50 pounds – in the long run I receive back, in exchange for this 100 pounds no more commodities than I did before for 50; because the cost of production has fallen by 1/2, or because I can furnish double the product at the same cost.

Finally, in whatsoever proportion the capitalist class, whether of one country or of the entire world-market, distribute the net revenue of production among themselves, the total amount of this net revenue always consists exclusively of the amount by which accumulated labour has been increased from the proceeds of direct labour. This whole amount, therefore, grows in the same proportion in which labour augments capital – i.e., in the same proportion in which profit rises as compared with wages.

VII

The Interests of Capital and Wage-Labour Are Diametrically Opposed: Effect of Growth of Productive Capital on Wages

We thus see that, even if we keep ourselves within the relation of capital and wage-labour, the interests of capitals and the interests of wage-labour are diametrically opposed to each other.

A rapid growth of capital is synonymous with a rapid growth of profits. Profits can grow rapidly only when the price of labour – the relative wages – decrease just as rapidly. Relative wages may fall, although real wages rise simultaneously with nominal wages, with the money value of labour, provided only that the real wage does not rise in the same proportion as the profit. If, for instance, in good business years wages rise 5 per cent, while profits rise 30 per cent, the proportional, the relative wage has not increased, but decreased.

If, therefore, the income of the worker increased with the rapid growth of capital, there is at the same time a widening of the social chasm that divides the worker from the capitalist, and increase in the power of capital over labour, a greater dependence of labour upon capital.

To say that "the worker has an interest in the rapid growth of capital", means only this: that the more speedily the worker augments the wealth of the capitalist, the larger will be the crumbs which fall to him, the greater will be the number of workers than can be called into existence, the more can the mass of slaves dependent upon capital be increased.

We have thus seen that even the most favourable situation for the working class, namely, the most rapid growth of capital, however much it may improve the material life of the worker, does not abolish the antagonism between his interests and the interests of the capitalist. Profit and wages remain as before, in inverse proportion.

If capital grows rapidly, wages may rise, but the profit of capital rises disproportionately faster. The material position of the worker has improved, but at the cost of his social position. The social chasm that separates him from the capitalist has widened.

Finally, to say that "the most favourable condition for wage-labour is the fastest possible growth of productive capital", is the same as to say: the quicker the working class multiplies and augments the power inimical to it – the wealth of another which lords over that class – the more favourable will be the conditions under which it will be permitted to toil anew at the multiplication of bourgeois wealth, at the enlargement of the power of capital, content thus to forge for itself the golden chains by which the bourgeoisie drags it in its train.

Growth of productive capital and rise of wages, are they really so indissolubly united as the bourgeois economists maintain? We must not believe their mere words. We dare not believe them even when they claim that the fatter capital is the more will its slave be pampered. The bourgeoisie is too much enlightened, it keeps its accounts much too carefully, to share the prejudices of the feudal lord, who makes an ostentatious display of the magnificence of his retinue. The conditions of existence of the bourgeoisie compel it to attend carefully to its bookkeeping. We must therefore examine more closely into the following question:

VIII

In What Manner Does the Growth of Productive Capital Affect Wages?

If as a whole, the productive capital of bourgeois society grows, there takes place a more many-sided accumulation of labour. The individual capitals increase in number and in magnitude. The multiplications of individual capitals increases the competition among capitalists. The increasing magnitude of increasing capitals provides the means of leading more powerful armies of workers with more gigantic instruments of war upon the industrial battlefield.

The one capitalist can drive the other from the field and carry off his capital only by selling more cheaply. In order to sell more cheaply without ruining himself, he must produce more cheaply – i.e., increase the productive forces of labour as much as possible.

But the productive forces of labour is increased above all by a greater division of labour and by a more general introduction and constant improvement of machinery. The larger the army of workers among whom the labour is subdivided, the more gigantic the scale upon which machinery is introduced, the more in proportion does the cost of production decrease, the more fruitful is the labour. And so there arises among the capitalists a universal rivalry for the increase of the division of labour and of machinery and for their exploitation upon the greatest possible scale.

If, now, by a greater division of labour, by the application and improvement of new machines, by a more advantageous exploitation of the forces of nature on a larger scale, a capitalist has found the means of producing with the same amount of labour (whether it be direct or accumulated labour) a larger amount of products of commodities than his competitors – if, for instance, he can produce a whole yard of linen in the same labour-time in which his competitors weave half-a-yard – how will this capitalist act?

He could keep on selling half-a-yard of linen at old market price; but this would not have the effect of driving his opponents from the field and enlarging his own market. But his need of a market has increased in the same measure in which his productive power has extended. The more powerful and costly means of production that he has called into existence enable him, it is true, to sell his wares more cheaply, but they compel him at the same time to sell more wares, to get control of a very much greater market for his commodities; consequently, this capitalist will sell his half-yard of linen more cheaply than his competitors.

But the capitalist will not sell the whole yard so cheaply as his competitors sell the half-yard, although the production of the whole yard costs him no more than does that of the half-yard to the others. Otherwise, he would make no extra profit, and would get back in exchange only the cost of production. He might obtain a greater income from having set in motion a larger capital, but not from having made a greater profit on his capital than the others. Moreover, he attains the object he is aiming at if he prices his goods only a small percentage lower than his competitors. He drives them off the field, he wrests from them at least part of their market, by underselling them.

And finally, let us remember that the current price always stands either above or below the cost of production, according as the sale of a commodity takes place in the favourable or unfavourable period of the industry. According as the market price of the yard of linen stands above or below its former cost of production, will the percentage vary at which the capitalist who has made use of the new and more faithful means of production sell above his real cost of production.

But the privilege of our capitalist is not of long duration. Other competing capitalists introduce the same machines, the same division of labour, and introduce them upon the same or even upon a greater scale. And finally this introduction becomes so universal that the price of the linen is lowered not only below its old, but even below its new cost of production.

The capitalists therefore find themselves, in their mutual relations, in the same situation in which they were before the introduction of the new means of production; and if they are by these means enabled to offer double the product at the old price, they are now forced to furnish double the product for less than the old price. Having arrived at the new point, the new cost of production, the battle for supremacy in the market has to be fought out anew. Given more division of labour and more machinery, and there results a greater scale upon which division of labour and machinery are exploited. And competition again brings the same reaction against this result.

IX

Effect of Capitalist Competition on the Capitalist Class, the Middle Class and the Working Class

We thus see how the method of production and the means of production are constantly enlarged, revolutionized, how division of labour necessarily draws after it greater division of labour, the employment of machinery greater employment of machinery, work upon a large scale work upon a still greater scale. This is the law that continually throws capitalist production out of its old ruts and compels capital to strain ever more the productive forces of labour for the very reason that it has already strained them – the law that grants it no respite, and constantly shouts in its ear: March! march! This is no other law than that which, within the periodical fluctuations of commerce, necessarily adjusts the price of a commodity to its cost of production.

No matter how powerful the means of production which a capitalist may bring into the field, competition will make their adoption general; and from the moment that they have been generally adopted, the sole result of the greater productiveness of his capital will be that he must furnish at the same price, 10, 20, 100 times as much as before. But since he must find a market for, perhaps, 1,000 times as much, in order to outweigh the lower selling price by the greater quantity of the sale; since now a more extensive sale is necessary not only to gain a greater profit, but also in order to replace the cost of production (the instrument of production itself grows always more costly, as we have seen), and since this more extensive sale has become a question of life and death not only for him, but also for his rivals, the old struggle must begin again, and it is all the more violent the more powerful the means of production already invented are. The division of labour and the application of machinery will therefore take a fresh start, and upon an even greater scale.

Whatever be the power of the means of production which are employed, competition seeks to rob capital of the golden fruits of this power by reducing the price of commodities to the cost of production; in the same measure in which production is cheapened - i.e., in the same measure in which more can be produced with the same amount of labour – it compels by a law which is irresistible a still greater cheapening of production, the sale of ever greater masses of product for smaller prices. Thus the capitalist will have gained nothing more by his efforts than the obligation to furnish a greater product in the same labour-time; in a word, more difficult conditions for the profitable employment of his capital. While competition, therefore, constantly pursues him with its law of the cost of production and turns against himself every weapon that he forges against his rivals, the capitalist continually seeks to get the best of competition by restlessly introducing further subdivision of labour and new machines, which, though more expensive, enable him to produce more cheaply, instead of waiting until the new machines shall have been rendered obsolete by competition.

If we now conceive this feverish agitation as it operates in the market of the whole world, we shall be in a position to comprehend how the growth, accumulation, and concentration of capital bring in their train an ever more detailed subdivision of labour, an ever greater improvement of old machines, and a constant application of new machine – a process which goes on uninterruptedly, with feverish haste, and upon an ever more gigantic scale.

But what effect do these conditions, which are inseparable from the growth of productive capital, have upon the determination of wages?

The greater division of labour enables one labourer to accomplish the work of five, 10, or 20 labourers; it therefore increases competition among the labourers fivefold, tenfold, or twentyfold. The labourers compete not only by selling themselves one cheaper than the other, but also by one doing the work of five, 10, or 20; and they are forced to compete in this manner by the division of labour, which is introduced and steadily improved by capital.

Furthermore, to the same degree in which the division of labour increases, is the labour simplified. The special skill of the labourer becomes worthless. He becomes transformed into a simple monotonous force of production, with neither physical nor mental elasticity. His work becomes accessible to all; therefore competitors press upon him from all sides. Moreover, it must be remembered that the more simple, the more easily learned the work is, so much the less is its cost to production, the expense of its acquisition, and so much the lower must the wages sink – for, like the price of any other commodity, they are determined by the cost of production. Therefore, in the same manner in which labour becomes more unsatisfactory, more repulsive, do competition increase and wages decrease.

The labourer seeks to maintain the total of his wages for a given time by performing more labour, either by working a great number of hours, or by accomplishing more in the same number of hours. Thus, urged on by want, he himself multiplies the disastrous effects of division of labour. The result is: the more he works, the less wages he receives. And for this simple reason: the more he works, the more he competes against his fellow workmen, the more he compels them to compete against him, and to offer themselves on the same wretched conditions as he does; so that, in the last analysis, he competes against himself as a member of the working class.

Machinery produces the same effects, but upon a much larger scale. It supplants skilled labourers by unskilled, men by women, adults by children; where newly introduced, it throws workers upon the streets in great masses; and as it becomes more highly developed and more productive it discards them in additional though smaller numbers.

We have hastily sketched in broad outlines the industrial war of capitalists among themselves. This war has the peculiarity that the battles in it are won less by recruiting than by discharging the army of workers. The generals (the capitalists) vie with one another as to who can discharge the greatest number of industrial soldiers.

The economists tell us, to be sure, that those labourers who have been rendered superfluous by machinery find new venues of employment. They dare not assert directly that the same labourers that have been discharged find situations in new branches of labour. Facts cry out too loudly against this lie. Strictly speaking, they only maintain that new means of employment will be found for other sections of the working class; for example, for that portion of the young generation of labourers who were about to enter upon that branch of industry which had just been abolished. Of course, this is a great satisfaction to the disabled labourers. There will be no lack of fresh exploitable blood and muscle for the Messrs. Capitalists – the dead may bury their dead. This consolation seems to be intended more for the comfort of the capitalists themselves than their labourers. If the whole class of the wage-labourer were to be annihilated by machinery, how terrible that would be for capital, which, without wage-labour, ceases to be capital!

But even if we assume that all who are directly forced out of employment by machinery, as well as all of the rising generation who were waiting for a chance of employment in the same branch of industry, do actually find some new employment – are we to believe that this new employment will pay as high wages as did the one they have lost? If it did, it would be in contradiction to the laws of political economy. We have seen how modern industry always tends to the substitution of the simpler and more subordinate employments for the higher and more complex ones. How, then, could a mass of workers thrown out of one branch of industry by machinery find refuge in another branch, unless they were to be paid more poorly?

An exception to the law has been adduced, namely, the workers who are employed in the manufacture of machinery itself. As soon as there is in industry a greater demand for and a greater consumption of machinery, it is said that the number of machines must necessarily increase; consequently, also, the manufacture of machines; consequently, also, the employment of workers in machine manufacture; and the workers employed in this branch of industry are skilled, even educated, workers.

Since the year 1840 this assertion, which even before that date was only half-true, has lost all semblance of truth; for the most diverse machines are now applied to the manufacture of the machines themselves on quite as extensive a scale as in the manufacture of cotton yarn, and the labourers employed in machine factories can but play the role of very stupid machines alongside of the highly ingenious machines.

But in place of the man who has been dismissed by the machine, the factory may employ, perhaps, three children and one woman! And must not the wages of the man have previously sufficed for the three children and one woman? Must not the minimum wages have sufficed for the preservation and propagation of the race? What, then, do these beloved bourgeois phrases prove? Nothing more than that now four times as many workers' lives are used up as there were previously, in order to obtain the livelihood of one working family.

To sum up: the more productive capital grows, the more it extends the division of labour and the application of machinery; the more the division of labour and the application of machinery extend, the more does competition extend among the workers, the more do their wages shrink together.

In addition, the working class is also recruited from the higher strata of society; a mass of small business men and of people living upon the interest of their capitals is precipitated into the ranks of the working class, and they will have nothing else to do than to stretch out their arms alongside of the arms of the workers. Thus the forest of outstretched arms, begging for work, grows ever thicker, while the arms themselves grow every leaner.

It is evident that the small manufacturer cannot survive in a struggle in which the first condition of success is production upon an ever greater scale. It is evident that the small manufacturers and thereby increasing the number of candidates for the proletariat – all this requires no further elucidation.

Finally, in the same measure in which the capitalists are compelled, by the movement described above, to exploit the already existing gigantic means of production on an ever-increasing scale, and for this purpose to set in motion all the mainsprings of credit, in the same measure do they increase the industrial earthquakes, in the midst of which the commercial world can preserve itself only by sacrificing a portion of its wealth, its products, and even its forces of production, to the gods of the lower world – in short, the crises increase. They become more frequent and more violent, if for no other reason, than for this alone, that in the same measure in which the mass of products grows, and therefore the needs for extensive markets, in the same measure does the world market shrink ever more, and ever fewer markets remain to be exploited, since every previous crisis has subjected to the commerce of the world a hitherto unconquered or but superficially exploited market.

But capital not only lives upon labour. Like a master, at once distinguished and barbarous, it drags with it into its grave the corpses of its slaves, whole hecatombs of workers, who perish in the crises.

We thus see that if capital grows rapidly, competition among the workers grows with even greater rapidity – i.e., the means of employment and subsistence for the working class decrease in proportion even more rapidly; but, this notwithstanding, the rapid growth of capital is the most favourable condition for wage-labour.

Value, Price and Profit

Karl Marx

Preface

The circumstances under which this paper was read are narrated at the beginning of the work. The paper was never published during the lifetime of Marx. It was found amongst his papers after the death of Engels. Among many other characteristics of Marx, this paper shows two especially. These are his patient willingness to make the meaning of his ideas plain to the humblest student, and the extraordinary clearness of those ideas. In a partial sense the present volume is an epitome of the first volume of Capital. More than one of us have attempted to analyze and simplify that volume, with not too much success perhaps. In fact, a witty friend and commentator has suggested that what is now required is an explanation by Marx of our explanations of him. I am often asked what is the best succession of books for the student to acquire the fundamental principles of Socialism. The question is a difficult one to answer. But, by way of suggestion, one might say, first, Engels' *Socialism: Scientific And Utopian*, then the present work, the first volume of Capital, and the Student's Marx. My small part in the preparation of this work has been reading the manuscript, making a few suggestions as to English forms of expression, dividing the work up into chapters and naming the chapters, and revising the proofs for press. All the rest, and by far the most important part, of the work has been done by her whose name appears on the title page. The present volume has already been translated into German.

Edward Aveling

Preliminary

CITIZENS,

Before entering into the subject-matter, allow me to make a few preliminary remarks. There reigns now on the Continent a real epidemic of strikes, and a general clamour for a rise of wages. The question will turn up at our Congress. You, as the head of the International Association, ought to have settled convictions upon this paramount question. For my own part, I considered it therefore my duty to enter fully into the matter, even at the peril of putting your patience to a severe test.

Another preliminary remark I have to make in regard to Citizen Weston. He has not only proposed to you, but has publicly defended, in the interest of the working class, as he thinks, opinions he knows to be most unpopular with the working class. Such an exhibition of moral courage all of us must highly honour. I hope that, despite the unvarnished style of my paper, at its conclusion he will find me agreeing with what appears to me the just idea lying at the bottom of his theses, which, however, in their present form, I cannot but consider theoretically false and practically dangerous.

I shall now at once proceed to the business before us.

I

Production and Wages

Citizen Weston's argument rested, in fact, upon two premises: firstly, the amount of national production is a fixed thing, a constant quantity or magnitude, as the mathematicians would say; secondly, that the amount of real wages, that is to say, of wages as measured by the quantity of the commodities they can buy, is a fixed amount, a constant magnitude.

Now, his first assertion is evidently erroneous. Year after year you will find that the value and mass of production increase, that the productive powers of the national labour increase, and that the amount of money necessary to circulate this increasing production continuously changes. What is true at the end of the year, and for different years compared with each other, is true for every average day of the year. The amount or magnitude of national production changes continuously. It is not a constant but a variable magnitude, and apart from changes in population it must be so, because of the continuous change in the accumulation of capital and the productive powers of labour. It is perfectly true that if a rise in the general rate of wages should take place today, that rise, whatever its ulterior effects might be, would, by itself, not immediately change the amount of production. It would, in the first instance, proceed from the existing state of things. But if before the rise of wages the national production was variable, and not fixed, it will continue to be variable and not fixed after the rise of wages.

But suppose the amount of national production to be constant instead of variable. Even then, what our friend Weston considers a logical conclusion would still remain a gratuitous assertion. If I have a given number, say eight, the absolute limits of this number do not prevent its parts from changing their relative limits. If profits were six and wages two, wages might increase to six and profits decrease to two, and still the total amount remain eight. The fixed amount of production would by no means prove the fixed amount of wages. How then does our friend Weston prove this fixity? By asserting it.

But even conceding him his assertion, it would cut both ways, while he presses it only in one direction. If the amount of wages is a constant magnitude, then it can be neither increased nor diminished. If then, in enforcing a temporary rise of wages, the working men act foolishly, the capitalists, in enforcing a temporary fall of wages, would act not less foolishly. Our friend Weston does not deny that, under certain circumstances, the working men *can* enforce a rise of wages, but their amount being naturally fixed, there must follow a reaction. On the other hand, he knows also that the capitalists *can* enforce a fall of wages, and, indeed, continuously try to enforce it. According to the principle of the constancy of wages, a reaction ought to follow in this case not less than in the former. The working men, therefore, reacting against the attempt at, or the act of, lowering wages, would act rightly. They would, therefore, act rightly in enforcing *a rise of wages*, because every *reaction* against the lowering of wages is an *action* for raising wages. According to Citizen Weston's own principle of the *constancy of wages*, the working men ought, therefore, under certain circumstances, to combine and struggle for a rise of wages. If he denies this conclusion, he must give up the premise from which it flows. He must not say that the amount of wages is a *constant quantity*, but that, although it cannot and must not *rise*, it can and must *fall*, whenever capital pleases to lower it. If the capitalist pleases to feed you upon potatoes instead of upon meat, and upon oats instead of upon wheat, you must accept his will as a law of political economy, and submit to it. If in one country the rate of wages is higher than in another, in the United States, for example, than in England, you must explain this difference in the rate of wages by a difference between the will of the American capitalist and the will of the English capitalist, a method which would certainly very much simplify, not only the study of economic phenomena, but of all other phenomena.

But even then, we might ask, *why* the will of the American capitalist differs from the will of the English capitalist? And to answer the question you must go beyond the domain of *will*. A person may tell me that God wills one thing in France, and another thing in England. If I summon him to explain this duality of will, he might have the brass to answer me that God wills to have one will in France and another will in England. But our friend Weston is certainly the last man to make an argument of such a complete negation of all reasoning.

The *will* of the capitalist is certainly to take as much as possible. What we have to do is not to talk about his *will*, but to enquire into his *power*, the *limits of that power*, and the *character of those limits*.

II

Production, Wages, Profits

The address Citizen Weston read to us might have been compressed into a nutshell.

All his reasoning amounted to this: If the working class forces the capitalist class to pay five shillings instead of four shillings in the shape of money wages, the capitalist will return in the shape of commodities four shillings' worth instead of five shillings' worth. The working class would have to pay five shillings for what, before the rise of wages, they bought with four shillings. But why is this the case? Why does the capitalist only return four shillings' worth for five shillings? Because the amount of wages is fixed. But why is it fixed at four shillings' worth of commodities? Why not at three, or two, or any other sum? If the limit of the amount of wages is settled by an economical law, independent alike of the will of the capitalist and the will of the working man, the first thing Citizen Weston had to do was to state that law and prove it. He ought then, moreover, to have proved that the amount of wages actually paid at every given moment always corresponds exactly to the necessary amount of wages, and never deviates from it. If, on the other hand, the given limit of the amount of wages is founded on the *mere will* of the capitalist, or the limits of his avarice, it is an arbitrary limit. There is nothing necessary in it. It may be changed *by* the will of the capitalist, and may, therefore, be changed *against* his will.

Citizen Weston illustrated his theory by telling you that a bowl contains a certain quantity of soup, to be eaten by a certain number of persons, an increase in the broadness of the spoons would produce no increase in the amount of soup. He must allow me to find this illustration rather spoony. It reminded me somewhat of the simile employed by Menenius Agrippa. When the Roman plebeians struck against the Roman patricians, the patrician Agrippa told them that the patrician belly fed the plebeian members of the body politic. Agrippa failed to show that you feed the members of one man by filling the belly of another. Citizen Weston, on his part, has forgotten that the bowl from which the workmen eat is filled with the whole produce of national labour, and that what prevents them fetching more out of it is neither the narrowness of the bowl nor the scantiness of its contents, but only the smallness of their spoons.

By what contrivance is the capitalist enabled to return four shillings' worth for five shillings? By raising the price of the commodity he sells. Now, does a rise and more generally a change in the prices of commodities, do the prices of commodities themselves, depend on the mere will of the capitalist? Or are, on the contrary, certain circumstances wanted to give effect to that will? If not, the ups and downs, the incessant fluctuations of market prices, become an insoluble riddle.

As we suppose that no change whatever has taken place either in the productive powers of labour, or in the amount of capital and labour employed, or in the value of the money wherein the values of products are estimated, but *only a change in the rate of wages*, how could that *rise of wages* affect the *prices of commodities*? Only by affecting the actual proportion between the demand for, and the supply of these commodities.

It is perfectly true that, considered as a whole, the working class spends, and must spend, its income upon *necessaries*. A general rise in the rate of wages would, therefore, produce a rise in the demand for, and consequently in the *market prices of necessaries*. The capitalists who produce these necessaries would be compensated for the risen wages by the rising market prices of their commodities. But how with the other capitalists who do *not* produce necessaries? And you must not fancy them a small body. If you consider that two-thirds of the national produce are consumed by one-fifth of the population – a member of the House of Commons stated it recently to be but one-seventh of the population – you will understand what an immense proportion of the national produce must be produced in the shape of luxuries, or be *exchanged* for luxuries, and what an immense amount of the necessaries themselves must be wasted upon flunkeys, horses, cats, and so forth, a waste we know from experience to become always much limited with the rising prices of necessaries.

Well, what would be the position of those capitalists who do *not* produce necessaries? For the *fall in the rate of profit*, consequent upon the general rise of wages, they could not compensate themselves by a *rise in the price of their commodities*, because the demand for those commodities would not have increased. Their income would have decreased, and from this decreased income they would have to pay more for the same amount of higher-priced necessaries. But this would not be all. As their income had diminished they would have less to spend upon luxuries, and therefore their mutual demand for their respective commodities would diminish. Consequent upon this diminished demand the prices of their commodities would fall. In these branches of industry, therefore, *the rate of profit would fall,* not only in simple proportion to the general rise in the rate of wages, but in the compound ratio of the general rise of wages, the rise in the prices of necessaries, and the fall in the prices of luxuries.

What would be the consequence of *this difference in the rates of profit* for capitals employed in the different branches of industry? Why, the consequence that generally obtains whenever, from whatever reason, the *average rate of profit* comes to differ in different spheres of production. Capital and labour would be transferred from the less remunerative to the more remunerative branches; and this process of transfer would go on until the supply in the one department of industry would have risen proportionately to the increased demand, and would have sunk in the other departments according to the decreased demand. This change effected, the general rate of profit would again be *equalized* in the different branches. As the whole derangement originally arose from a mere change in the proportion of the demand for, and supply of, different commodities, the cause ceasing, the effect would cease, and *prices* would return to their former level and equilibrium. Instead of being limited to some branches of industry, *the fall in the rate of profit* consequent upon the rise of wages would have become general. According to our supposition, there would have taken place no change in the productive powers of labour, nor in the aggregate amount of production, but *that given amount of production would have changed its form.* A greater part of the produce would exist in the shape of necessaries, a lesser part in the shape of luxuries, or what comes to the same, a lesser part would be exchanged for foreign luxuries, and be consumed in its original form, or, what again comes to the same, a greater part of the native produce would be exchanged for foreign necessaries instead of for luxuries. The general rise in the rate of wages would, therefore, after a temporary disturbance of market prices, only result in a general fall of the rate of profit without any permanent change in the prices of commodities. If I am told that in the previous argument I assume the whole surplus wages to be spent upon necessaries, I answer that I have made the supposition most advantageous to the opinion of Citizen Weston. If the surplus wages were spent upon articles formerly not entering into the consumption of the working men, the real increase of their purchasing power would need no proof. Being, however, only derived from an advance of wages, that increase of their purchasing power must exactly correspond to the decrease of the purchasing power of the capitalists. The *aggregate demand* for commodities would, therefore, not *increase*, but the constituent parts of that demand would *change*. The increasing demand on the one side would be counterbalanced by the decreasing demand on the other side. Thus the aggregate demand remaining stationary, no change whatever could take place in the market prices of commodities. You arrive, therefore, at this dilemma: Either the surplus wages are equally spent upon all articles of consumption – then the expansion of demand on the part of the working class must be compensated by the contraction of demand on the part of the capitalist class – or the surplus wages are only spent upon some articles whose market prices will temporarily rise. The consequent rise in the rate of profit in some, and the consequent fall in the rate of profit in other branches of industry will produce a change in the distribution of capital and labour, going on until the supply is brought up to the increased demand in the one department of industry, and brought down to the diminished demand in the other departments of industry. On the one supposition there will occur no change in the prices of commodities. On the other supposition, after some fluctuations of market prices, the exchangeable values of commodities will subside to the former level. On both suppositions the general rise in the rate of wages will ultimately result in nothing else but a general fall in the rate of profit.

To stir up your powers of imagination Citizen Weston requested you to think of the difficulties which a general rise of English agricultural wages from nine shillings to eighteen shillings would produce. Think, he exclaimed, of the immense rise in the demand for necessaries, and the consequent fearful rise in their prices! Now, all of you know that the average wages of the American agricultural labourer amount to more than double that of the English agricultural labourer, although the prices of agricultural produce are lower in the United States than in the United Kingdom, although the general relations of capital and labour obtain in the United States the same as in England, and although the annual amount of production is much smaller in the United States than in England. Why, then, does our friend ring this alarm bell? Simply to shift the real question before us. A sudden rise of wages from nine shillings to eighteen shillings would be a sudden rise to the amount of 100 percent. Now, we are not at all discussing the question whether the general rate of wages in England could be suddenly increased by 100 percent. We have nothing at all to do with the *magnitude* of the rise, which in every practical instance must depend on, and be suited to, given circumstances. We have only to inquire how a general rise in the rate of wages, even if restricted to one percent, will act.

Dismissing friend Weston's fancy rise of 100 percent, I propose calling your attention to the real rise of wages that took place in Great Britain from 1849 to 1859.

You are all aware of the Ten Hours Bill, or rather Ten-and-a-half Hours Bill, introduced since 1848. This was one of the greatest economical changes we have witnessed. It was a sudden and compulsory rise of wages, not in some local trades, but in the leading industrial branches by which England sways the markets of the world. It was a rise of wages under circumstances singularly unpropitious. Dr. Ure, Professor Senior, and all the other official economical mouthpieces of the middle class, [The aristocracy was the upper class of Great Britain, while the capitalists composed what was known to Marx as the middle class] *proved*, and I must say upon much stronger grounds than those of our friend Weston, that it would sound the death-knell of English industry. They proved that it not only amounted to a simple rise of wages, but to a rise of wages initiated by, and based upon, a diminution of the quantity of labour employed. They asserted that the twelfth hour you wanted to take from the capitalist was exactly the only hour from which he derived his profit. They threatened a decrease of accumulation, rise of prices, loss of markets, stinting of production, consequent reaction upon wages, ultimate ruin. In fact, they declared Maximillian Robespierre's Maximum Laws[1] to be a small affair compared to it; and they were right in a certain sense. Well, what was the result? A rise in the money wages of the factory operatives, despite the curtailing of the working day, a great increase in the number of factory hands employed, a continuous fall in the prices of their products, a marvellous development in the productive powers of their labour, an unheard-of progressive expansion of the markets for their commodities. In Manchester, at the meeting, in 1860, of the Society for the Advancement of Science, I myself heard Mr. Newman confess that he, Dr. Ure, Senior, and all other official propounders of economical science had been wrong, while the instinct of the people had been right. I mention Mr. W. Newman, not

Professor Francis Newman, because he occupies an eminent position in economical science, as the contributor to, and editor of, Mr. Thomas Tooke's *History Of Prices*, that magnificent work which traces the history of prices from 1793 to 1856. If our friend Weston's fixed idea of a fixed amount of wages, a fixed amount of production, a fixed degree of the productive power of labour, a fixed and permanent will of the capitalist, and all his other fixedness and finality were correct, Professor Senior's woeful forebodings would been right, and Robert Owen[2], who already in 1816 proclaimed a general limitation of the working day the first preparatory step to the emancipation of the working class, and actually in the teeth of the general prejudice inaugurated it on his own hook in his cotton factory at New Lanark, would have been wrong.

In the very same period during which the introduction of the Ten Hours Bill, and the rise of wages consequent upon it, occurred, there took place in Great Britain, for reasons which it would be out of place to enumerate here, *a general rise in agricultural wages*. Although it is not required for my immediate purpose, in order not to mislead you, I shall make some preliminary remarks.

If a man got two shillings weekly wages, and if his wages rose to four shillings, the *rate of wages* would have risen by 100 per cent. This would seem a very magnificent thing if expressed as a rise in the *rate of wages*, although the *actual amount of wages*, four shillings weekly, would still remain a wretchedly small, a starvation pittance. You must not, therefore, allow yourselves to be carried away by the high sounding per cents in *rate* of wages. You must always ask: What was the *original* amount?

Moreover, you will understand, that if there were ten men receiving each 2s. per week, five men receiving each 5s., and five men receiving 11s. weekly, the twenty men together would receive 100s., or 5 Pounds, weekly. If then a rise, say by 20 per cent, upon the *aggregate* sum of their weekly wages took place, there would be an advance from 5 Pounds to 6 Pounds. Taking the average, we might say that the *general rate of wages* had risen by 25 per cent, although, in fact, the wages of the ten men had remained stationary, the wages of the one lot of five men had risen from 5s. to 6s. only, and the wages of the other lot of five from 55s. to 70s. [3] One half of the men would not have improved at all their position, one quarter would have improved it in an imperceptible degree, and only one quarter would have bettered it really. Still, reckoning by the *average*, the total amount of the wages of those twenty men would have increased by 25 per cent, and as far as the aggregate capital that employs them, and the prices of the commodities they produce, are concerned, it would be exactly the same as if all of them had equally shared in the average rise of wages. In the case of agricultural labour, the standard wages being very different in the different counties of England and Scotland, the rise affected them very unequally.

Lastly, during the period when that rise of wages took place counteracting influences were at work such as the new taxes consequent upon the Russian war, the extensive demolition of the dwelling-houses of the agricultural labourers, and so forth. Having premised so much, I proceed to state that from 1849 to 1859 there took place a *rise of about 40 percent* in the average rate of the agricultural wages of Great Britain. I could give you ample details in proof of my assertion, but for the present purpose think it sufficient to refer you to the conscientious and critical paper read in 1860 by the late Mr. John C. Morton at the London Society of Arts on "The Forces used in Agriculture." Mr. Morton gives the returns, from bills and other authentic documents, which he had collected from about one hundred farmers, residing in twelve Scotch and thirty-five English counties.

According to our friend Weston's opinion, and taken together with the simultaneous rise in the wages of the factory operatives, there ought to have occurred a tremendous rise in the prices of agricultural produce during the period 1849 to 1859. But what is the fact? Despite the Russian war, and the consecutive unfavourable harvests from 1854 to 1856, the average price of wheat, which is the leading agricultural produce of England, fell from about 3 Pounds per quarter for the years 1838 to 1848 to about 2 Pounds 10 Shillings per quarter for the years 1849 to 1859. This constitutes a fall in the price of wheat of more than 16 percent simultaneously with an average rise of agricultural wages of 40 percent. During the same period, if we compare its end with its beginning, 1859 with 1849, there was a decrease of official pauperism from 934,419 to 860,470, the difference being 73,949; a very small decrease, I grant, and which in the following years was again lost, but still a decrease.

It might be said that, consequent upon the abolition of the Corn Laws, the import of foreign corn was more than doubled during the period from 1849 to 1859, as compared with the period from 1838 to 1848. And what of that? From Citizen Weston's standpoint one would have expected that this sudden, immense, and continuously increasing demand upon foreign markets must have sent up the prices of agricultural produce there to a frightful height, the effect of increased demand remaining the same, whether it comes from without or from within. What was the fact? Apart from some years of failing harvests, during all that period the ruinous fall in the price of corn formed a standing theme of declamation in France; the Americans were again and again compelled to burn their surplus produce; and Russia, if we are to believe Mr. Urquhart, prompted the Civil War in the United States because her agricultural exports were crippled by the Yankee competition in the markets of Europe.

Reduced to its abstract form, Citizen Weston's argument would come to this: Every rise in demand occurs always on the basis of a given amount of production. It can, therefore, *never increase the supply of the articles demanded*, but can *only enhance their money prices*. Now the most common observation shows than an increased demand will, in some instances, leave the market prices of commodities altogether unchanged, and will, in other instances, cause a temporary rise of market prices followed by an increased supply, followed by a reduction of the prices to their original level, and in many cases *below* their original level. Whether the rise of demand springs from surplus wages, or from any other cause, does not at all change the conditions of the problem. From Citizen Weston's standpoint the general phenomenon was as difficult to explain as the phenomenon occurring under the exceptional circumstances of a rise of wages. His argument had, therefore, no peculiar bearing whatever upon the subject we treat. It only expressed his perplexity at accounting for the laws by which an increase of demand produces an increase of supply, instead of an ultimate rise of market prices.

III

Wages and Currency

On the second day of the debate our friend Weston clothed his old assertions in new forms. He said: Consequent upon a general rise in money wages, more currency will be wanted to pay the same wages. The currency being *fixed*, how can you pay with this fixed currency increased money wages? First the difficulty arose from the fixed amount of commodities accruing to the working man despite his increase of money wages; now it arises from the increased money wages, despite the fixed amount of commodities. Of course, if you reject his original dogma, his secondary grievance will disappear. However, I shall show that this currency question has nothing at all to do with the subject before us.

In your country the mechanism of payments is much more perfected than in any other country of Europe. Thanks to the extent and concentration of the banking system, much less currency is wanted to circulate the same amount of values, and to transact the same or a greater amount of business. For example, as far as wages are concerned, the English factory operative pays his wages weekly to the shopkeeper, who sends them weekly to the banker, who returns them weekly to the manufacturer, who again pays them away to his working men, and so forth. By this contrivance the yearly wages of an operative, say of 52 Pounds, may be paid by one single Sovereign turning round every week in the same circle. Even in England the mechanism is less perfect than in Scotland, and is not everywhere equally perfect; and therefore we find, for example, that in some agricultural districts, much more currency is wanted to circulate a much smaller amount of values.

If you cross the Channel you will find that the *money wages* are much lower than in England, but that they are circulated in Germany, Italy, Switzerland, and France by a *much larger amount of currency*. The same Sovereign will not be so quickly intercepted by the banker or returned to the industrial capitalist; and, therefore, instead of one Sovereign circulating 52 Pounds yearly, you want, perhaps, three Sovereigns to circulate yearly wages to the amount of 25 Pounds. Thus, by comparing continental countries with England, you will see at once that low money wages may require a much larger currency for their circulation than high money wages, and that this is, in fact, a merely technical point, quite foreign to our subject.

According to the best calculations I know, the yearly income of the working class of this country may be estimated at 250,000,000 Pounds. This immense sum is circulated by about three million Pounds. Suppose a rise of wages of fifty per cent to take place. Then, instead of three millions of currency, four and a half millions would be wanted. As a very considerable part of the working-man's daily expenses is laid out in silver and copper, that is to say, in mere tokens, whose relative value to gold is arbitrarily fixed by law, like that of inconvertible money paper, a rise of money wages by fifty per cent would, in the extreme case, require and additional circulation of Sovereigns, say to the amount of one million. One million, now dormant, in the shape of bullion or coin, in the cellars of the Bank of England, or of private bankers would circulate. But even the trifling expense resulting from the additional minting or the additional wear and tear of that million might be spared, and would actually be spared, if any friction should arise from the want of the additional currency. All of you know that the currency of this country is divided into two great departments. One sort, supplied by bank-notes of different descriptions, is used in the transactions between dealers and dealers, and the larger payments from consumers to dealers, while another sort of currency, metallic coin, circulates in the retail trade. Although distinct, these two sorts of currency intermix with each other. Thus gold coin, to a very great extent, circulates even in larger payments for all the odd sums under 5 Pounds. If tomorrow 4 Pound notes, or 3 Pound notes, or 2 Pound notes were issued, the gold filling these channels of circulation would at once be driven out of them, and flow into those channels where they would be needed from the increase of money wages. Thus the additional million required by an advance of wages by fifty per cent would be supplied without the addition of one single Sovereign. The same effect might be produced, without one additional bank-note, by an additional bill circulation, as was the case in Lancashire for a very considerable time.

If a general rise in the rate of wages, for example, of 100 per cent, as Citizen Weston supposed it to take place in agricultural wages, would produce a great rise in the prices of necessaries, and, according to his views, require an additional amount of currency not to be procured, *a general fall in wages* must produce the same effect, on the same scale, in the opposite direction. Well! All of you know that the years 1858 to 1860 were the most prosperous years for the cotton industry, and that peculiarly the year 1860 stands in that respect unrivalled in the annals of commerce, while at the same time all other branches of industry were most flourishing. The wages of the cotton operatives and of all the other working men connected with their trade stood, in 1860, higher than ever before. The American crisis came, and those aggregate wages were suddenly reduced to about one-fourth of their former amount. This would have been in the opposite direction a rise of 400 per cent. If wages rise from five to twenty, we say that they rise by 400 per cent; if they fall from twenty to five, we say that they fall by seventy-five per cent; but the amount of rise in the one and the amount of fall in the other case would be the same, namely, fifteen shillings. This, then, was a sudden change in the rate of wages unprecedented, and at the same time extending over a number of operatives which, if we count all the operatives not only directly engaged in but indirectly dependent upon the cotton trade, was larger by one-half than the number of agricultural labourers. Did the price of wheat fall? It *rose* from the annual average of 47 shillings 8d per quarter during the three years of 1858-1860 to the annual average of 55 shillings 10d per quarter during the three years 1861-1863. As to the currency, there were coined in the mint in 1861 8,673,323 Pounds, against 3,378,792 Pounds in 1860. That is to say, there were coined 5,294,440 Pounds more in 1861 than in 1860. It is true the bank-note circulation was in 1861 less by 1,319,000 Pounds than in 1860. Take this off. There remains still a surplus of currency for the year 1861, as compared with the prosperity year, 1860, to the amount of 3,975,440 Pounds, or about 4,000,000 Pounds; but the bullion reserve in the Bank of England had simultaneously decreased, not quite to the same, but in an approximating proportion.

Compare the year 1862 with 1842. Apart from the immense increase in the value and amount of commodities circulated, in 1862 the capital paid in regular transactions for shares, loans, etc. for the railways in England and Wales amounted alone to 320,000,000 Pounds, a sum that would have appeared fabulous in 1842. Still, the aggregate amounts in currency in 1862 and 1842 were pretty nearly equal, and generally you will find a tendency to a progressive diminution of currency in the face of enormously increasing value, not only of commodities, but of monetary transactions generally. From our friend Weston's standpoint this is an unsolvable riddle. Looking somewhat deeper into this matter, he would have found that, quite apart from wages, and supposing them to be fixed, the value and mass of the commodities to be circulated, and generally the amount of monetary transactions to be settled, vary daily; that the amount of bank-notes issued varies daily; that the amount of payments realized without the intervention of any money, by the instrumentality of bills, cheques, book-credits, clearing houses, varies daily; that, as far as actual metallic currency is required, the proportion between the coin in circulation and the coin and bullion in reserve or sleeping in the cellars of banks varies daily; that the amount of bullion absorbed by the national circulation and the amount being sent abroad for international circulation vary daily. He would have found that this dogma of a fixed currency is a monstrous error, incompatible with our everyday movement. He would have inquired into the laws which enable a currency to adapt itself to circumstances so continually changing, instead of turning his misconception of the laws of currency into an argument against a rise of wages.

IV
Supply and Demand

Our friend Weston accepts the Latin proverb that "*repetitio est mater studiorum*," that is to say, that repetition is the mother of study, and consequently he repeated his original dogma again under the new form, that the contraction of currency, resulting from an enhancement of wages, would produce a diminution of capital, and so forth. Having already dealt with his currency crotchet, I consider it quite useless to enter upon the imaginary consequences he fancies to flow from his imaginary currency mishap. I shall proceed to at once reduce his *one and the same dogma*, repeated in so many different shapes, to its simplest theoretical form.

The uncritical way in which he has treated his subject will become evident from one single remark. He pleads against a rise of wages or against high wages as the result of such a rise. Now, I ask him: What are high wages and what are low wages? Why constitute, for example, five shillings weekly low, and twenty shillings weekly high wages? If five is low as compared with twenty, twenty is still lower as compared with two hundred. If a man was to lecture on the thermometer, and commenced by declaiming on high and low degrees, he would impart no knowledge whatever. He must first tell me how the freezing-point is found out, and how the boiling-point, and how these standard points are settled by natural laws, not by the fancy of the sellers or makers of thermometers. Now, in regard to wages and profits, Citizen Weston has not only failed to deduce such standard points from economical laws, but he has not even felt the necessity to look after them. He satisfied himself with the acceptance of the popular slang terms of low and high as something having a fixed meaning, although it is self-evident that wages can only be said to be high or low as compared with a standard by which to measure their magnitudes.

He will be unable to tell me why a certain amount of money is given for a certain amount of labour. If he should answer me, "This was settled by the law of supply and demand," I should ask him, in the first instance, by what law supply and demand are themselves regulated. And such an answer would at once put him out of court. The relations between the supply and demand of labour undergo perpetual change, and with them the market prices of labour. If the demand overshoots the supply wages rise; if the supply overshoots the demand wages sink, although it might in such circumstances be necessary to *test* the real state of demand and supply by a strike, for example, or any other method. But if you accept supply and demand as the law regulating wages, it would be as childish as useless to declaim against a rise of wages, because, according to the supreme law you appeal to, a periodical rise of wages is quite as necessary and legitimate as a periodical fall of wages. If you do *not* accept supply and demand as the law regulating wages, I again repeat the question, why a certain amount of money is given for a certain amount of labour?

But to consider matters more broadly: You would be altogether mistaken in fancying that the value of labour or any other commodity whatever is ultimately fixed by supply and demand. Supply and demand regulate nothing but the temporary *fluctuations* of market prices. They will explain to you why the market price of a commodity rises above or sinks below its *value*, but they can never account for the *value* itself. Suppose supply and demand to equilibrate, or, as the economists call it, to cover each other. Why, the very moment these opposite forces become equal they paralyze each other, and cease to work in the one or other direction. At the moment when supply and demand equilibrate each other, and therefore cease to act, the *market price* of a commodity coincides with its *real value*, with the standard price round which its market prices oscillate. In inquiring into the nature of that VALUE, we have therefore nothing at all to do with the temporary effects on market prices of supply and demand. The same holds true of wages and of the prices of all other commodities.

V
Wages and Prices

Reduced to their simplest theoretical expression, all our friend's arguments resolve themselves into this one dogma: "*The prices of commodities are determined or regulated by wages.*"

I might appeal to practical observation to bear witness against this antiquated and exploded fallacy. I might tell you that the English factory operatives, miners, shipbuilders, and so forth, whose labour is relatively high-priced, undersell by the cheapness of their produce all other nations; while the English agricultural labourer, for example, whose labour is relatively low-priced, is undersold by almost every other nation because of the dearness of his produce. By comparing article with article in the same country, and the commodities of different countries, I might show, apart from some exceptions more apparent than real, that on an average the high-priced labour produces the low-priced, and low priced labour produces the high-priced commodities. This, of course, would not prove that the high price of labour in the one, and its low price in the other instance, are the respective causes of those diametrically opposed effects, but at all events it would prove that the prices of commodities are not ruled by the prices of labour. However, it is quite superfluous for us to employ this empirical method.

It might, perhaps, be denied that Citizen Weston has put forward the dogma: "*The prices of commodities are determined or regulated by wages.*" In point of fact, he has never formulated it. He said, on the contrary, that profit and rent also form constituent parts of the prices of commodities, because it is out of the prices of commodities that not only the working man's wages, but also the capitalist's profits and the landlord's rents must be paid. But how in his idea are prices formed? First by wages. Then an additional percentage is joined to the price on behalf of the capitalist, and another additional percentage on behalf of the landlord. Suppose the wages of the labour employed in the production of a commodity to be ten. If the rate of profit was 100 per cent, to the wages advanced the capitalist would add ten, and if the rate of rent was also 100 per cent upon the wages, there would be added ten more, and the aggregate price of the commodity would amount to thirty. But such a determination of prices would be simply their determination by wages. If wages in the above case rose to twenty, the price of the commodity would rise to sixty, and so forth. Consequently all the superannuated writers on political economy who propounded the dogma that wages regulate prices, have tried to prove it by treating profit and rent *as mere additional percentages upon wages*. None of them were, of course, able to reduce the limits of those percentages to any economic law. They seem, on the contrary, to think profits settled by tradition, custom, the will of the capitalist, or by some other equally arbitrary and inexplicable method. If they assert that they are settled by the competition between the capitalists, they say nothing. That competition is sure to equalize the different rates of profit in different trades, or reduce them to one average level, but it can never determine the level itself, or the general rate of profit.

What do we mean by saying that the prices of the commodities are determined by wages? Wages being but a name for the price of labour, we mean that the prices of commodities are regulated by the price of labour. As "price" is exchangeable value – and in speaking of value I speak always of exchangeable value – is exchangeable *value expressed in money*, the proposition comes to this, that "the *value of commodities* is determined by the value of labour," or that "the *value of labour is the general measure of value*."

But how, then, is the "*value of labour*" itself determined? Here we come to a standstill. Of course, we come to a standstill if we try reasoning logically, yet the propounders of that doctrine make short work of logical scruples. Take our friend Weston, for example. First he told us that wages regulate the price of commodities and that consequently when wages rise prices must rise. Then he turned round to show us that a rise of wages will be no good because the prices of commodities had risen, and because wages were indeed measured by the prices of the commodities upon which they are spent. Thus we begin by saying that the value of labour determines the value of commodities, and we wind up by saying that the value of commodities determines the value of labour. Thus we move to and fro in the most vicious circle, and arrive at no conclusion at all.

On the whole, it is evident that by making the value of one commodity, say labour, corn, or any other commodity, the general measure and regulator of value, we only shift the difficulty, since we determine one value by another, which on its side wants to be determined.

The dogma that "wages determine the price of commodities," expressed in its most abstract terms, comes to this, that "value is determined by value," and this tautology means that, in fact, we know nothing at all about value. Accepting this premise, all reasoning about the general laws of political economy turns into mere twaddle. It was, therefore, the great merit of Ricardo that in his work on *the principles of political economy*, published in 1817, he fundamentally destroyed the old popular, and worn-out fallacy that "wages determine prices," a fallacy which Adam Smith and his French predecessors had spurned in the really scientific parts of their researches, but which they reproduced in their more exoterical and vulgarizing chapters.

1. The Maximum Law was introduced during the Great French Revolution in 1792, fixing definite price limits for commodities and standard rates of wages. The chief supporters of the Maximum Law were the so-called "madmen" who represented the interests of the urban and village poor. Robespierre, the leader of the Jacobin Party, introduced this law at a time when the Jacobins as a result of tactical considerations had formed a bloc with the "madmen." – *Ed.*

2. Robert Owen (1771-1858) was a British manufacturer who became a utopian socialist. He introduced in his factory the ten-hour day, and also organised sickness insurance, consumers' co-operative societies, etc. – *Ed.*

3. These figures, 55s.-70s., refer to the total wages of the group of five men. The wage of each man in the group would increase from 11s. to 14s. – *Ed*

VI
Value and Labour

Citizens, I have now arrived at a point where I must enter upon the real development of the question. I cannot promise to do this in a very satisfactory way, because to do so I should be obliged to go over the whole field of political economy. I can, as the French would say, but "effleurer la question," touch upon the main points. The first question we have to put is: What is the *value* of a commodity? How is it determined?

At first sight it would seem that the value of a commodity is a thing quite *relative*, and not to be settled without considering one commodity in its relations to all other commodities. In fact, in speaking of the value, the value in exchange of a commodity, we mean the proportional quantities in which it exchanges with all other commodities. But then arises the question: How are the proportions in which commodities exchange with each other regulated? We know from experience that these proportions vary infinitely. Taking one single commodity, wheat, for instance, we shall find that a quarter of wheat exchanges in almost countless variations of proportion with different commodities. Yet, *its value remaining always the same*, whether expressed in silk, gold, or any other commodity, it must be something distinct from, and independent of, these *different rates of exchange* with different articles. It must be possible to express, in a very different form, these various equations with various commodities.

Besides, if I say a quarter of wheat exchanges with iron in a certain proportion, or the value of a quarter of wheat is expressed in a certain amount of iron, I say that the value of wheat and its equivalent in iron are equal to *some third thing*, which is neither wheat nor iron, because I suppose them to express the same magnitude in two different shapes. Either of them, the wheat or the iron, must, therefore, independently of the other, be reducible to this third thing which is their common measure.

To elucidate this point I shall recur to a very simple geometrical illustration. In comparing the areas of triangles of all possible forms and magnitudes, or comparing triangles with rectangles, or any other rectilinear figure, how do we proceed? We reduce the area of any triangle whatever to an expression quite different from its visible form. Having found from the nature of the triangle that its area is equal to half the product of its base by its height, we can then compare the different values of all sorts of triangles, and of all rectilinear figures whatever, because all of them may be resolved into a certain number of triangles.

The same mode of procedure must obtain with the values of commodities. We must be able to reduce all of them to an expression common to all, and distinguishing them only by the proportions in which they contain that identical measure.

As the *exchangeable values* of commodities are only *social functions* of those things, and have nothing at all to do with the *natural* qualities, we must first ask: What is the common *social substance* of all commodities? It is *labour*. To produce a commodity a certain amount of labour must be bestowed upon it, or worked up in it. And I say not only *labour*, but *social labour*. A man who produces an article for his own immediate use, to consume it himself, creates a *product*, but not a *commodity*. As a self-sustaining producer he has nothing to do with society. But to produce a *commodity*, a man must not only produce an article satisfying some *social* want, but his labour itself must form part and parcel of the total sum of labour expended by society. It must be subordinate to the *division of labour within society*. It is nothing without the other divisions of labour, and on its part is required to *integrate* them.

If we consider *commodities as values*, we consider them exclusively under the single aspect of *realized, fixed*, or, if you like, *crystallized social labour*. In this respect they can *differ* only by representing greater or smaller quantities of labour, as, for example, a greater amount of labour may be worked up in a silken handkerchief than in a brick. But how does one measure *quantities of labour*? By the *time the labour lasts*, in measuring the labour by the hour, the day, etc. Of course, to apply this measure, all sorts of labour are reduced to average or simple labour as their unit. We arrive, therefore, at this conclusion. A commodity has *a value*, because it is a *crystallization of social labour*. The *greatness* of its value, or its *relative* value, depends upon the greater or less amount of that social substance contained in it; that is to say, on the relative mass of labour necessary for its production. The *relative values of commodities* are, therefore, determined by the *respective quantities or amounts of labour, worked up, realized, fixed in them*. The *correlative* quantities of commodities which can be produced in the *same time of labour* are *equal*. Or the value of one commodity is to the value of another commodity as the quantity of labour fixed in the one is to the quantity of labour fixed in the other.

I suspect that many of you will ask: Does then, indeed, there exist such a vast or any difference whatever, between determining the values of commodities by *wages*, and determining them by the *relative quantities of labour* necessary for their production? You must, however, be aware that the *reward* for labour, and *quantity* of labour, are quite disparate things. Suppose, for example, *equal quantities of labour* to be fixed in one quarter of wheat and one ounce of gold. I resort to the example because it was used by Benjamin Franklin in his first Essay published in 1721, and entitled *A Modest Enquiry into the Nature and Necessity of a Paper Currency*, where he, one of the first, hit upon the true nature of value.

Well. We suppose, then, that one quarter of wheat and one ounce of gold are *equal values* or *equivalents*, because they are *crystallizations of equal amounts of average labour*, of so many days' or so many weeks' labour respectively fixed in them. In thus determining the relative values of gold and corn, do we refer in any way whatever to the *wages* of the agricultural labourer and the miner? Not a bit. We leave it quite *indeterminate* how their day's or their week's labour was paid, or even whether wage labour was employed at all. If it was, wages may have been very unequal. The labourer whose labour is realized in the quarter of wheat may receive two bushels only, and the labourer employed in mining may receive one-half of the ounce of gold. Or, supposing their wages to be equal, they may deviate in all possible proportions from the values of the commodities produced by them. They may amount to one-fourth, one-fifth, or any other proportional part of the one quarter of corn or the one ounce of gold. Their *wages* can, of course, not *exceed*, not be *more* than the values of the commodities they produced, but they can be *less* in every possible degree. Their *wages* will be *limited* by the *values* of the products, but the *values of their products* will not be limited by the wages. And above all, the values, the relative values of corn and gold, for example, will have been settled without any regard whatever to the value of the labour employed, that is to say, to *wages*. To determine the values of commodities by the *relative quantities of labour fixed in them*, is, therefore, a thing quite different from the tautological method of determining the values of commodities by the value of labour, or by *wages.* This point, however, will be further elucidated in the progress of our inquiry.

In calculating the exchangeable value of a commodity we must add to the quantity of labour *previously* worked up in the raw material of the commodity, and the labour bestowed on the implements, tools, machinery, and buildings, with which such labour is assisted. For example, the value of a certain amount of cotton yarn is the crystallization of the quantity of labour added to the cotton during the spinning process, the quantity of labour previously realized in the cotton itself, the quantity of labour realized in the coal, oil, and other auxiliary substances used, the quantity of labour fixed in the steam-engine, the spindles, the factory building, and so forth. Instruments of production properly so-called, such as tools, machinery, buildings, serve again and again for longer or shorter period during repeated processes of production. If they were used up at once, like the raw material, their whole value would at once be transferred to the commodities they assist in producing. But as a spindle, for example, is but gradually used up, an average calculation is made, based upon the average time it lasts, and its average waste or wear and tear during a certain period, say a day. In this way we calculate how much of the value of the spindle is transferred to the yarn daily spin, and how much, therefore, of the total amount of labour realized in a pound of yarn, for example, is due to the quantity of labour previously realized in the spindle. For our present purpose it is not necessary to dwell any longer upon this point.

It might seem that if the value of a commodity is determined by the *quantity of labour bestowed upon its production,* the lazier a man, or the clumsier a man, the more valuable his commodity, because the greater the time of labour required for finishing the commodity. This, however, would be a sad mistake. You will recollect that I used the word "*social* labour," and many points are involved in this qualification of "*social.*" In saying that the value of a commodity is determined by the *quantity of labour* worked up or crystallized in it, we mean *the quantity of labour necessary* for its production in a given state of society, under certain social average conditions of production, with a given social average intensity, and average skill of the labour employed. When, in England, the power-loom came to compete with the hand-loom, only half the former time of labour was wanted to convert a given amount of yarn into a yard of cotton or cloth. The poor hand-loom weaver now worked seventeen or eighteen hours daily, instead of the nine or ten hours he had worked before. Still the product of twenty hours of his labour represented now only ten social hours of labour, or ten hours of labour socially necessary for the conversion of a certain amount of yarn into textile stuffs. His product of twenty hours had, therefore, no more value than his former product of ten hours.

If then the quantity of socially necessary labour realized in commodities regulates their exchangeable values, every increase in the quantity of labour wanted for the production of a commodity must augment its value, as every diminution must lower it.

If the respective quantities of labour necessary for the production of the respective commodities remained constant, their relative values also would be constant. But such is not the case. The quantity of labour necessary for the production of a commodity changes continuously with the changes in the productive powers of labour, the more produce is finished in a given time of labour; and the smaller the productive powers of labour, the less produce is finished in the same time. If, for example, in the progress of population it should become necessary to cultivate less fertile soils, the same amount of produce would be only attainable by a greater amount of labour spent, and the value of agricultural produce would consequently rise. On the other hand, if, with the modern means of production, a single spinner converts into yarn, during one working day, many thousand times the amount of cotton which he could have spun during the same time with the spinning wheel, it is evident that every single pound of cotton will absorb many thousand times less of spinning labour than it did before, and consequently, the value added by spinning to every single pound of cotton will be a thousand times less than before. The value of yarn will sink accordingly.

Apart from the different natural energies and acquired working abilities of different peoples, the productive powers of labour must principally depend: –

Firstly. Upon the *natural* conditions of labour, such as fertility of soil, mines, and so forth.

Secondly. Upon the progressive improvement of the *social powers of labour*, such as are derived from production on a grand scale, concentration of capital and combination of labour, subdivision of labour, machinery, improved methods, appliance of chemical and other natural agencies, shortening of time and space by means of communication and transport, and every other contrivance by which science presses natural agencies into the service of labour, and by which the social or co-operative character of labour is developed. The greater the productive powers of labour, the less labour is bestowed upon a given amount of produce; hence the smaller the value of the produce. The smaller the productive powers of labour, the more labour is bestowed upon the same amount of produce; hence the greater its value. As a general law we may, therefore, set it down that: –

The values of commodities are directly as the times of labour employed in their production, and are inversely as the productive powers of the labour employed.

Having till now only spoken of *value*, I shall add a few words about *price*, which is a peculiar form assumed by value.

Price, taken by itself, is nothing but the *monetary expression of value*. The values of all commodities of the country, for example, are expressed in gold prices, while on the Continent they are mainly expressed in silver prices. The value of gold or silver, like that of all other commodities is regulated by the quantity of labour necessary for getting them. You exchange a certain amount of your national products, in which a certain amount of your national labour is crystallized, for the produce of the gold and silver producing countries, in which a certain quantity of *their* labour is crystallized. It is in this way, in fact by barter, that you learn to express in gold and silver the values of all commodities, that is the respective quantities of labour bestowed upon them. Looking somewhat closer into the *monetary expression of value*, or what comes to the same, the conversion of value into price, you will find that it is a process by which you give to the *values* of all commodities an *independent* and *homogeneous form*, or by which you express them as quantities of equal social labour. So far as it is but the monetary expression of value, price has been called *natural price* by Adam Smith, *"prix necessaire"* by the French physiocrats.

What then is the relation between *value* and *market prices*, or between *natural prices* and *market prices*? You all know that the *market price* is the *same* for all commodities of the same kind, however the conditions of production may differ for the individual producers. The market price expresses only the *average amount of social labour* necessary, under the average conditions of production, to supply the market with a certain mass of a certain article. It is calculated upon the whole lot of a commodity of a certain description.

So far the *market price* of a commodity coincides with its *value*. On the other hand, the oscillations of market prices, rising now over, sinking now under the value or natural price, depend upon the fluctuations of supply and demand. The deviations of market prices from values are continual, but as Adam Smith says:

"The natural price is the central price to which the prices of commodities are continually gravitating. Different accidents may sometimes keep them suspended a good deal above it, and sometimes force them down even somewhat below it. But whatever may be the obstacles which hinder them from settling in this centre of repose and continuance, they are constantly tending towards it."

I cannot now sift this matter. It suffices to say the *if* supply and demand equilibrate each other, the market prices of commodities will correspond with their natural prices, that is to say with their values, as determined by the respective quantities of labour required for their production. But supply and demand *must* constantly tend to equilibrate each other, although they do so only by compensating one fluctuation by another, a rise by a fall, and *vice versa*. If instead of considering only the daily fluctuations you analyze the movement of market prices for longer periods, as Mr. Tooke, for example, has done in his *History of Prices*, you will find that the fluctuations of market prices, their deviations from values, their ups and downs, paralyze and compensate each other; so that apart from the effect of monopolies and some other modifications I must now pass by, all descriptions of commodities are, on average, sold at their respective *values* or natural prices. The average periods during which the fluctuations of market prices compensate each other are different for different kinds of commodities, because with one kind it is easier to adapt supply to demand than with the other.

If then, speaking broadly, and embracing somewhat longer periods, all descriptions of commodities sell at their respective values, it is nonsense to suppose that profit, not in individual cases; but that the constant and usual profits of different trades spring from the prices of commodities, or selling them at a price over and above their *value*. The absurdity of this notion becomes evident if it is generalized. What a man would constantly win as a seller he would constantly lose as a purchaser. It would not do to say that there are men who are buyers without being sellers, or consumers without being producers. What these people pay to the producers, they must first get from them for nothing. If a man first takes your money and afterwards returns that money in buying your commodities, you will never enrich yourselves by selling your commodities too dear to that same man. This sort of transaction might diminish a loss, but would never help in realizing a profit. To explain, therefore, the *general nature of profits*, you must start from the theorem that, on an average, commodities are *sold at their real values*, and that *profits are derived from selling them at their values*, that is, in proportion to the quantity of labour realized in them. If you cannot explain profit upon this supposition, you cannot explain it at all. This seems paradox and contrary to every-day observation. It is also paradox that the earth moves round the sun, and that water consists of two highly inflammable gases. Scientific truth is always paradox, if judged by every-day experience, which catches only the delusive appearance of things.

VII
Labour Power

Having now, as far as it could be done in such a cursory manner, analyzed the nature of *value*, of the *value of any commodity whatever*, we must turn our attention to the specific *value of labour*. And here, again, I must startle you by a seeming paradox. All of you feel sure that what they daily sell is their Labour; that, therefore, Labour has a price, and that, the price of a commodity being only the monetary expression of its value, there must certainly exist such a thing as the *value of labour*. However, there exists no such thing as the *value of labour* in the common acceptance of the word. We have seen that the amount of necessary labour crystallized in a commodity constitutes its value. Now, applying this notion of value, how could we define, say, the value of a ten hours working day? How much labour is contained in that day? Ten hours' labour.

To say that the value of a ten hours working day is equal to ten hours' labour, or the quantity of labour contained in it, would be a tautological and, moreover, a nonsensical expression. Of course, having once found out the true but hidden sense of the expression *"value of labour,"* we shall be able to interpret this irrational, and seemingly impossible application of value, in the same way that, having once made sure of the real movement of the celestial bodies, we shall be able to explain their apparent or merely phenomenal movements.

What the working man sells is not directly his *labour*, but his *labouring power*, the temporary disposal of which he makes over to the capitalist. This is so much the case that I do not know whether by the English Laws, but certainly by some Continental Laws, the *maximum time* is fixed for which a man is allowed to sell his labouring power. If allowed to do so for any indefinite period whatever, slavery would be immediately restored. Such a sale, if it comprised his lifetime, for example, would make him at once the lifelong slave of his employer.

One of the oldest economists and most original philosophers of England – Thomas Hobbes – has already, in his Leviathan, instinctively hit upon this point overlooked by all his successors. He says: *"the value or worth of a man* is, as in all other things, his *price*: that is so much as would be given for the *use of his power.*" Proceeding from this basis, we shall be able to determine the *value of labour* as that of all other commodities.

But before doing so, we might ask, how does this strange phenomenon arise, that we find on the market a set of buyers, possessed of land, machinery, raw material, and the means of subsistence, all of them, save land in its crude state, the *products of labour*, and on the other hand, a set of sellers who have nothing to sell except their labouring power, their working arms and brains? That the one set buys continually in order to make a profit and enrich themselves, while the other set continually sells in order to earn their livelihood? The inquiry into this question would be an inquiry into what the economists call "*previous or original accumulation*," but which ought to be called *original expropriation*. We should find that this so-called *original accumulation* means nothing but a series of historical processes, resulting in a *decomposition* of the *original union* existing between the labouring Man and his Instruments of Labour. Such an inquiry, however, lies beyond the pale of my present subject. The *separation* between the Man of Labour and the Instruments of Labour once established, such a state of things will maintain itself and reproduce itself upon a constantly increasing scale, until a new and fundamental revolution in the mode of production should again overturn it, and restore the original union in a new historical form.

What, then, is the *value of labouring power*?

Like that of every other commodity, its value is determined by the quantity of labour necessary to produce it. The labouring power of a man exists only in his living individuality. A certain mass of necessaries must be consumed by a man to grow up and maintain his life. But the man, like the machine, will wear out, and must be replaced by another man. Beside the mass of necessaries required for *his own* maintenance, he wants another amount of necessaries to bring up a certain quota of children that are to replace him on the labour market and to perpetuate the race of labourers. Moreover, to develop his labouring power, and acquire a given skill,another amount of values must be spent. For our purpose it suffices to consider only *average* labour, the costs of whose education and development are vanishing magnitudes. Still I must seize upon this occasion to state that, as the costs of producing labouring powers of different quality differ, so much differ the values of the labouring powers employed in different trades. The cry for an *equality of wages* rests, therefore, upon a mistake, is an inane wish never to be fulfilled. It is an offspring of that false and superficial radicalism that accepts premises and tries to evade conclusions. Upon the basis of the wages system the value of labouring power is settled like that of every other commodity; and as different kinds of labouring power have different values, or require different quantities of labour for their production, they *must* fetch different prices in the labour market. To clamour for *equal or even equitable retribution* on the basis of the wages system is the same as to clamour for *freedom* on the basis of the slavery system. What you think just or equitable is out of the question. The question is: What is necessary and unavoidable with a given system of production? After what has been said, it will be seen that the *value of labouring power* is determined by the *value of the necessaries* required to produce, develop, maintain, and perpetuate the labouring power.

VIII
Production of Surplus Value

Now suppose that the average amount of the daily necessaries of a labouring man require *six hours of average labour* for their production. Suppose, moreover, six hours of average labour to be also realized in a quantity of gold equal to 3s. Then 3s. would be the *price*, or the monetary expression of the *daily value* of that man's *labouring power*. If he worked daily six hours he would daily produce a value sufficient to buy the average amount of his daily necessaries, or to maintain himself as a labouring man.

But our man is a wages labourer. He must, therefore, sell his labouring power to a capitalist. If he sells it at 3s. daily, or 18s. weekly, he sells it at its value. Suppose him to be a spinner. If he works six hours daily he will add to the cotton a value of 3s. daily. This value, daily added by him, would be an exact equivalent for the wages, or the price of his labouring power, received daily. But in that case *no surplus value* or *surplus produce* whatever would go to the capitalist. Here, then, we come to the rub.

In buying the labouring power of the workman, and paying its value, the capitalist, like every other purchaser, has acquired the right to consume or use the commodity bought. You consume or use the labouring power of a man by making him work, as you consume or use a machine by making it run. By buying the daily or weekly value of the labouring power of the workman, the capitalist has, therefore, acquired the right to use or make that labouring power during the *whole day or week*. The working day or the working week has, of course, certain limits, but those we shall afterwards look more closely at.

For the present I want to turn your attention to one decisive point. The *value* of the labouring power is determined by the quantity of labour necessary to maintain or reproduce it, but the *use* of that labouring power is only limited by the active energies and physical strength of the labourer. The daily or weekly *value* of the labouring power is quite distinct from the daily or weekly exercise of that power, the same as the food a horse wants and the time it can carry the horseman are quite distinct. The quantity of labour by which the *value* of the workman's labouring power is limited forms by no means a limit to the quantity of labour which his labouring power is apt to perform. Take the example of our spinner. We have seen that, to daily reproduce his labouring power, he must daily reproduce a value of three shillings, which he will do by working six hours daily. But this does not disable him from working ten or twelve or more hours a day. But by paying the daily or weekly *value* of the spinner's labouring power the capitalist has acquired the right of using that labouring power during *the whole day or week*. He will, therefore, make him work say, daily, *twelve hours*. Over and above the six hours required to replace his wages, or the value of his labouring power, he will, therefore, have to work *six other hours*, which I shall call hours of *surplus labour*, which surplus labour will realize itself in a *surplus value* and a *surplus produce*. If our spinner, for example, by his daily labour of six hours, added three shillings' value to the cotton, a value forming an exact equivalent to his wages, he will, in twelve hours, add six shillings' worth to the cotton, and produce *a proportional surplus of yarn*. As he has sold his labouring power to the capitalist, the whole value of produce created by him belongs to the capitalist, the owner *pro tem.* of his labouring power. By advancing three shillings, the capitalist will, therefore, realize a value of six shillings, because, advancing a value in which six hours of labour are crystallized, he will receive in return a value in which twelve hours of labour are crystallized. By repeating this same process daily, the capitalist will daily advance three shillings and daily pocket six shillings, one half of which will go to pay wages anew, and the other half of which will form *surplus value*, for which the capitalist pays no equivalent. It is this *sort of exchange between capital and labour* upon which capitalistic production, or the wages system, is founded, and which must constantly result in reproducing the working man as a working man, and the capitalist as a capitalist.

The rate of surplus value, all other circumstances remaining the same, will depend on the proportion between that part of the working day necessary to reproduce the value of the labouring power and the *surplus time* or *surplus labour* performed for the capitalist. It will, therefore, depend on the *ratio in which the working day is prolonged over and above that extent*, by working which the working man would only reproduce the value of his labouring power, or replace his wages.

IX
Value of Labour

We must now return to the expression, "*value, or price of labour.*" We have seen that, in fact, it is only the value of the labouring power, measured by the values of commodities necessary for its maintenance. But since the workman receives his wages *after* his labour is performed, and knows, moreover, that what he actually gives to the capitalist is his labour, the value or price of his labouring power necessarily appears to him as the *price* or *value of his labour itself.* If the price of his labouring power is three shillings, in which six hours of labour are realized, and if he works twelve hours, he necessarily considers these three shillings as the value or price of twelve hours of labour, although these twelve hours of labour realize themselves in a value of six shillings. A double consequence flows from this.

Firstly. The *value or price of the labouring power* takes the semblance of the *price or value of labour itself*, although, strictly speaking, value and price of labour are senseless terms.

Secondly. Although one part only of the workman's daily labour is *paid*, while the other part is *unpaid*, and while that unpaid or surplus labour constitutes exactly the fund out of which *surplus value* or *profit* is formed, it seems as if the aggregate labour was paid labour.

This false appearance distinguishes *wages labour* from other *historical* forms of labour. On the basis of the wages system even the *unpaid* labour seems to be *paid* labour. With the *slave*, on the contrary, even that part of his labour which is paid appears to be unpaid. Of course, in order to work the slave must live, and one part of his working day goes to replace the value of his own maintenance. But since no bargain is struck between him and his master, and no acts of selling and buying are going on between the two parties, all his labour seems to be given away for nothing.

Take, on the other hand, the peasant serf, such as he, I might say, until yesterday existed in the whole of East of Europe. This peasant worked, for example, three days for himself on his own field or the field allotted to him, and the three subsequent days he performed compulsory and gratuitous labour on the estate of his lord. Here, then, the paid and unpaid parts of labour were sensibly separated, separated in time and space; and our Liberals overflowed with moral indignation at the preposterous notion of making a man work for nothing.

In point of fact, however, whether a man works three days of the week for himself on his own field and three days for nothing on the estate of his lord, or whether he works in the factory or the workshop six hours daily for himself and six for his employer, comes to the same, although in the latter case the paid and unpaid portions of labour are inseparably mixed up with each other, and the nature of the whole transaction is completely masked by the *intervention of a contract* and the *pay* received at the end of the week. The gratuitous labour appears to be voluntarily given in the one instance, and to be compulsory in the other. That makes all the difference.

In using the word "*value of labour*," I shall only use it as a popular slang term for "*value of labouring power*."

X

Profit Is Made by Selling a Commodity at Its Value

Suppose an average hour of labour to be realized in a value equal to sixpence, or twelve average hours of labour to be realized in six shillings. Suppose, further, the value of labour to be three shillings or the produce of six hours' labour. If, then, in the raw material, machinery, and so forth, used up in a commodity, twenty-four hours of average labour were realized, its value would amount to twelve shillings. If, moreover, the workman employed by the capitalist added twelve hours of labour to those means of production, these twelve hours would be realized in an additional value of six shillings. The *total value of the product* would, therefore, amount to thirty-six hours of realized labour, and be equal to eighteen shillings. But as the value of labour, or the wages paid to the workman, would be three shillings only, no equivalent would have been paid by the capitalist for the six hours of surplus labour worked by the workman, and realized in the value of the commodity. By selling this commodity at its value for eighteen shillings, the capitalist would, therefore, realize a value of three shillings, for which had paid no equivalent. These three shillings would constitute the surplus value or profit pocketed by him. The capitalist would consequently realize the profit of three shillings, not by selling his commodity at a price *over and above* its value, but by selling it *at its real value*.

The value of a commodity is determined by the *total quantity of labour* contained in it. But part of that quantity of labour is realized in a value for which and equivalent has been paid in the form of wages; part of it is realized in a value for which NO equivalent has been paid. Part of the labour contained in the commodity is *paid* labour; part is *unpaid* labour. By selling, therefore, the commodity *at its value*, that is, as the crystallization of the *total quantity of labour* bestowed upon it, the capitalist must necessarily sell it at a profit. He sells not only what has cost him an equivalent, but he sells also what has cost him nothing, although it has cost his workman labour. The cost of the commodity to the capitalist and its real cost are different things.

I repeat, therefore, that normal and average profits are made by selling commodities not *above*, but *at their real values*.

XI

The Different Parts into Which Surplus Value Is Decomposed

The *surplus value*, or that part of the total value of the commodity in which the *surplus labour* or *unpaid labour* of the working man is realized, I call *profit*. The whole of that profit is not pocketed by the employing capitalist. The monopoly of land enables the landlord to take one part of that *surplus value*, under the name of *rent*, whether the land is used for agricultural buildings or railways, or for any other productive purpose. On the other hand, the very fact that the possession of the *instruments of labour* enables the employing capitalist to produce a *surplus value*, or, what comes to the same, to *appropriate to himself a certain amount of unpaid labour*, enables the owner of the means of labour, which he lends wholly or partly to the employing capitalist – enables, in one word, the money-lending capitalist to claim for himself under the name of *interest* another part of that surplus value, so that there remains to the employing capitalist *as such* only what is called *industrial* or *commercial profit*.

By what laws this division of the total amount of surplus value amongst the three categories of people is regulated is a question quite foreign to our subject. This much, however, results from what has been stated.

Rent, interest, and industrial profit are only different names for different parts of the *surplus value* of the commodity, or the *unpaid labour enclosed in it*, and they are *equally derived from this source and from this source alone*. They are not derived from *land* as such or from *capital* as such, but land and capital enable their owners to get their respective shares out of the surplus value extracted by the employing capitalist from the labourer. For the labourer himself it is a matter of subordinate importance whether that surplus value, the result of his surplus labour, or unpaid labour, is altogether pocketed by the employing capitalist, or whether the latter is obliged to pay portions of it, under the name of rent and interest, away to third parties. Suppose the employing capitalist to use only his own capital and to be his own landlord, then the whole surplus value would go into his pocket.

It is the employing capitalist who immediately extracts from the labourer this surplus value, whatever part of it he may ultimately be able to keep for himself. Upon this relation, therefore between the employing capitalist and the wages labourer the whole wages system and the whole present system of production hinge. Some of the citizens who took part in our debate were, there, wrong in trying to mince matters, and to treat this fundamental relation between the employing capitalist and the working man as a secondary question, although they were right in stating that, under given circumstances, a rise of prices might affect in very unequal degrees the employing capitalist, the landlord, the moneyed capitalist, and, if you please, the tax-gatherer.

Another consequence follows from what has been stated.

That part of the value of the commodity which represents only the value of the raw materials, the machinery, in one word, the value of the means of production used up, forms *no revenue* at all, but replaces *only capital*. But, apart from this, it is false that the other part of the value of the commodity *which forms revenue*, or may be spent in the form of wages, profits, rent, interest, is *constituted* by the value of wages, the value of rent, the value of profits, and so forth. We shall, in the first instance, discard wages, and only treat industrial profits, interest, and rent. We have just seen that the *surplus value* contained in the *commodity*, or that part of its value in which *unpaid labour* is realized, resolves itself into different fractions, bearing three different names.

But it would be quite the reverse of the truth to say that its value is *composed* of, or *formed* by, the *addition* of the *independent values of these three constituents*.

If one hour of labour realizes itself in a value of sixpence, if the working day of the labourer comprises twelve hours, if half of this time is unpaid labour, that surplus labour will add to the commodity a *surplus value* of three shillings, that is of value for which no equivalent has been paid. This surplus value of three shillings constitutes the *whole fund* which the employing capitalist may divide, in whatever proportions, with the landlord and the money-lender. The value of these three shillings constitutes the limit of the value they have to divide amongst them. But it is not the employing capitalist who adds to the value of the commodity an arbitrary value for his profit, to which another value is added for the landlord, and so forth, so that the addition of these arbitrarily fixed values would constitute the total value. You see, therefore, the fallacy of the popular notion, which confounds the *decomposition of a given value* into three parts, with the *formation* of that value by the addition of three *independent* values, thus converting the aggregate value, from which rent, profit, and interest are derived, into an arbitrary magnitude.

If the total profit realized by a capitalist is equal to 100 Pounds, we call this sum, considered as *absolute* magnitude, the *amount of profit*. But if we calculate the ratio which those 100 Pounds bear to the capital advanced, we call this *relative* magnitude, the *rate of profit*. It is evident that this rate of profit may be expressed in a double way.

Suppose 100 Pounds to be the capital *advanced in wages*. If the surplus value created is also 100 Pounds – and this would show us that half the working day of the labourer consists of *unpaid* labour – and if we measured this profit by the value of the capital advanced in wages, we should say that the *rate of profit* amounted to one hundred percent, because the value advanced would be one hundred and the value realized would be two hundred.

If, on the other hand, we should not only consider the *capital advanced in wages*, but the *total capital* advanced, say, for example, 500 Pounds, of which 400 Pounds represented the value of raw materials, machinery, and so forth, we should say that the *rate of profit* amounted only to twenty percent, because the profit of one hundred would be but the fifth part of the *total* capital advanced.

The first mode of expressing the rate of profit is the only one which shows you the real ratio between paid and unpaid labour, the real degree of the *exploitation* (you must allow me this French word) *of labour*. The other mode of expression is that in common use, and is, indeed, appropriate for certain purposes. At all events, it is very useful for concealing the degree in which the capitalist extracts gratuitous labour from the workman.

In the remarks I have still to make I shall use the word *profit* for the whole amount of the surplus value extracted by the capitalist without any regard to the division of that surplus value between different parties, and in using the words *rate of profit*, I shall always measure profits by the value of the capital advanced in wages.

XII

General Relation of Profits, Wages, and Prices

Deduct from the value of a commodity the value replacing the value of the raw materials and other means of production used upon it, that is to say, deduct the value representing the *past* labour contained in it, and the remainder of its value will resolve into the quantity of labour added by the working man *last* employed. If that working man works twelve hours daily, if twelve hours of average labour crystallize themselves in an amount of gold equal to six shillings, this additional value of six shillings is the *only* value his labour will have created. This given value, determined by the time of his labour, is the only fund from which both he and the capitalist have to draw their respective shares or dividends, the only value to be divided into wages and profits. It is evident that this value itself will not be altered by the variable proportions in which it may be divided amongst the two parties. There will also be nothing changed if in the place of one working man you put the whole working population, twelve million working days, for example, instead of one.

Since the capitalist and workman have only to divide this limited value, that is, the value measured by the total labour of the working man, the more the one gets the less will the other get, and *vice versa*. Whenever a quantity is given, one part of it will increase inversely as the other decreases. If the wages change, profits will change in an opposite direction. If wages fall, profits will rise; and if wages rise, profits will fall. If the working man, on our former supposition, gets three shillings, equal to one half of the value he has created, or if his whole working day consists half of paid, half of unpaid labour, the *rate of profit* will be 100 percent, because the capitalist would also get three shillings. If the working man receives only two shillings, or works only one third of the whole day for himself, the capitalist will get four shillings, and the rate of profit will be 200 per cent. If the working man receives four shillings, the capitalist will only receive two, and the rate of profit would sink to 50 percent, but all these variations will not affect the value of the commodity. A general rise of wages would, therefore, result in a fall of the general rate of profit, but not affect values.

But although the values of commodities, which must ultimately regulate their market prices, are exclusively determined by the total quantities of labour fixed in them, and not by the division of that quantity into paid and unpaid labour, it by no means follows that the values of the single commodities, or lots of commodities, produced during twelve hours, for example, will remain constant. The *number* or mass of commodities produced in a given time of labour, or by a given quantity of labour, depends upon the *productive power* of the labour employed, and not upon its *extent* or length. With one degree of the productive power of spinning labour, for example, a working day of twelve hours may produce twelve pounds of yarn, with a lesser degree of productive power only two pounds. If then twelve hours' average labour were realized in the value of six shillings in the one case, the twelve pounds of yarn would cost six shillings, in the other case the two pounds of yarn would also cost six shillings. One pound of yarn would, therefore, cost sixpence in the one case, and three shillings in the other. The difference of price would result from the difference in the productive powers of labour employed. One hour of labour would be realized in one pound of yarn with the greater productive power, while with the smaller productive power, six hours of labour would be realized in one pound of yarn. The price of a pound of yarn would, in the one instance, be only sixpence, although wages were relatively high and the rate of profit low; it would be three shillings in the other instance, although wages were low and the rate of profit high. This would be so because the price of the pound of yarn is regulated by the *total amount of labour worked up in it*, and not by the *proportional division of that total amount into paid and unpaid labour*. The fact I have mentioned before that high-price labour may produce cheap, and low-priced labour may produce dear commodities, loses, therefore, its paradoxical appearance. It is only the expression of the general law that the value of a commodity is regulated by the quantity of labour worked up in it, and the the quantity of labour worked up in it depends altogether upon the productive powers of labour employed, and will therefore, vary with every variation in the productivity of labour.

XIII

Main Cases of Attempts at Raising Wages or Resisting Their Fall

Let us now seriously consider the main cases in which a rise of wages is attempted or a reduction of wages resisted.

1. We have seen that the *value of the labouring power*, or in more popular parlance, the *value of labour*, is determined by the value of necessaries, or the quantity of labour required to produce them.

If, then, in a given country the value of the daily average necessaries of the labourer represented six hours of labour expressed in three shillings, the labourer would have to work six hours daily to produce an equivalent for this daily maintenance. If the whole working day was twelve hours, the capitalist would pay him the value of his labour by paying him three shillings. Half the working day would be unpaid labour, and the rate of profit would amount to 100 percent. But now suppose that, consequent upon a decrease of productivity, more labour should be wanted to produce, say, the same amount of agricultural produce, so that the price of the average daily necessaries should rise from three to four shillings. In that case the *value* of labour would rise by one third, or 33 1/3 percent. Eight hours of the working day would be required to produce an equivalent for the daily maintenance of the labourer, according to his old standard of living. The surplus labour would therefore sink from six hours to four, and the rate of profit from 100 to 50 percent. But in insisting upon a rise of wages, the labourer would only insist upon getting the *increased value of his labour*, like every other seller of a commodity, who, the costs of his commodities having increased, tries to get its increased value paid. If wages did not rise, or not sufficiently rise, to compensate for the increased values of necessaries, the *price* of labour would sink below the *value of labour*, and the labourer's standard of life would deteriorate.

But a change might also take place in an opposite direction. By virtue of the increased productivity of labour, the same amount of the average daily necessaries might sink from three to two shillings, or only four hours out of the working day, instead of six, be wanted to reproduce an equivalent for the value of the daily necessaries. The working man would now be able to buy with two shillings as many necessaries as he did before with three shillings. Indeed, the *value of labour* would have sunk, but diminished value would command the same amount of commodities as before. Then profits would rise from three to four shillings, and the rate of profit from 100 to 200 percent. Although the labourer's absolute standard of life would have remained the same, his *relative* wages, and therewith his relative social position, as compared with that of the capitalist, would have been lowered. If the working man should resist that reduction of relative wages, he would only try to get some share in the increased productive powers of his own labour, and to maintain his former relative position in the social scale. Thus, after the abolition of the Corn Laws, and in flagrant violation of the most solemn pledges given during the anti-corn law agitation, the English factory lords generally reduced wages ten per cent. The resistance of the workmen was at first baffled, but, consequent upon circumstances I cannot now enter upon, the ten per cent lost were afterwards regained.

2. The *values* of necessaries, and consequently the *value of labour*, might remain the same, but a change might occur in their *money prices*, consequent upon a previous change in the *value of money*. By the discovery of more fertile mines and so forth, two ounces of gold might, for example, cost no more labour to produce than one ounce did before. The *value* of gold would then be depreciated by one half, or fifty per cent. As the *values* of all other commodities would then be expressed in twice their former *money prices*, so also the same with the *value of labour*. Twelve hours of labour, formerly expressed in six shillings, would now be expressed in twelve shillings. If the working man's wages should remain three shillings, instead of rising to six shillings, the *money price of his labour* would only be equal to *half the value of his labour*, and his standard of life would fearfully deteriorate. This would also happen in a greater or lesser degree if his wages should rise, but not proportionately to the fall in the value of gold. In such a case nothing would have been changed, either in the productive powers of labour, or in supply and demand, or in values.

Nothing would have changed except the money *names* of those values. To say that in such a case the workman ought not to insist upon a proportionate rise of wages, is to say that he must be content to be paid with names, instead of with things. All past history proves that whenever such a depreciation of money occurs, the capitalists are on the alert to seize this opportunity for defrauding the workman. A very large school of political economists assert that, consequent upon the new discoveries of gold lands, the better working of silver mines, and the cheaper supply of quicksilver, the value of precious metals has again depreciated. This would explain the general and simultaneous attempts on the Continent at a rise of wages.

3. We have till now supposed that the *working day* has given limits. The working day, however, has, by itself, no constant limits. It is the constant tendency of capital to stretch it to its utmost physically possible length, because in the same degree surplus labour, and consequently the profit resulting therefrom, will be increased. The more capital succeeds in prolonging the working day, the greater the amount of other peoples' labour it will appropriate.

During the seventeenth and even the first two thirds of the eighteenth century a ten hours' working day was the normal working day all over England. During the anti-Jacobin war, which was in fact a war waged by the British barons against the British working masses, capital celebrated its bacchanalia, and prolonged the working day from ten to twelve, fourteen, eighteen hours. Malthus, by no means a man whom you would suspect of a maudlin sentimentalism declared in a pamphlet, published about 1815, that if this sort of thing was to go on the life of the nation would be attacked at its very source. A few years before the general introduction of newly-invented machinery, about 1765, a pamphlet appeared in England under the title, *An Essay On Trade*. The anonymous author, an avowed enemy of the working classes, declaims on the necessity of expanding the limits of the working day. Amongst other means to this end, he proposes *working houses*, which, he says, ought to be "Houses of Terror." And what is the length of the working he prescribes for these "Houses of Terror"? *Twelve hours*, the very same time which in 1832 was declared by capitalists, political economists, and ministers to be not only the existing but the necessary time of labour for a child under twelve years.

By selling his labouring power, and he must do so under the present system, the working man makes over to the capitalist the consumption of that power, but within certain rational limits. He sells his labouring power in order to maintain it, apart from its natural wear and tear, but not to destroy it. In selling his labouring power at its daily or weekly value, it is understood that in one day or one week that labouring power shall not be submitted to two days' or two weeks' waste or wear and tear. Take a machine worth 1000 Pounds. If it is used up in ten years it will add to the value of the commodities in whose production it assists 100 Pounds yearly. If it is used up in five years it will add 200 Pounds yearly, or the value of its annual wear and tear is in inverse ratio to the quickness with which it is consumed. But this distinguishes the working man from the machine. Machinery does not wear out exactly in the same ratio in which it is used. Man, on the contrary, decays in a greater ratio than would be visible from the mere numerical addition of work.

In their attempts at reducing the working day to its former rational dimensions, or, where they cannot enforce a legal fixation of a normal working day, at checking overwork by a rise of wages, a rise not only in proportion to the surplus time exacted, but in a greater proportion, working men fulfill only a duty to themselves and their race. They only set limits to the tyrannical usurpations of capital. Time is the room of human development. A man who has no free time to dispose of, whose whole lifetime, apart from the mere physical interruptions by sleep, meals, and so forth, is absorbed by his labour for the capitalist, is less than a beast of burden. He is a mere machine for producing Foreign Wealth, broken in body and brutalized in mind. Yet the whole history of modern industry shows that capital, if not checked, will recklessly and ruthlessly work to cast down the whole working class to this utmost state of degradation.

In prolonging the working day the capitalist may pay *higher wages* and still lower the *value of labor*, if the rise of wages does not correspond to the greater amount of labour extracted, and the quicker decay of the labouring power thus caused. This may be done in another way. Your middle-class statisticians will tell you, for instance, that the average wages of factory families in Lancashire has risen. They forget that instead of the labour of the man, the head of the family, his wife and perhaps three or four children are now thrown under the Juggernaut wheels of capital, and that the rise of the aggregate wages does not correspond to the aggregate surplus labour extracted from the family.

Even with given limits of the working day, such as they now exist in all branches of industry subjected to the factory laws, a rise of wages may become necessary, if only to keep up the old standard *value of labour*. By increasing the *intensity* of labour, a man may be made to expend as much vital force in one hour as he formerly did in two. This has, to a certain degree, been effected in the trades, placed under the Factory Acts, by the acceleration of machinery, and the greater number of working machines which a single individual has now to superintend. If the increase in the intensity of labour or the mass of labour spent in an hour keeps some fair proportion to the decrease in the extent of the working day, the working man will still be the winner. If this limit is overshot, he loses in one form what he has gained in another, and ten hours of labour may then become as ruinous as twelve hours were before. In checking this tendency of capital, by struggling for a rise of wages corresponding to the rising intensity of labour, the working man only resists the depreciation of his labour and the deterioration of his race.

4. All of you know that, from reasons I have not now to explain, capitalistic production moves through certain periodical cycles. It moves through a state of quiescence, growing animation, prosperity, overtrade, crisis, and stagnation. The market prices of commodities, and the market rates of profit, follow these phases, now sinking below their averages, now rising above them.

Considering the whole cycle, you will find that one deviation of the market price is being compensated by the other, and that, taking the average of the cycle, the market prices of commodities are regulated by their values. Well! During the phases of sinking market prices and the phases of crisis and stagnation, the working man, if not thrown out of employment altogether, is sure to have his wages lowered. Not to be defrauded, he must, even with such a fall of market prices, debate with the capitalist in what proportional degree a fall of wages has become necessary. If, during the phases of prosperity, when extra profits are made, he did not battle for a rise of wages, he would, taking the average of one industrial cycle, not even receive his *average wages*, or the *value* of his labour. It is the utmost height of folly to demand, that while his wages are necessarily affected by the adverse phases of the cycle, he should exclude himself from compensation during the prosperous phases of the cycle. Generally, the *values* of all commodities are only realized by the compensation of the continuously changing market prices, springing from the continuous fluctuations of demand and supply. On the basis of the present system labour is only a commodity like others. It must, therefore, pass through the same fluctuations to fetch an average price corresponding to its value.

It would be absurd to treat it on the one hand as a commodity, and to want on the other hand to exempt it from the laws which regulate the prices of commodities. The slave receives a permanent and fixed amount of maintenance; the wage-labourer does not. He must try to get a rise of wages in the one instance, if only to compensate for a fall of wages in the other. If he resigned himself to accept the will, the dictates of the capitalist as a permanent economical law, he would share in all the miseries of the slave, without the security of the slave.

5. In all the cases I have considered, and they form ninety-nine out of a hundred, you have seen that a struggle for a rise of wages follows only in the track of *previous* changes, and is the necessary offspring of previous changes in the amount of production, the productive powers of labour, the value of labour, the value of money, the extent or the intensity of labour extracted, the fluctuations of market prices, dependent upon the fluctuations of demand and supply, and consistent with the different phases of the industrial cycle; in one word, as reactions of labour against the previous action of capital. By treating the struggle for a rise of wages independently of all these circumstances, by looking only upon the change of wages, and overlooking all other changes from which they emanate, you proceed from a false premise in order to arrive at false conclusions.

XIV

The Struggle between Capital and Labour and Its Results

1. Having shown that the periodical resistance on the part of the working men against a reduction of wages, and their periodical attempts at getting a rise of wages, are inseparable from the wages system, and dictated by the very fact of labour being assimilated to commodities, and therefore subject to the laws, regulating the general movement of prices; having furthermore, shown that a general rise of wages would result in a fall in the general rate of profit, but not affect the average prices of commodities, or their values, the question now ultimately arises, how far, in this incessant struggle between capital and labour, the latter is likely to prove successful.

I might answer by a generalization, and say that, as with all other commodities, so with labour, its *market price* will, in the long run, adapt itself to its *value*; that, therefore, despite all the ups and downs, and do what he may, the working man will, on an average, only receive the value of his labour, which resolves into the value of his labouring power, which is determined by the value of the necessaries required for its maintenance and reproduction, which value of necessaries finally is regulated by the quantity of labour wanted to produce them.

But there are some peculiar features which distinguish the *value of the labouring power, or the value of labour*, from the values of all other commodities. The value of the labouring power is formed by two elements -- the one merely physical, the other historical or social. Its *ultimate limit* is determined by the *physical* element, that is to say, to maintain and reproduce itself, to perpetuate its physical existence, the working class must receive the necessaries absolutely indispensable for living and multiplying. The *value* of those indispensable necessaries forms, therefore, the ultimate limit of the *value of labour*. On the other hand, the length of the working day is also limited by ultimate, although very elastic boundaries. Its ultimate limit is given by the physical force of the labouring man. If the daily exhaustion of his vital forces exceeds a certain degree, it cannot be exerted anew, day by day.

However, as I said, this limit is very elastic. A quick succession of unhealthy and short-lived generations will keep the labour market as well supplied as a series of vigorous and long-lived generations. Besides this mere physical element, the value of labour is in every country determined by a *traditional standard of life*. It is not mere physical life, but it is the satisfaction of certain wants springing from the social conditions in which people are placed and reared up. The English standard of life may be reduced to the Irish standard; the standard of life of a German peasant to that of a Livonian peasant. The important part which historical tradition and social habitude play in this respect, you may learn from Mr. Thornton's work on *over-population*, where he shows that the average wages in different agricultural districts of England still nowadays differ more or less according to the more or less favourable circumstances under which the districts have emerged from the state of serfdom.

This historical or social element, entering into the value of labour, may be expanded, or contracted, or altogether extinguished, so that nothing remains but the *physical limit*. During the time of the anti-Jacobin war, undertaken, as the incorrigible tax-eater and sinecurist, old George Rose, used to say, to save the comforts of our holy religion from the inroads of the French infidels, the honest English farmers, so tenderly handled in a former chapter of ours, depressed the wages of the agricultural labourers even beneath that *mere physical minimum*, but made up by Poor Laws the remainder necessary for the physical perpetuation of the race. This was a glorious way to convert the wages labourer into a slave, and Shakespeare's proud yeoman into a pauper.

By comparing the standard wages or values of labour in different countries, and by comparing them in different historical epochs of the same country, you will find that the *value of labour* itself is not a fixed but a variable magnitude, even supposing the values of all other commodities to remain constant.

A similar comparison would prove that not only the *market rates* of profit change, but its *average* rates.

But as to *profits*, there exists no law which determines their *minimum*. We cannot say what is the ultimate limit of their decrease. And why cannot we fix that limit? Because, although we can fix the *minimum* of wages, we cannot fix their *maximum*.

We can only say that, the limits of the working day being given, the *maximum of profit* corresponds to the *physical minimum of wages*; and that wages being given, the *maximum of profit* corresponds to such a prolongation of the working day as is compatible with the physical forces of the labourer. The maximum of profit is therefore limited by the physical minimum of wages and the physical maximum of the working day. It is evident that between the two limits of the *maximum rate of profit* an immense scale of variations is possible. The fixation of its actual degree is only settled by the continuous struggle between capital and labour, the capitalist constantly tending to reduce wages to their physical minimum, and to extend the working day to its physical maximum, while the working man constantly presses in the opposite direction.

The matter resolves itself into a question of the respective powers of the combatants.

2. As to the *limitation of the working day* in England, as in all other countries, it has never been settled except by *legislative interference*. Without the working men's continuous pressure from without that interference would never have taken place. But at all events, the result was not to be attained by private settlement between the working men and the capitalists. This very necessity of *general political action* affords the proof that in its merely economical action capital is the stronger side.

As to the *limits* of the *value of labour*, its actual settlement always depends upon supply and demand, I mean the demand for labour on the part of capital, and the supply of labour by the working men. In colonial countries the law of supply and demand favours the working man. Hence the relatively high standard of wages in the United States. Capital may there try its utmost. It cannot prevent the labour market from being continuously emptied by the continuous conversion of wages labourers into independent, self-sustaining peasants. The position of a wages labourer is for a very large part of the American people but a probational state, which they are sure to leave within a longer or shorter term. To mend this colonial state of things the paternal British Government accepted for some time what is called the modern colonization theory, which consists in putting an artificial high price upon colonial land, in order to prevent the too quick conversion of the wages labourer into the independent peasant.

But let us now come to old civilized countries, in which capital domineers over the whole process of production. Take, for example, the rise in England of agricultural wages from 1849 to 1859. What was its consequence? The farmers could not, as our friend Weston would have advised them, raise the value of wheat, nor even its market prices. They had, on the contrary, to submit to their fall. But during these eleven years they introduced machinery of all sorts, adopted more scientific methods, converted part of arable land into pasture, increased the size of farms, and with this the scale of production, and by these and other processes diminishing the demand for labour by increasing its productive power, made the agricultural population again relatively redundant. This is the general method in which a reaction, quicker or slower, of capital against a rise of wages takes place in old, settled countries. Ricardo has justly remarked that machinery is in constant competition with labour, and can often be only introduced when the price of labour has reached a certain height, but the appliance of machinery is but one of the many methods for increasing the productive powers of labour. The very same development which makes common labour relatively redundant simplifies, on the other hand, skilled labour, and thus depreciates it.

The same law obtains in another form. With the development of the productive powers of labour the accumulation of capital will be accelerated, even despite a relatively high rate of wages. Hence, one might infer, as Adam Smith, in whose days modern industry was still in its infancy, did infer, that the accelerated accumulation of capital must turn the balance in favour of the working man, by securing a growing demand for his labour. From this same standpoint many contemporary writers have wondered that English capital having grown in that last twenty years so much quicker than English population, wages should not have been more enhanced. But simultaneously with the progress of accumulation there takes place a *progressive change in the composition of capital*. That part of the aggregate capital which consists of fixed capital, machinery, raw materials, means of production in all possible forms, progressively increases as compared with the other part of capital, which is laid out in wages or in the purchase of labour. This law has been stated in a more or less accurate manner by Mr. Barton, Ricardo, Sismondi, Professor Richard Jones, Professor Ramsey, Cherbuilliez, and others.

If the proportion of these two elements of capital was originally one to one, it will, in the progress of industry, become five to one, and so forth. If of a total capital of 600, 300 is laid out in instruments, raw materials, and so forth, and 300 in wages, the total capital wants only to be doubled to create a demand for 600 working men instead of for 300. But if of a capital of 600, 500 is laid out in machinery, materials, and so forth and 100 only in wages, the same capital must increase from 600 to 3,600 in order to create a demand for 600 workmen instead of 300. In the progress of industry the demand for labour keeps, therefore, no pace with the accumulation of capital. It will still increase, but increase in a constantly diminishing ratio as compared with the increase of capital.

These few hints will suffice to show that the very development of modern industry must progressively turn the scale in favour of the capitalist against the working man, and that consequently the general tendency of capitalistic production is not to raise, but to sink the average standard of wages, or to push the *value of labour* more or less to its *minimum limit*. Such being the tendency of *things* in this system, is this saying that the working class ought to renounce their resistance against the encroachments of capital, and abandon their attempts at making the best of the occasional chances for their temporary improvement? If they did, they would be degraded to one level mass of broken wretches past salvation. I think I have shown that their struggles for the standard of wages are incidents inseparable from the whole wages system, that in 99 cases out of 100 their efforts at raising wages are only efforts at maintaining the given value of labour, and that the necessity of debating their price with the capitalist is inherent to their condition of having to sell themselves as commodities. By cowardly giving way in their everyday conflict with capital, they would certainly disqualify themselves for the initiating of any larger movement.

At the same time, and quite apart from the general servitude involved in the wages system, the working class ought not to exaggerate to themselves the ultimate working of these everyday struggles. They ought not to forget that they are fighting with effects, but not with the causes of those effects; that they are retarding the downward movement, but not changing its direction; that they are applying palliatives, not curing the malady. They ought, therefore, not to be exclusively absorbed in these unavoidable guerrilla fights incessantly springing up from the never ceasing encroachments of capital or changes of the market. They ought to understand that, with all the miseries it imposes upon them, the present system simultaneously engenders the *material conditions* and the *social forms* necessary for an economical reconstruction of society. Instead of the *conservative* motto: "*A fair day's wage for a fair day's work!*" they ought to inscribe on their banner the *revolutionary* watchword: "*Abolition of the wages system!*"

After this very long and, I fear, tedious exposition, which I was obliged to enter into to do some justice to the subject matter, I shall conclude by proposing the following resolutions:

Firstly. A general rise in the rate of wages would result in a fall of the general rate of profit, but, broadly speaking, not affect the prices of commodities.

Secondly. The general tendency of capitalist production is not to raise, but to sink the average standard of wages.

Thirdly. Trades Unions work well as centres of resistance against the encroachments of capital. They fail partially from an injudicious use of their power. They fail generally from limiting themselves to a guerilla war against the effects of the existing system, instead of simultaneously trying to change it, instead of using their organized forces as a lever for the final emancipation of the working class that is to say the ultimate abolition of the wages system.

"Left-Wing" Communism: an Infantile Disorder

V I Lenin

I

In What Sense We Can Speak of the International Significance of the Russian Revolution

In the first months after the proletariat in Russia had won political power (25th October [7th November], 1917), it might have seemed that the enormous difference between backward Russia and the advanced countries of Western Europe would lead to the proletarian revolution in the latter countries bearing very little resemblance to ours. We now possess quite considerable international experience, which shows very definitely that certain fundamental features of our revolution have a significance that is not local, or peculiarly national, or Russian alone, but international. I am not speaking here of international significance in the broad sense of the term: not merely several but all the primary features of our revolution, and many of its secondary features, are of international significance in the meaning of its effect on all countries. I am speaking of it in the narrowest sense of the word, taking international significance to mean the international validity or the historical inevitability of a repetition, on an international scale, of what has taken place in our country. It must be admitted that certain fundamental features of our revolution do possess that significance.

It would, of course, be grossly erroneous to exaggerate this truth and to extend it beyond certain fundamental features of our revolution. It would also be erroneous to lose sight of the fact that, soon after the victory of the proletarian revolution in at least one of the advanced countries, a sharp change will probably come about: Russia will cease to be the model and will once again become a backward country (in the "Soviet" and the socialist sense).

At the present moment in history, however, it is the Russian model that reveals to *all* countries something – and something highly significant – of their near and inevitable future. Advanced workers in all lands have long realised this; more often than not, they have grasped it with their revolutionary class instinct rather than realised it. Herein lies the international "significance" (in the narrow sense of the word) of Soviet power, and of the fundamentals of Bolshevik theory and tactics. The "revolutionary" leaders of the Second International, such as Kautsky in Germany and Otto Bauer and Friedrich Adler in Austria, have failed to understand this, which is why they have proved to be reactionaries and advocates of the worst kind of opportunism and social treachery. Incidentally, the anonymous pamphlet entitled *The World Revolution* (*Weltrevolution*), which appeared in Vienna in 1919 (*Sozialistische Bücherei*, Heft 11; Ignaz Brand), very clearly reveals their entire thinking and their entire range of ideas, or, rather, the full extent of their stupidity, pedantry, baseness and betrayal of working-class interests – and that, moreover, under the guise of "defending" the idea of "world revolution".

We shall, however, deal with this pamphlet in greater detail some other time. We shall here note only one more point: in bygone days, when he was still a Marxist and not a renegade, Kautsky, dealing with the question as an historian, foresaw the possibility of a situation arising in which the revolutionary spirit of the Russian proletariat would provide a model to Western Europe. This was in 1902, when Kautsky wrote an article for the revolutionary *Iskra*[1], entitled "The Slavs and Revolution". Here is what he wrote in the article:

> "At the present time [in contrast with 1848] it would seem that not only have the Slavs entered the ranks of the revolutionary nations, but that the centre of revolutionary thought and revolutionary action is shifting more and more to the Slavs. The revolutionary centre is shifting from the West to the East. In the first half of the nineteenth century it was located in France, at times in England. In 1848 Germany too joined the ranks of the revolutionary nations. . . . The new century has begun with events which suggest the idea that we are approaching a further shift of the revolutionary centre, namely, to Russia. . . . Russia, which has borrowed so much revolutionary initiative from the West, is now perhaps herself ready to serve the West as a source of revolutionary energy. The Russian revolutionary movement that is now flaring up will perhaps prove to be the most potent means of exorcising the spirit of flabby philistinism and coldly calculating politics that is beginning to spread in our midst, and it may cause the fighting spirit and the passionate devotion to our great ideals to flare up again. To Western Europe, Russia has long ceased to be a bulwark of reaction and absolutism. I think the reverse is true today. Western Europe is becoming Russia's bulwark of reaction and absolutism. . . . The Russian revolutionaries might perhaps have coped with the tsar long ago had they not been compelled at the same time to fight his ally – European

capital. Let us hope that this time they will succeed in coping with both enemies, and that the new 'Holy Alliance' will collapse more rapidly than its predecessors did. However the present struggle in Russia may end, the blood and suffering of the martyrs whom, unfortunately, it will produce in too great numbers, will not have been in vain. They will nourish the shoots of social revolution throughout the civilised world and make them grow more luxuriantly and rapidly. In 1848 the Slavs were a killing frost which blighted the flowers of the people's spring. Perhaps they are now destined to be the storm that will break the ice of reaction and irresistibly bring with it a new and happy spring for the nations" (Karl Kautsky, "The Slavs and Revolution", *Iskra*, Russian Social-Democratic revolutionary newspaper, No. 18, March 10, 1902).

How well Karl Kautsky wrote eighteen years ago!

Footnotes

[Numbered footnotes by Julius Katzer, translator; star-numbered footnotes by Lenin himself.]

[1] The old *Iskra* – the first illegal Marxist newspaper in Russia. It was founded by V. I. Lenin in 1900, and played a decisive role in the formation of revolutionary Marxist party of the working class in Russia. Iskra's first issue appeared in Leipzig in December 1900, the following issues being brought out in Munich, and then beginning with July 1902 – in London, and after the spring of 1903 – in Geneva.

On Lenin's initiative and with his participation, the editorial staff drew up a draft of the Party's Programme (published in *Iskra No. 21*), and prepared the Second Congress of the R.S.D.L.P., at which the Russian revolutionary Marxist party was actually founded.

Soon after the Second Congress, the Mensheviks, supported by Plekhanov, won control of Iskra. Beginning with issue No. 52, Iskra ceased to be an organ of the revolutionary Marxists.

II

An Essential Condition of the Bolsheviks' Success

It is, I think, almost universally realised at present that the Bolsheviks could not have retained power for two and a half months, let alone two and a half years, without the most rigorous and truly iron discipline in our Party, or without the fullest and unreserved support from the entire mass of the working class, that is, from all thinking, honest, devoted and influential elements in it, capable of leading the backward strata or carrying the latter along with them.

The dictatorship of the proletariat means a most determined and most ruthless war waged by the new class against a *more powerful* enemy, the bourgeoisie, whose resistance is increased *tenfold* by their overthrow (even if only in a single country), and whose power lies, not only in the strength of international capital, the strength and durability of their international connections, but also in the *force of habit*, in the strength of *small-scale production*. Unfortunately, small-scale production is still widespread in the world, and small-scale production *engenders* capitalism and the bourgeoisie continuously, daily, hourly, spontaneously, and on a mass scale. All these reasons make the dictatorship of the proletariat necessary, and victory over the bourgeoisie is impossible without a long, stubborn and desperate life-and-death struggle which calls for tenacity, discipline, and a single and inflexible will.

I repeat: the experience of the victorious dictatorship of the proletariat in Russia has clearly shown even to those who are incapable of thinking or have had no occasion to give thought to the matter that absolute centralisation and rigorous discipline of the proletariat are an essential condition of victory over the bourgeoisie.

This is often dwelt on. However, not nearly enough thought is given to what it means, and under what conditions it is possible. Would it not be better if the salutations addressed to the Soviets and the Bolsheviks were *more frequently* accompanied by a *profound analysis* of the reasons *why* the Bolsheviks have been able to build up the discipline needed by the revolutionary proletariat?

As a current of political thought and as a political party, Bolshevism has existed since 1903. Only the history of Bolshevism during the *entire* period of its existence can satisfactorily explain why it has been able to build up and maintain, under most difficult conditions, the iron discipline needed for the victory of the proletariat.

The first questions to arise are: how is the discipline of the proletariat's revolutionary party maintained? How is it tested? How is it reinforced? First, by the class-consciousness of the proletarian vanguard and by its devotion to the revolution, by its tenacity, self-sacrifice and heroism. Second, by its ability to link up, maintain the closest contact, and – if you wish – merge, in certain measure, with the broadest masses of the working people – primarily with the proletariat, *but also with the non-proletarian* masses of working people. Third, by the correctness of the political leadership exercised by this vanguard, by the correctness of its political strategy and tactics, provided the broad masses have seen, *from their own experience*, that they are correct. Without these conditions, discipline in a revolutionary party really capable of being the party of the advanced class, whose mission it is to overthrow the bourgeoisie and transform the whole of society, cannot be achieved. Without these conditions, all attempts to establish discipline inevitably fall flat and end up in phrase-mongering and clowning. On the other hand, these conditions cannot emerge at once. They are created only by prolonged effort and hard-won experience. Their creation is facilitated by a correct revolutionary theory, which, in its turn, is not a dogma, but assumes final shape only in close connection with the practical activity of a truly mass and truly revolutionary movement.

The fact that, in 1917–20, Bolshevism was able, under unprecedentedly difficult conditions, to build up and successfully maintain the strictest centralisation and iron discipline was due simply to a number of historical peculiarities of Russia.

On the one hand, Bolshevism arose in 1903 on a very firm foundation of Marxist theory. The correctness of this revolutionary theory, and of it alone, has been proved, not only by world experience throughout the nineteenth century, but especially by the experience of the searching and vacillations, the errors and disappointments of revolutionary thought in Russia. For about half a century – approximately from the forties to the nineties of the last century – progressive thought in Russia, oppressed by a most brutal and reactionary tsarism, searched eagerly for a correct revolutionary theory, and followed with the utmost diligence and thoroughness each and every "last word" in this sphere in Europe and America. Russia achieved Marxism – the only correct revolutionary theory – through the *agony* she experienced in the course of half a century of unparalleled torment and sacrifice, of unparalleled revolutionary heroism, incredible energy, devoted searching, study, practical trial, disappointment. verification, and comparison with European experience. Thanks to the political emigration caused by tsarism, revolutionary Russia, in the second half of the nineteenth century, acquired a wealth of international links and excellent information on the forms and theories of the world revolutionary movement, such as no other country possessed.

On the other hand, Bolshevism, which had arisen on this granite foundation of theory, went through fifteen years of practical history (1903–17) unequalled anywhere in the world in its wealth of experience. During those fifteen years, no other country knew anything even approximating to that revolutionary experience, that rapid and varied succession of different forms of the movement – legal and illegal, peaceful and stormy, underground and open, local circles and mass movements, and parliamentary and terrorist forms. In no other country has there been concentrated, in so brief a period, such a wealth of forms, shades, and methods of struggle of *all* classes of modern society, a struggle which, owing to the backwardness of the country and the severity of the tsarist yoke, matured with exceptional rapidity, and assimilated most eagerly and successfully the appropriate "last word" of American and European political experience.

III

The Principal Stages in the History of Bolshevism

The years of preparation for revolution (1903–05)

The approach of a great storm was sensed everywhere. All classes were in a state of ferment and preparation. Abroad, the press of the political exiles discussed the theoretical aspects of *all* the fundamental problems of the revolution. Representatives of the three main classes, of the three principal political trends – the liberal-bourgeois, the petty-bourgeois-democratic (concealed behind "social-democratic" and "social-revolutionary" labels)², and the proletarian-revolutionary – anticipated and prepared the impending open class struggle by waging a most bitter struggle on issues of programme and tactics. *All* the issues on which the masses waged an armed struggle in 1905–07 and 1917–20 can (and should) be studied, in their embryonic form, in the press of the period. Among these three main trends there were, of course, a host of intermediate, transitional or half-hearted forms. It would be more correct to say that those political and ideological trends which were genuinely of a class nature crystallised in the struggle of press organs, parties, factions and groups; the classes were forging the requisite political and ideological weapons for the impending battles.

The years of revolution (1905–07)

All classes came out into the open. All programmatical and tactical views were tested by the action of the masses. In its extent and acuteness, the strike struggle had no parallel anywhere in the world. The economic strike developed into a political strike, and the latter into insurrection. The relations between the proletariat, as the leader, and the vacillating and unstable peasantry, as the led, were tested in practice. The Soviet form of organisation came into being in the spontaneous development of the struggle. The controversies of that period over the significance of the Soviets anticipated the great struggle of 1917–20. The alternation of parliamentary and non-parliamentary forms of struggle, of the tactics of boycotting parliament and that of participating in parliament, of legal and illegal forms of struggle, and likewise their interrelations and connections – all this was marked by an extraordinary wealth of content. As for teaching the fundamentals of political science to masses and leaders, to classes and parties alike, each month of this period was equivalent to an entire year of "peaceful" and "constitutional" development. Without the "dress rehearsal" of 1905, the victory of the October Revolution in 1917 would have been impossible.

The years of reaction (1907–10)

Tsarism was victorious. All the revolutionary and opposition parties were smashed. Depression, demoralisation, splits, discord, defection, and pornography took the place of politics. There was an ever greater drift towards philosophical idealism; mysticism became the garb of counter-revolutionary sentiments. At the same time, however, it was this great defeat that taught the revolutionary parties and the revolutionary class a real and very useful lesson, a lesson in historical dialectics, a lesson in an understanding of the political struggle, and in the art and science of waging that struggle. It is at moments of need that one learns who one's friends are. Defeated armies learn their lesson.

Victorious tsarism was compelled to speed up the destruction of the remnants of the pre-bourgeois, patriarchal mode of life in Russia. The country's development along bourgeois lines proceeded apace. Illusions that stood outside and above class distinctions, illusions concerning the possibility of avoiding capitalism, were scattered to the winds. The class struggle manifested itself in a quite new and more distinct way.

The revolutionary parties had to complete their education. They were learning how to attack. Now they had to realise that such knowledge must be supplemented with the knowledge of how to retreat in good order. They had to realise – and it is from bitter experience that the revolutionary class learns to realise this – that victory is impossible unless one has learned how to attack and retreat properly. Of all the defeated opposition and revolutionary parties, the Bolsheviks effected the most orderly retreat, with the least loss to their "army", with its core best preserved, with the least significant splits (in point of depth and incurability), with the least demoralisation, and in the best condition to resume work on the broadest scale and in the most correct and energetic manner. The Bolsheviks achieved this only because they ruthlessly exposed and expelled the revolutionary phrase-mongers, those who did not wish to understand that one had to retreat, that one had to know how to retreat, and that one had absolutely to learn how to work legally in the most reactionary of parliaments, in the most reactionary of trade unions, co-operative and insurance societies and similar organisations.

The years of revival (1910–14)

At first progress was incredibly slow, then, following the Lena events of 1912, it became somewhat more rapid. Overcoming unprecedented difficulties, the Bolsheviks thrust back the Mensheviks, whose role as bourgeois agents in the working-class movement was clearly realised by the entire bourgeoisie after 1905, and whom the bourgeoisie therefore supported in a thousand ways against the Bolsheviks. But the Bolsheviks would never have succeeded in doing this had they not followed the correct tactics of combining illegal work with the utilisation of "legal opportunities", which they made a point of doing. In the elections to the arch-reactionary Duma, the Bolsheviks won the full support of the worker curia.

The First Imperialist World War (1914–17)

Legal parliamentarianism, with an extremely reactionary "parliament", rendered most useful service to the Bolsheviks, the party of the revolutionary proletariat. The Bolshevik deputies were exiled to Siberia.[3] All shades of social-imperialism social-chauvinism, social-patriotism, inconsistent and consistent internationalism, pacifism, and the revolutionary repudiation of pacifist illusions found full expression in the Russian émigré press. The learned fools and the old women of the Second International, who had arrogantly and contemptuously turned up their noses at the abundance of "factions" in the Russian socialist movement and at the bitter struggle they were waging among themselves, were unable – when the war deprived them of their vaunted "legality" in *all* the advanced countries – to organise anything even approximating such a free (illegal) interchange of views and such a free (illegal) evolution of correct views as the Russian revolutionaries did in Switzerland and in a number of other countries. That was why both the avowed social-patriots and the "Kautskyites" of all countries proved to be the worst traitors to the proletariat. One of the principal reasons why Bolshevism was able to achieve victory in 1917–20 was that, since the end of 1914, it has been ruthlessly exposing the baseness and vileness of social-chauvinism and "Kautskyism" (to which Longuetism[4,5] in France, the views of the Fabians[6] and the leaders of the Independent Labour Party[7] in Britain, of Turati in Italy, etc., correspond), the masses later becoming more and more convinced, from their own experience, of the correctness of the Bolshevik views.

The second revolution in Russia (February to October 1917)

Tsarism's senility and obsoleteness had (with the aid of the blows and hardships of a most agonising war) created an incredibly destructive force directed against it. Within a few days Russia was transformed into a democratic bourgeois republic, freer – in war conditions – than any other country in the world. The leaders of the opposition and revolutionary parties began to set up a government, just as is done in the most "strictly parliamentary" republics; the fact that a man had been a leader of an opposition party in parliament – even in a most reactionary parliament – *facilitated* his subsequent role in the revolution.

In a few weeks the Mensheviks and Socialist-Revolutionaries thoroughly assimilated all the methods and manners, the arguments and sophistries of the European heroes of the Second International, of the ministerialists[8] and other opportunist riff-raff. Everything we now read about the Scheidemanns and Noskes, about Kautsky and Hilferding, Renner and Austerlitz, Otto Bauer and Fritz Adler, Turati and Longuet, about the Fabians and the leaders of the Independent Labour Party of Britain – all this seems to us (and indeed is) a dreary repetition, a reiteration, of an old and familiar refrain. We have already witnessed all this in the instance of the Mensheviks. As history would have it, the opportunists of a backward country became the forerunners of the opportunists in a number of advanced countries.

If the heroes of the Second International have all gone bankrupt and have disgraced themselves over the question of the significance and role of the Soviets and Soviet rule; if the leaders of the three very important parties which have now left the Second International (namely, the German Independent Social-Democratic Party[9], the French Longuetists and the British Independent Labour Party) have disgraced themselves and become entangled in this question in a most "telling" fashion; if they have all shown themselves slaves to the prejudices of petty-bourgeois democracy (fully in the spirit of the petty-bourgeois of 1848 who called themselves "Social-Democrats") – then we can only say that we have *already* witnessed *all this* in the instance of the Mensheviks. As history would have it, the Soviets came into being in Russia in 1905; from February to October 1917 they were turned to a false use by the Mensheviks, who went bankrupt because of their inability to understand the role and significance of the Soviets; today the idea of Soviet power has emerged *throughout the world* and is spreading among the proletariat of all countries with extraordinary speed. Like our Mensheviks, the old heroes of the Second International are *everywhere* going bankrupt, because they are incapable of understanding the role and significance of the Soviets. Experience has proved that, on certain very important questions of the proletarian revolution, *all* countries will inevitably have to do what Russia has done.

Despite views that are today often to be met with in Europe and America, the Bolsheviks began their victorious struggle against the parliamentary and (in fact) bourgeois republic and against the Mensheviks in a very cautious manner, and the preparations they made for it were by no means simple. At the beginning of the period mentioned, we did *not* call for the overthrow of the government but explained that it was impossible to overthrow it *without* first changing the composition and the temper of the Soviets. We did not proclaim a boycott of the bourgeois parliament, the Constituent Assembly, but said – and following the April (1917) Conference of our Party began to state officially in the name of the Party – that a bourgeois republic with a Constituent Assembly would be better than a bourgeois republic without a Constituent Assembly, but that a "workers' and peasants' " republic, a Soviet republic, would be better than any bourgeois-democratic, parliamentary republic. Without such thorough, circumspect and long preparations, we could not have achieved victory in October 1917, or have consolidated that victory.

Footnotes

[2] The reference is to the Mensheviks (who formed the Right and opportunist wing of Social-Democracy in the R.S.D.L.P.), and to the Socialist-Revolutionaries.

[3] The reference is to the Bolshevik deputies to the Fourth Duma, namely, A. Y. Badayev, M. K. Muranov, G. I. Petrovsky, F. N. Samoilov and N. R. Shagov. At the Duma's session of 26th July (8th August), 1914, at which the representatives of all the bourgeois-landowner Duma groups approved tsarist Russia's entry into the imperialist war, the Bolshevik Duma group declared a firm protest; they refused to vote for war credits and launched revolutionary propaganda among the people. In November 1914 the Bolshevik deputies were arrested, in February 1915 they were brought to trial, and exiled for life to Turukhansk Territory in Eastern Siberia. The courageous speeches made by the Bolshevik deputies at their trial, exposing the autocracy, played an important part in anti-war propaganda and in revolutionising the toiling masses.

[4,5] Longuetism – the Centrist trend within the French Socialist Party, headed by Jean Longuet. During the First World War of 1914–18, the Longuetists conducted a policy of conciliation with the social-chauvinists. They rejected the revolutionary struggle and came out for "defence of country" in the imperialist war. Lenin called them petty-bourgeois nationalists. After the victory of the October Socialist Revolution in Russia, the Longuetists called themselves supporters of the proletarian dictatorship, but in fact they remained opposed to it. In December 1920 the Longuetists, together with the avowed reformists, broke away from the Party and joined the so-called Two-and-a-Half International.

[6] Fabians – members of the Fabian Society, a British reformist organisation founded in 1884. The membership consisted, in the main, of bourgeois intellectuals. The Fabians denied the necessity of the proletariat's class struggle and the socialist revolution, and contended that the transition from capitalism to socialism was possible only through petty reforms and the gradual reorganisation of society. In 1900 the Fabian Society joined the Labour Party. The Fabians are characterised by Lenin in "British Pacifism and British Dislike of Theory" (see *LCW*, Vol. 21, pp. 260–65) and elsewhere.

[7] The Independent Labour Party of Britain (I.L.P.) – a reformist organisation founded in 1893 by leaders of the "new trade unions", in conditions of a revival of the strike struggle and the mounting movement for British working-class independence of the bourgeois parties. The I.L.P. included members of the "new trade unions" and those of a number of the old trade unions, as well as intellectuals and petty bourgeoisie who were under the influence of the Fabians. The I.L.P. was headed by James Keir Hardie and Ramsay MacDonald. From its very inception, the I.L.P. took a bourgeois-reformist stand, laying particular stress on parliamentary forms of struggle and parliamentary deals with the Liberals. Lenin wrote of the I.L.P. that "in reality it is an opportunist party always dependent on the bourgeoisie".

[8] Ministerialism (or "ministerial socialism", or else Millerandism) – the opportunist tactic of socialists' participation in reactionary bourgeois governments. The term appeared when in 1899, the French socialist Millerand joined the bourgeois government of Waldeck-Rousseau.

[9] The Independent Social-Democratic Party of Germany – a Centrist party founded in April 1917.

A split took place at the Congress of the Independent Social-Democratic Party, held in Halle in October 1920, the majority joining the Communist Party of Germany in December 1920. The Right wing formed a separate party, retaining the old name of the Independent Social-Democratic Party. In 1922 the "Independents" re-joined the German Social-Democratic Party.

IV

The Struggle against Enemies within the Working-Class Movement Helped Bolshevism Develop, Gain Strength, and Become Steeled

First and foremost, the struggle against opportunism which in 1914 definitely developed into social-chauvinism and definitely sided with the bourgeoisie, against the proletariat. Naturally, this was Bolshevism's principal enemy within the working-class movement. It still remains the principal enemy on an international scale. The Bolsheviks have been devoting the greatest attention to this enemy. This aspect of Bolshevik activities is now fairly well known abroad too.

It was, however, different with Bolshevism's other enemy within the working-class movement. Little is known in other countries of the fact that Bolshevism took shape, developed and became steeled in the long years of struggle against *petty-bourgeois revolutionism*, which smacks of anarchism, or borrows something from the latter and, in all essential matters, does not measure up to the conditions and requirements of a consistently proletarian class struggle. Marxist theory has established – and the experience of all European revolutions and revolutionary movements has fully confirmed – that the petty proprietor, the small master (a social type existing on a very extensive and even mass scale in many European countries), who, under capitalism, always suffers oppression and very frequently a most acute and rapid deterioration in his conditions of life, and even ruin, easily goes to revolutionary extremes, but is incapable of perseverance, organisation, discipline and steadfastness. A petty bourgeois driven to frenzy by the horrors of capitalism is a social phenomenon which, like anarchism, is characteristic of all capitalist countries. The instability of such revolutionism, its barrenness, and its tendency to turn rapidly into submission, apathy, phantasms, and even a frenzied infatuation with one bourgeois fad or another – all this is common knowledge. However, a theoretical or abstract recognition of these truths does not at all rid revolutionary parties of old errors, which always crop up at unexpected occasions, in somewhat new forms, in a hitherto unfamiliar garb or surroundings, in an unusual – a more or less unusual – situation.

Anarchism was not infrequently a kind of penalty for the opportunist sins of the working-class movement. The two monstrosities complemented each other. And if in Russia – despite the more petty-bourgeois composition of her population as compared with the other European countries – anarchism's influence was negligible during the two revolutions (of 1905 and 1917) and the preparations for them, this should no doubt stand partly to the credit of Bolshevism, which has always waged a most ruthless and uncompromising struggle against opportunism. I say "partly", since of still greater importance in weakening anarchism's influence in Russia was the circumstance that in the past (the seventies of the nineteenth century) it was able to develop inordinately and to reveal its absolute erroneousness, its unfitness to serve the revolutionary class as a guiding theory.

When it came into being in 1903, Bolshevism took over the tradition of a ruthless struggle against petty-bourgeois, semi-anarchist (or dilettante-anarchist) revolutionism, a tradition which had always existed in revolutionary Social-Democracy and had become particularly strong in our country during the years 1900–03, when the foundations for a mass party of the revolutionary proletariat were being laid in Russia. Bolshevism took over and carried on the struggle against a party which, more than any other, expressed the tendencies of petty-bourgeois revolutionism, namely, the "Socialist-Revolutionary" Party, and waged that struggle on three main issues. First, that party, which rejected Marxism, stubbornly refused (or, it might be more correct to say: was unable) to understand the need for a strictly objective appraisal of the class forces and their alignment, before taking any political action. Second, this party considered itself particularly "revolutionary", or "Left", because of its recognition of individual terrorism, assassination – something that we Marxists emphatically rejected. It was, of course, only on grounds of expediency that we rejected individual terrorism, whereas people who were capable of condemning "on principle" the terror of the Great French Revolution, or, in general, the terror employed by a victorious revolutionary party which is besieged by the bourgeoisie of the whole world, were ridiculed and laughed to scorn by Plekhanov in 1900–03, when he was a Marxist and a revolutionary. Third, the "Socialist-Revolutionaries" thought it very "Left" to sneer at the comparatively insignificant opportunist sins of the German Social-Democratic Party, while they themselves imitated the extreme opportunists of that party, for example, on the agrarian question, or on the question of the dictatorship of the proletariat.

History, incidentally, has now confirmed on a vast and world-wide scale the opinion we have always advocated, namely, that German *revolutionary* Social-Democracy (note that as far back as 1900–03 Plekhanov demanded Bernstein's expulsion from the Party, and in 1913 the Bolsheviks, always continuing this tradition, exposed Legien's[10] baseness, vileness and treachery) *came closest* to being the party the revolutionary proletariat needs in order to achieve victory. Today, in 1920, after all the ignominious failures and crises of the war period and the early post-war years, it can be plainly seen that, of all the Western parties, the German revolutionary Social-Democrats produced the finest leaders, and recovered and gained new strength more rapidly than the others did. This may be seen in the instances both of the Spartacists[11] and the Left, proletarian wing of the Independent Social-Democratic Party of Germany, which is waging an incessant struggle against the opportunism and spinelessness of the Kautskys, Hilferdings, Ledebours and Crispiens. If we now cast a glance to take in a complete historical period, namely, from the Paris Commune to the first Socialist Soviet Republic, we shall find that Marxism's attitude to anarchism in general stands out most definitely and unmistakably. In the final analysis, Marxism proved to be correct, and although the anarchists rightly pointed to the opportunist views on the state prevalent among most of the socialist parties, it must be said, first, that this opportunism was connected with the distortion, and even deliberate suppression, of Marx's views on the state (in my book, *The State and Revolution*, I pointed out that for thirty-six years, from 1875 to 1911, Bebel withheld a letter by Engels[12], which very clearly, vividly, bluntly and definitively exposed the opportunism of the current Social-Democratic views on the state); second, that the rectification of these opportunist views, and the recognition of Soviet power and its superiority to bourgeois parliamentary democracy proceeded most rapidly and extensively among those trends in the socialist parties of Europe and America that were most Marxist.

The struggle that Bolshevism waged against "Left" deviations within its own Party assumed particularly large proportions on two occasions: in 1908, on the question of whether or not to participate in a most reactionary "parliament" and in the legal workers' societies, which were being restricted by most reactionary laws; and again in 1918 (the Treaty of Brest-Litovsk)[13], on the question of whether one "compromise" or another was permissible.

In 1908 the "Left" Bolsheviks were expelled from our Party for stubbornly refusing to understand the necessity of participating in a most reactionary "parliament".[14] The "Lefts" – among whom there were many splendid revolutionaries who subsequently were (and still are) commendable members of the Communist Party – based themselves particularly on the successful experience of the 1905 boycott. When, in August 1905, the tsar proclaimed the convocation of a consultative "parliament"[15], the Bolsheviks called for its boycott, in the teeth of all the opposition parties and the Mensheviks, and the "parliament" was in fact swept away by the revolution of October 1905.[16] The boycott proved correct at the time, not because nonparticipation in reactionary parliaments is correct in general, but because we accurately appraised the objective situation, which was leading to the rapid development of the mass strikes first into a political strike, then into a revolutionary strike, and finally into an uprising. Moreover, the struggle centred at that time on the question of whether the convocation of the first representative assembly should be left to the tsar, or an attempt should be made to wrest its convocation from the old regime. When there was not, and could not be, any certainty that the objective situation was of a similar kind, and when there was no certainty of a similar trend and the same rate of development, the boycott was no longer correct.

The Bolsheviks' boycott of "parliament" in 1905 enriched the revolutionary proletariat with highly valuable political experience and showed that, when legal and illegal parliamentary and non-parliamentary forms of struggle are combined, it is sometimes useful and even essential to reject parliamentary forms. It would, however, be highly erroneous to apply this experience blindly, imitatively and uncritically to *other* conditions and *other* situations. The Bolsheviks' boycott of the Duma in 1906 was a mistake, although a minor and easily remediable one.[*] The boycott of the Duma in 1907, 1908 and subsequent years was a most serious error and difficult to remedy, because, on the one hand, a very rapid rise of the revolutionary tide and its conversion into an uprising was not to be expected, and, on the other hand, the entire historical situation attendant upon the renovation of the bourgeois monarchy called for legal and illegal activities being combined. Today, when we look back at this fully completed historical period, whose connection with subsequent periods has now become quite clear, it becomes most obvious that in 1908–14 the Bolsheviks *could not have* preserved (let alone strengthened and developed) the core of the revolutionary party of the proletariat, had they not upheld, in a most strenuous struggle, the viewpoint that it was *obligatory* to combine legal and illegal forms of struggle, and that it was *obligatory* to participate even in a most reactionary parliament and in a number of other institutions hemmed in by reactionary laws (sick benefit societies, etc.).

In 1918 things did not reach a split. At that time the "Left" Communists formed only a separate group or "faction" within our Party, and that not for long. In the same year, 1918, the most prominent representatives of "Left Communism", for example, Comrades Radek and Bukharin, openly acknowledged their error. It had seemed to them that the Treaty of Brest-Litovsk was a compromise with the imperialists, which was inexcusable on principle and harmful to the party of the revolutionary proletariat. It was indeed a compromise with the imperialists, but it was a compromise which, under the circumstances, *had to be made*.

Today, when I hear our tactics in signing the Brest-Litovsk Treaty being attacked by the Socialist-Revolutionaries, for instance, or when I hear Comrade Lansbury say, in a conversation with me, "Our British trade union leaders say that if it was permissible for the Bolsheviks to compromise, it is permissible for them to compromise too", I usually reply by first of all giving a simple and "popular" example:

Imagine that your car is held up by armed bandits. You hand them over your money, passport, revolver and car. In return you are rid of the pleasant company of the bandits. That is unquestionably a compromise. "*Do ut des*" (I "give" you money, fire-arms and a car "so that you give" me the opportunity to get away from you with a whole skin). It would, however, be difficult to find a sane man who would declare such a compromise to be "inadmissible on principle", or who would call the compromiser an accomplice of the bandits (even though the bandits might use the car and the firearms for further robberies). Our compromise with the bandits of German imperialism was just that kind of compromise.

But when, in 1914–18 and then in 1918–20, the Mensheviks and Socialist-Revolutionaries in Russia, the Scheidemannites (and to a large extent the Kautskyites) in Germany, Otto Bauer and Friedrich Adler (to say nothing of the Renners and Co.) in Austria, the Renaudels and Longuets and Co. in France, the Fabians, the Independents and the Labourites in Britain entered into *compromises* with the bandits of their own bourgeoisie, and sometimes of the "Allied" bourgeoisie, and *against* the revolutionary proletariat of their own countries, all these gentlemen were actually acting as *accomplices in banditry*.

The conclusion is clear: to reject compromises "on principle", to reject the permissibility of compromises in general, no matter of what kind, is childishness, which it is difficult even to consider seriously. A political leader who desires to be useful to the revolutionary proletariat must be able to distinguish *concrete* cases of compromises that are inexcusable and are an expression of opportunism and *treachery*; he must direct all the force of criticism, the full intensity of merciless exposure and relentless war, against *these concrete* compromises, and not allow the past masters of "practical" socialism and the parliamentary Jesuits to dodge and wriggle out of responsibility by means of disquisitions on "compromises in general". It is in this way that the "leaders" of the British trade unions, as well as of the Fabian society and the "Independent" Labour Party, dodge responsibility *for the treachery they have perpetrated*, for having made *a compromise* that is really tantamount to the worst kind of opportunism, treachery and betrayal.

There are different kinds of compromises. One must be able to analyse the situation and the concrete conditions of each compromise, or of each variety of compromise. One must learn to distinguish between a man who has given up his money and fire-arms to bandits so as to lessen the evil they can do and to facilitate their capture and execution, and a man who gives his money and fire-arms to bandits so as to share in the loot. In politics this is by no means always as elementary as it is in this childishly simple example. However, anyone who is out to think up for the workers some kind of recipe that will provide them with cut-and-dried solutions for all contingencies, or promises that the policy of the revolutionary proletariat will never come up against difficult or complex situations, is simply a charlatan.

To leave no room for misinterpretation, I shall attempt to outline, if only very briefly, several fundamental rules for the analysis of concrete compromises.

The party which entered into a compromise with the German imperialists by signing the Treaty of Brest-Litovsk had been evolving its internationalism in practice ever since the end of 1914. It was not afraid to call for the defeat of the tsarist monarchy and to condemn "defence of country" in a war between two imperialist robbers. The parliamentary representatives of this party preferred exile in Siberia to taking a road leading to ministerial portfolios in a bourgeois government. The revolution that overthrew tsarism and established a democratic republic put this party to a new and tremendous test – it did not enter into any agreements with its "own" imperialists, but prepared and brought about their overthrow. When it had assumed political power, this party did not leave a vestige of either landed or capitalist ownership. After making public and repudiating the imperialists' secret treaties, this party proposed peace to *all* nations, and yielded to the violence of the Brest-Litovsk robbers only after the Anglo-French imperialists had torpedoed the conclusion of a peace, and after the Bolsheviks had done everything humanly possible to hasten the revolution in Germany and other countries. The absolute correctness of this compromise, entered into by such a party in such a situation, is becoming ever clearer and more obvious with every day.

The Mensheviks and the Socialist-Revolutionaries in Russia (like all the leaders of the Second International throughout the world, in 1914–20) began with treachery – by directly or indirectly justifying "defence of country", i.e., the defence of *their own* predatory bourgeoisie. They continued their treachery by entering into a coalition with the bourgeoisie of *their own* country, and fighting, together with *their own* bourgeoisie, against the revolutionary proletariat of their own country. Their bloc, first with Kerensky and the Cadets, and then with Kolchak and Denikin in Russia – like the bloc of their *confrères* abroad with the bourgeoisie of *their* respective countries – was in fact desertion to the side of the bourgeoisie, against the proletariat. From beginning to end, *their* compromise with the bandits of imperialism meant their becoming *accomplices* in imperialist banditry.

Footnotes

[10] Lenin is referring probably to his article "What Should Not Be Copied from the German Labour Movement", published in the Bolshevik magazine *Prosveshcheniye* in April 1914 (see *Lenin Collected Works* [*LCW*], Vol. 20, pp. 254–58). Here Lenin exposed the treacherous behaviour of Karl Legien, the German Social-Democrat who in 1912, in addressing the Congress of the U.S.A., praised U.S. official circles and bourgeois parties.

[11] Spartacists – members of the Spartacus League founded in January 1916, during the First World War, under the leadership of Karl Liebknecht, Rosa Luxemburg, Franz Mehring and Clara Zetkin. The Spartacists conducted revolutionary anti-war propaganda among the masses, and exposed the expansionist policy of German imperialism and the treachery of the Social-Democratic leaders. However, the Spartacists – the German Left wing – did not get rid of their semi-Menshevik errors on the most important questions of theory and tactics. A criticism of the German Left-wing's mistakes is given in Lenin's works "On Junius's Pamphlet" (see *LCW, Vol. 22*, pp. 297–305), "A Caricature of Marxism and Imperialist Economism" (see Vol. 23, pp. 28–76) and elsewhere.

In April 1917, the Spartacists joined the Centrist Independent Social-Democratic Party of Germany, preserving their organisational independence. After the November 1918 revolution in Germany, the Spartacists broke away from the "Independents", and in December of the same year founded the Communist Party of Germany.

[12] The reference is to Frederick Engels's letter to August Bebel, written on 18-28th March, 1875.

[13] The Treaty of Brest-Litovsk was signed between Soviet Russia and the powers of the Quadruple Alliance (Germany, Austria-Hungary, Bulgaria and Turkey) on March 3, 1918, at Brest-Litovsk and ratified on March 15 by the Fourth (Extraordinary) All-Russia Congress of Soviets. The peace terms were very harsh for Soviet Russia. According to the treaty, Poland, almost all the Baltic states, and part of Byelorussia were placed under the control of Germany and Austria-Hungary. The Ukraine was separated from Soviet Russia, becoming a state dependent on Germany. Turkey gained control of the cities of Kars, Batum and Ardagan. In August 1918, Germany imposed on Soviet Russia a supplementary treaty and a financial agreement containing new and exorbitant demands.

The treaty prevented further needless loss of life, and gave the R.S.F.S.R. the ability to shift its attention to urgent domestic matters. The signing of the Treaty of Brest-Litovsk promoted the struggle for peace among the broad masses of all the warring nations, and denounced the war as a struggle between imperialist powers. On 13th November, 1918, following the November revolution in Germany, which overthrew the monarchist regime, the All-Russia Central Executive Committee annulled the predatory Treaty of Brest-Litovsk.

[14] The reference is to the otzovists [the term otzovist derives from the Russian verb "otozvat" meaning "to recall". – Ed.] and ultimatumists, the struggle against whom developed in 1908, and in 1909 resulted in the expulsion of A. Bogdanov, the otzovist leader, from the Bolshevik Party. Behind a screen of revolutionary phrases, the otzovists demanded the recall of the Social-Democrat deputies from the Third Duma and the cessation of activities in legal organisations such as the trade unions, the co-operatives, etc. Ultimatumism was a variety of otzovism. The ultimatumists did not realise the necessity of conducting persistent day-by-day work with the Social-Democrat deputies, so as to make them consistent revolutionary parliamentarians. They proposed that an ultimatum should be presented to the Social-Democratic group in the Duma, demanding their absolute subordination to decisions of the Party's Central Committee; should the deputies fail to comply, they were to be recalled from the Duma. A conference of the enlarged editorial board of the Bolshevik paper *Proletary*, held in June 1909, pointed out in its decision that "Bolshevism, as a definite trend in the R.S.D.L.P., had nothing in common either with otzovism or with ultimatumism". The conference urged the Bolsheviks "to wage a most resolute struggle against these deviations from the path of revolutionary Marxism" (KPSS v rezolutsiyakh i resheniyakh syezdov, konferentsii i plenumov TsK [The C.P.S.U. in the Resolutions and Decisions of Its Congresses, Conferences and Plenums of the Central Committee], Part I, 1954, p. 221).

[15] On 6th (19th) August, 1905, the tsar's manifesto was made public, proclaiming the law on the setting up of the Duma and the election procedures. This body was known as the Bulygin Duma, after A.G. Bulygin, the Minister of the Interior, whom the tsar entrusted with drawing up the Duma draft. According to the latter, the Duma had no legislative functions, but could merely discuss certain questions as a consultative body under the tsar. The Bolsheviks called upon the workers and peasants to actively boycott the Bulygin Duma, and concentrate all agitation on the slogans of an armed uprising, a revolutionary army, and a provisional revolutionary government. The boycott campaign against the Bulygin Duma was used by the Bolsheviks to mobilise all the

revolutionary forces, organise mass political strikes, and prepare for an armed uprising. Elections to the Bulygin Duma were not held and the government was unable to convene it. The Duma was swept away by the mounting tide of the revolution and the all-Russia October political strike of 1905.

16 Lenin is referring to the all-Russia October political strike of 1905, during the first Russian revolution. This strike, which involved over two million people, was conducted under the slogan of the overthrow of the tsarist autocracy, an active boycott of the Bulygin Duma, the summoning of a Constituent Assembly and the establishment of a democratic republic. The all-Russia political strike showed the strength of the working-class movement, fostered the development of the revolutionary struggle in the countryside, the army and the navy. The October strike led the proletariat to the December armed uprising. Concerning the October strike, see the article by V. I. Lenin "The All-Russia Political Strike" (*LCW, Vol. 9*, pp. 392–95).

* What applies to individuals also applies – with necessary modifications – to politics and parties. It is not he who makes no mistakes that is intelligent. There are no such men, nor can there be. It is he whose errors are not very grave and who is able to rectify them easily and quickly that is intelligent.

V

"Left-Wing" Communism in Germany: The Leaders, the Party, the Class, the Masses

The German Communists we must now speak of call themselves not "Left-wingers" but, if I am not mistaken, an "opposition on principle".[17] From what follows below it will, however, be seen that they reveal all the symptoms of the "infantile disorder of Leftism".

Published by the "local group in Frankfurt am Main", a pamphlet reflecting the point of view of this opposition, and entitled *The Split in the Communist Party of Germany (The Spartacus League)* sets forth the substance of this opposition's views most saliently, and with the utmost clarity and concision. A few quotations will suffice to acquaint the reader with that substance:

"The Communist Party is the party of the most determined class struggle. . . ."

". . . Politically, the transitional period [between capitalism and socialism] is one of the proletarian dictatorship. . . ."

". . . The question arises: who is to exercise this dictatorship: the Communist Party or the proletarian class? . . . Fundamentally, should we strive for a dictatorship of the Communist Party, or for a dictatorship of the proletarian class? . . ."

(All italics as in the original)

The author of the pamphlet goes on to accuse the Central Committee of the Communist Party of Germany of seeking ways of achieving a *coalition with the Independent Social-Democratic Party of Germany*, and of raising *"the question of recognising, in principle, all political means"* of struggle, including parliamentarianism, with the sole purpose of concealing its actual and main efforts to form a coalition with the Independents. The pamphlet goes on to say:

"The opposition have chosen another road. They are of the opinion that the question of the rule of the Communist Party and of the dictatorship of the Party is merely one of tactics. In any case, rule by the Communist Party is the ultimate form of any party rule. Fundamentally, we must work for the dictatorship of the proletarian class. And all the measures of the Party, its organisations, methods of struggle, strategy and tactics should be directed to that end. Accordingly, all compromise with other parties, all reversion to parliamentary forms of struggle which have become historically and politically obsolete, and any policy of manoeuvring and compromise must be emphatically rejected." "Specifically proletarian methods of revolutionary struggle must be strongly emphasised. New forms of organisation must be created on the widest basis and with the widest scope in order to enlist the most extensive proletarian circles and strata to take part in the revolutionary struggle under the leadership of the Communist Party. A Workers' Union, based on factory organisations, should be the rallying point for all revolutionary elements. This should unite all workers who follow the slogan: 'Get out of the trade unions!' It is here that the militant proletariat musters its ranks for battle. Recognition of the class struggle, of the Soviet system and of the dictatorship should be sufficient for enrolment. All subsequent political education of the fighting masses and their political orientation in the struggle are the task of the Communist Party, which stands outside the Workers' Union. . . .

". . . Consequently, two Communist parties are now arrayed against each other:

"One is a party of leaders, which is out to organise the revolutionary struggle and to direct it from above, accepting compromises and parliamentarianism so as to create a situation enabling it to join a coalition government exercising a dictatorship.

"The other is a mass party, which expects an upsurge of the revolutionary struggle from below, which knows and applies a single method in this struggle – a method which clearly leads to the goal – and rejects all parliamentary and opportunist methods. That single method is the unconditional overthrow of the bourgeoisie, so as then to set up the proletarian class dictatorship for the accomplishment of socialism. . . .

". . . There – the dictatorship of leaders; here – the dictatorship of the masses! That is our slogan."

Such are the main features characterising the views of the opposition in the German Communist Party.

Any Bolshevik who has consciously participated in the development of Bolshevism since 1903 or has closely observed that development will at once say, after reading these arguments, "What old and familiar rubbish! What 'Left-wing' childishness!"

But let us examine these arguments a little more closely.

The mere presentation of the question – "dictatorship of the party *or* dictatorship of the class; dictatorship (party) of the leaders, *or* dictatorship (party) of the masses?" – testifies to most incredibly and hopelessly muddled thinking. These people want to *invent* something quite out of the ordinary, and, in their effort to be clever, make themselves ridiculous. It is common knowledge that the masses are divided into classes, that the masses can be contrasted with classes only by contrasting the vast majority in general, regardless of division according to status in the social system of production, with categories holding a definite status in the social system of production; that as a rule and in most cases – at least in present-day civilised countries – classes are led by political parties; that political parties, as a general rule, are run by more or less stable groups composed of the most authoritative, influential and experienced members, who are elected to the most responsible positions, and are called leaders. All this is elementary. All this is clear and simple. Why replace this with some kind of rigmarole, some new Volapük? On the one hand, these people seem to have got muddled when they found themselves in a predicament, when the party's abrupt transition from legality to illegality upset the customary, normal and simple relations between leaders, parties and classes. In Germany, as in other European countries, people had become too accustomed to legality, to the free and proper election of "leaders" at regular party congresses, to the convenient method of testing the class composition of parties through parliamentary elections, mass meetings the press, the sentiments of the trade unions and other associations, etc. When, instead of this customary procedure, it became necessary, because of the stormy development of the revolution and the development of the civil war, to go over rapidly from legality to illegality, to combine the two, and to adopt the "inconvenient" and "undemocratic" methods of selecting, or forming, or preserving "groups of leaders" – people lost their bearings and began to think up some unmitigated nonsense. Certain members of the Communist Party of Holland, who were unlucky enough to be born in a small country with traditions and conditions of highly privileged and highly stable legality, and who had never seen a transition from legality to illegality, probably fell into confusion, lost their heads, and helped create these absurd inventions.

On the other hand, one can see simply a thoughtless and incoherent use of the now "fashionable" terms: "masses" and "leaders". These people have heard and memorised a great many attacks on "leaders", in which the latter have been contrasted with the "masses"; however, they have proved unable to think matters out and gain a clear understanding of what it was all about.

The divergence between "leaders" and "masses" was brought out with particular clarity and sharpness in all countries at the end of the imperialist war and following it. The principal reason for this was explained many times by Marx and Engels between the years 1852 and 1892, from the example of Britain. That country's exclusive position led to the emergence, from the "masses", of a semi–petty-bourgeois, opportunist "labour aristocracy". The leaders of this labour aristocracy were constantly going over to the bourgeoisie, and were directly or indirectly on its pay roll. Marx earned the honour of incurring the hatred of these disreputable persons by openly branding them as traitors. Present-day (twentieth-century) imperialism has given a few advanced countries an exceptionally privileged position, which, everywhere in the Second International, has produced a certain type of traitor, opportunist, and social-chauvinist leaders, who champion the interests of their own craft, their own section of the labour aristocracy. The opportunist parties have become separated from the "masses", i.e., from the broadest strata of the working people, their majority, the lowest-paid workers. The revolutionary proletariat cannot be victorious unless this evil is combated, unless the opportunist, social-traitor leaders are exposed, discredited and expelled. That is the policy the Third International has embarked on.

To go so far, in this connection, as to contrast, *in general*, the dictatorship of the masses with a dictatorship of the leaders is ridiculously absurd, and stupid. What is particularly amusing is that, in fact, instead of the old leaders, who hold generally accepted views on simple matters, *new leaders* are brought forth (under cover of the slogan "Down with the leaders!"), who talk rank stuff and nonsense. Such are Laufenberg, Wolffheim, Horner[18], Karl Schroder, Friedrich Wendel and Karl Erler[*2], in Germany. Erler's attempts to give the question more "profundity" and to proclaim that in general political parties are unnecessary and "bourgeois" are so supremely absurd that one can only shrug one's shoulders. It all goes to drive home the truth that a minor error can always assume monstrous proportions if it is persisted in, if profound justifications are sought for it, and if it is carried to its logical conclusion. Repudiation of the Party principle and of Party discipline – that is what the opposition has *arrived at*. And this is tantamount to completely disarming the proletariat in *the interests of the bourgeoisie*. It all adds up to that petty-bourgeois diffuseness and instability, that incapacity for sustained effort, unity and organised action, which, if encouraged, must inevitably destroy any proletarian revolutionary movement. From the standpoint of communism, repudiation of the Party principle means attempting to leap from the eve of capitalism's collapse (in Germany), not to the lower or the intermediate phase of communism, but to the higher. We in Russia (in the third year since the overthrow of the bourgeoisie) are making the first steps in the transition from capitalism to socialism or the lower stage of communism. Classes still remain, and will remain everywhere *for years after* the proletariat's conquest of power. Perhaps in Britain, where there is no peasantry (but where petty proprietors exist), this period may be shorter. The abolition of classes means, not merely ousting the landowners and the capitalists – that is something we accomplished with comparative ease; it also means *abolishing the small commodity producers*, and they *cannot be ousted*, or crushed; we *must learn to live* with them. They can (and must) be transformed and re-educated only by means of very prolonged, slow, and cautious organisational work. They surround the proletariat on every side with a petty-bourgeois atmosphere, which permeates and corrupts the proletariat, and constantly causes among the proletariat relapses into petty-bourgeois spinelessness, disunity, individualism, and alternating moods of exaltation and dejection. The strictest centralisation and discipline are required within the political party of the proletariat in order to counteract this, in order that the *organisational* role of the proletariat (and that is its *principal* role) may be exercised correctly, successfully and victoriously. The dictatorship of the proletariat means a persistent struggle – bloody and bloodless, violent and peaceful, military and economic, educational and administrative – against the forces and traditions of the old society. The force of habit in millions and tens of millions is a most formidable force. Without a party of iron that has been tempered in the struggle, a party enjoying the confidence of all honest people in the class in question, a party capable of watching and influencing the mood of the masses, such a struggle cannot be waged successfully. It is a thousand times easier to vanquish the centralised big bourgeoisie than to "vanquish" the millions upon millions of petty proprietors; however, through their ordinary, everyday, imperceptible, elusive and demoralising activities, they produce the *very* results which the bourgeoisie need and which tend to *restore* the bourgeoisie. Whoever brings about even the slightest weakening of the iron discipline of the party of the proletariat (especially during its dictatorship), is actually aiding the bourgeoisie against the proletariat.

Parallel with the question of the leaders – the party – the class – the masses, we must pose the question of the "reactionary" trade unions. But first I shall take the liberty of making a few concluding remarks based on the experience of our Party. There *have always been* attacks on the "dictatorship of leaders" in our Party. The first time I heard such attacks, I recall, was in 1895, when, officially, no party yet existed, but a central group was taking shape in St. Petersburg, which was to assume the leadership of the district groups.[20] At the Ninth Congress of our Party (April 1920)[21], there was a small opposition, which also spoke against the "dictatorship of leaders", against the "oligarchy", and so on. There is therefore nothing surprising, new, or terrible in the "infantile disorder" of "Left-wing communism" among the Germans. The ailment involves no danger, and after it the organism even becomes more robust. In our case, on the other hand, the rapid alternation of legal and illegal work, which made it necessary to keep the general staff – the leaders – under cover and cloak them in the greatest secrecy, sometimes gave rise to extremely dangerous consequences. The worst of these was that in 1912 the *agent provocateur* Malinovsky got into the Bolshevik Central Committee. He betrayed scores and scores of the best and most loyal comrades, caused them to be sentenced to penal servitude, and hastened the death of many of them. That he did not cause still greater harm was due to the correct balance between legal and illegal work. As member of the Party's Central Committee and Duma deputy, Malinovsky was forced, in order to gain our confidence, to help us establish legal daily papers, which even under tsarism were able to wage a struggle against the Menshevik opportunism and to spread the fundamentals of Bolshevism in a suitably disguised form. While, with one hand, Malinovsky sent scores and scores of the finest Bolsheviks to penal servitude and death, he was obliged, with the other, to assist in the education of scores and scores of thousands of new Bolsheviks through the medium of the legal press. Those German (and also British, American, French and Italian) comrades who are faced with the task of learning how to conduct revolutionary work within the reactionary trade unions would do well to give serious thought to this fact.[*3]

In many countries, including the most advanced, the bourgeoisie are undoubtedly sending *agents provocateurs* into the Communist parties and will continue to do so. A skilful combining of illegal and legal work is one of the ways to combat this danger.

Footnotes

[17] The "opposition on principle" – a group of German Left-wing Communists advocating anarcho-syndicalist views. When the Second Congress of the Communist Party of Germany, which was held in Heidelberg in October 1919, expelled the opposition, the latter formed the so-called Communist Workers' Party of Germany, in April 1920. To facilitate the unification of all German communist forces and win over the finest proletarian. elements in the C.W.P.G., the opposition was temporarily admitted into the Communist International in November 1920 with the rights of a sympathising member.

However, the Executive Committee of the Communist International still considered the United Communist Party of Germany to be the only authoritative section of the Comintern. C.W.P.G.'s representatives were admitted into the Comintern on the condition that they merged with the United Communist Party of Germany and supported all its activities. The C.W.P.G. leaders, however, failed to observe these conditions. The Third Congress of the Communist International, which was held in June–July 1921, and wanted solidarity with workers who still followed the C.W.P.G. leaders, resolved to give the C.W.P.G. two months to call a congress and settle the question of affiliation. The C.W.P.G. Leaders did not obey the Third Congress's resolution and thus placed themselves outside the Communist International. Later the C.W.P.G. degenerated into a small sectarian group without any support in the working class.

[18] Horner, Karl – Anton Pannekoek.

[19] The reference is to the League of Struggle for the Emancipation of the Working Class organised by V. I. Lenin in the autumn of 1895. The League of Struggle united about twenty Marxist circles in St. Petersburg. It was headed by the Central Group including V. I. Lenin, A. A. Vaneyev, P. K. Zaporozhets, G. M. Krzhizhanovsky, N. K. Krupskaya, L. Martov, M. A. Silvin, V. V. Starkov, and others; five members headed by V. I. Lenin directed the League's activities. The organisation was divided into district groups. Progressive workers such as I. V. Babushkin, V. A. Shelgunov and others linked these groups with the factories.

The St. Petersburg League of Struggle for the Emancipation of the Working Class was, in V. I. Lenin's words, the embryo of a revolutionary party based on the working-class movement and giving leadership to the class struggle of the proletariat.

[21] The Congress was held in Moscow from 29th March to 5th April, 1920. The Ninth Congress was more numerous than any previous Party congresses. It was attended by 715 delegates – 553 of them with full votes, and 162 with deliberative votes – representing a membership of 611,978. Represented were the Party organisations of Central Russia, the Ukraine, the Urals, Siberia and other regions recently liberated by the Red Army. Many of the delegates came to the Congress straight from the front.

The agenda of the Congress was as follows:

1. The report of the Central Committee.
2. The immediate tasks of economic construction.
3. The trade union movement.
4. Organisational questions.
5. The tasks of the Communist International.
6. The attitude towards the co-operatives.

7. The change-over to the militia system.
8. Elections to the Central Committee.
9. Miscellaneous.

The Congress was held under the guidance of V. I. Lenin, who was the main speaker on the political work of the Central Committee and replied to the debate on the report. He also spoke on economic construction and co-operation, made the speech at the closing of the Congress, and submitted a proposal on the list of candidates to the Party's Central Committee.

In the resolution "The Immediate Tasks of Economic Development" the Congress noted that "the basic condition of economic rehabilitation of the country is a steady implementation of the single economic plan for the coming historical epoch" (KPSS v rezolutsiyakh i resheniyakh syezdov, konferentsii i plenumov TsK [The C.P.S.U. in the Resolutions and Decisions of Its Congresses, Conferences and Plenums of the Central Committee], Part I, 1954, p. 478). The kingpin of the single economic plan was electrification, which V. I. Lenin considered a great programme for a period of 10 to 20 years. The directives of the Ninth Congress were the basis of the plan conclusively drawn up by the State Commission for the Electrification of Russia (the GOELRO plan) and approved by the All-Russia Congress of Soviets in December 1920.

The Congress paid particular attention to the organisation of industrial management. The resolution on this question called for the establishment of competent, firm and energetic one-man management. Taking its guidance from Lenin, the Congress especially stressed the necessity to extensively enlist old and experienced experts.

The anti-Party group of Democratic Centralists, consisting of Sapronov, Osinsky, V. Smirnov and others, came out against the Party line. Behind a cover of phrases about Democratic Centralism but in fact distorting that principle, they denied the need for one-man management at factories, came out against strict Party and state discipline, and alleged that the Central Committee did not give effect to the principle of collective leadership.

The group of Democratic Centralists was supported at the Congress by Rykov, Tomsky, Milyutin and Lomov. The Congress rebuffed the Democratic Centralists and rejected their proposals.

The Congress gave special attention to labour emulation and communist Subbotniks. To stimulate such emulation, the extensive application of the bonus system of wages was recommended. The Congress resolved that 1st May, the international proletarian holiday, which in 1920 fell on Saturday, should be a mass Subbotnik organised throughout Russia.

An important place in the work of the Congress was held by the question of trade unions, which was considered from the viewpoint of adapting the entire work of the trade unions to the accomplishment of the economic tasks. In a resolution on this question, the Congress distinctly defined the trade unions' role, their relations with the state and the Party, forms and methods of guidance of trade unions by the Communist Party, as well as forms of their participation in communist construction. The Congress decisively rebuffed the anarcho-syndicalist elements (Shlyapnikov, Lozovsky, Tomsky and Lutovinov), who advocated the "independence" of the trade unions and contraposed them to the Communist Party and the Soviet government.

At a closed meeting held on 4th April, the Congress elected a new Central Committee of 19 members and 12 candidate members. The former included V.I. Lenin, A. A. Andreyev, F. E. Dzerzhinsky, M. I. Kalinin, Y. E. Rudzutak, F. A. Sergeyev (Artyom), and J. V. Stalin. On 5th April the Congress concluded its work.

[*2] Karl Erler, "The Dissolution of the Party", *Kommunistische Arbeiterzeitung*,[20] Hamburg, 7th February, 1920, No. 32:

"The working class cannot destroy the bourgeois state without destroying bourgeois democracy, and it cannot destroy bourgeois democracy without destroying parties."

The more muddle-headed of the syndicalists and anarchists in the Latin countries may derive "satisfaction" from the fact that solid Germans, who evidently consider themselves Marxists (by their articles in the above-mentioned paper K. Erler and K. Horner have shown most plainly that they consider themselves sound Marxists, but talk incredible nonsense in a most ridiculous manner and reveal their failure to understand the ABC of Marxism), go to the length of making utterly inept statements. Mere acceptance of Marxism does not save one from errors. We Russians know this especially well, because Marxism has been very often the "fashion" in our country.

*3 Malinovsky was a prisoner of war in Germany. On his return to Russia when the Bolsheviks were in power he was instantly put on trial and shot by our workers. The Mensheviks attacked us most bitterly for our mistake – the fact that an agent provocateur had become a member of the Central Committee of our Party. But when, under Kerensky, we demanded the arrest and trial of Rodzyanko, the Chairman of the Duma, because he had known, even before the war, that Malinovsky was an agent provocateur and had not informed the Trudoviks and the workers in the Duma, neither the Mensheviks nor the Socialist-Revolutionaries in the Kerensky government supported our demand, and Rodzyanko remained at large and made off unhindered to join Denikin.

20 *Kommunistische Arbeiterzeitung* (The Communist Workers' Newspaper) – organ of the anarcho-syndicalist group of the German Leftwing Communists (see Note 17). The newspaper was published in Hamburg from 1919 till 1927. Karl Erler, who is mentioned by V. I. Lenin, was Heinrich Laufenberg's pen-name.

VI

Should Revolutionaries Work in Reactionary Trade Unions?

The German "Lefts" consider that, as far as they are concerned, the reply to this question is an unqualified negative. In their opinion, declamations and angry outcries (such as uttered by K. Horner in a particularly "solid" and particularly stupid manner) against "reactionary" and "counter-revolutionary" trade unions are sufficient "proof" that it is unnecessary and even inexcusable for revolutionaries and Communists to work in yellow, social-chauvinist, compromising and counter-revolutionary trade unions of the Legien type.

However firmly the German "Lefts" may be convinced of the revolutionism of such tactics, the latter are in fact fundamentally wrong, and contain nothing but empty phrases.

To make this clear, I shall begin with our own experience, in keeping with the general plan of the present pamphlet, which is aimed at applying to Western Europe whatever is universally practicable, significant and relevant in the history and the present-day tactics of Bolshevism.

In Russia today, the connection between leaders, party, class and masses, as well as the attitude of the dictatorship of the proletariat and its party to the trade unions, are concretely as follows: the dictatorship is exercised by the proletariat organised in the Soviets; the proletariat is guided by the Communist Party of Bolsheviks, which, according to the figures of the latest Party Congress (April 1920), has a membership of 611,000. The membership varied greatly both before and after the October Revolution, and used to be much smaller, even in 1918 and 1919.[22] We are apprehensive of an excessive growth of the Party, because careerists and charlatans, who deserve only to be shot, inevitably do all they can to insinuate themselves into the ranks of the ruling party. The last time we opened wide the doors of the Party – to workers and peasants only – was when (in the winter of 1919) Yudenich was within a few versts of Petrograd, and Denikin was in Orel (about 350 versts from Moscow), i.e., when the Soviet Republic was in mortal danger, and when adventurers, careerists, charlatans and unreliable persons generally could not possibly count on making a profitable career (and had more reason to expect the gallows and torture) by joining the Communists.[23] The Party, which holds annual congresses (the most recent on the basis of one delegate per 1,000 members), is directed by a Central Committee of nineteen elected at the Congress, while the current work in Moscow has to be carried on by still smaller bodies, known as the Organising Bureau and the Political Bureau, which are elected at plenary meetings of the Central Committee, five members of the Central Committee to each bureau. This, it would appear, is a full-fledged "oligarchy". No important political or organisational question is decided by any state institution in our republic without the guidance of the Party's Central Committee.

In its work, the Party relies directly on the *trade unions*, which, according to the data of the last congress (April 1920), now have a membership of over four million and are formally *non-Party*. Actually, all the directing bodies of the vast majority of the unions, and primarily, of course, of the all-Russia general trade union centre or bureau (the All-Russia Central Council of Trade Unions), are made up of Communists and carry out all the directives of the Party. Thus, on the whole, we have a formally non-communist, flexible and relatively wide and very powerful proletarian apparatus, by means of which the Party is closely linked up with the *class* and the *masses*, and by means of which, under the leadership of the Party, the *class dictatorship* is exercised. Without close contacts with the trade unions, and without their energetic support and devoted efforts, not only in economic, *but also in military* affairs, it would of course have been impossible for us to govern the country and to maintain the dictatorship for two and a half months, let alone two and a half years. In practice, these very close contacts naturally call for highly complex and diversified work in the form of propaganda, agitation, timely and frequent conferences, not only with the leading trade union workers, but with influential trade union workers generally; they call for a determined struggle against the Mensheviks, who still have a certain though very small following to whom they teach all kinds of counter-revolutionary machinations, ranging from an ideological defence of (*bourgeois*) democracy and the preaching that the trade unions should be "independent" (independent of proletarian state power!) to sabotage of proletarian discipline, etc., etc.

We consider that contacts with the "masses" through the trade unions are not enough. In the course of our revolution, practical activities have given rise to such institutions as *non-Party workers' and peasants' conferences*, and we strive by every means to support, develop and extend this institution in order to be able to observe the temper of the masses, come closer to them, meet their requirements, promote the best among them to state posts, etc. Under a recent decree on the transformation of the People's Commissariat of State Control into the Workers' and Peasants' Inspection, non-Party conferences of this kind have been empowered to select members of the State Control to carry out various kinds of investigations, etc.

Then, of course, all the work of the Party is carried on through the Soviets, which embrace the working masses irrespective of occupation. The district congresses of Soviets are *democratic* institutions, the like of which even the best of the democratic republics of the bourgeois world have never known; through these congresses (whose proceedings the Party endeavours to follow with the closest attention), as well as by continually appointing class-conscious workers to various posts in the rural districts, the proletariat exercises its role of leader of the peasantry, gives effect to the dictatorship of the urban proletariat wages a systematic struggle against the rich, bourgeois, exploiting and profiteering peasantry, etc.

Such is the general mechanism of the proletarian state power viewed "from above", from the standpoint of the practical implementation of the dictatorship. We hope that the reader will understand why the Russian Bolshevik who has known this mechanism for twenty-five years and has seen it develop out of small, illegal and underground circles, cannot help regarding all this talk about "from above" *or* "from below", about the dictatorship of leaders *or* the dictatorship of the masses, etc., as ridiculous and childish nonsense, something like discussing whether a man's left leg or right arm is of greater use to him.

We cannot but regard as equally ridiculous and childish nonsense the pompous, very learned, and frightfully revolutionary disquisitions of the German Lefts to the effect that Communists cannot and should not work in reactionary trade unions, that it is permissible to turn down such work, that it is necessary to withdraw from the trade unions and create a brand-new and immaculate "Workers' Union" invented by very pleasant (and, probably, for the most part very youthful) Communists, etc., etc.

Capitalism inevitably leaves socialism the legacy, on the one hand, of the old trade and craft distinctions among the workers, distinctions evolved in the course of centuries; on the other hand, trade unions, which only very slowly, in the course of years and years, can and will develop into broader industrial unions with less of the craft union about them (embracing entire industries, and not only crafts, trades and occupations), and later proceed, through these industrial unions, to eliminate the division of labour among people, to educate and school people, give them *all-round development and an all-round* training, so that they *are able to do everything*. Communism is advancing and must advance towards that goal, and *will reach* it, but only after very many years. To attempt in practice, today, to anticipate this future result of a fully developed, fully stabilised and constituted, fully comprehensive and mature communism would be like trying to teach higher mathematics to a child of four.

We can (and must) begin to build socialism, not with abstract human material, or with human material specially prepared by us, but with the human material bequeathed to us by capitalism. True, that is no easy matter, but no other approach to this task is serious enough to warrant discussion.

The trade unions were a tremendous step forward for the working class in the early days of capitalist development, inasmuch as they marked a transition from the workers' disunity and helplessness to the *rudiments* of class organisation. When the *revolutionary party of the proletariat*, the *highest* form of proletarian class organisation, began to take shape (and the Party will not merit the name until it learns to weld the leaders into one indivisible whole with the class and the masses) the trade unions inevitably began to reveal *certain* reactionary features, a certain craft narrow-mindedness, a certain tendency to be non-political, a certain inertness, etc. However, the development of the proletariat did not, and could not, proceed anywhere in the world otherwise than through the trade unions, through reciprocal action between them and the party of the working class. The proletariat's conquest of political power is a gigantic step forward for the proletariat as a class, and the Party must more than ever and in a new way, not only in the old, educate and guide the trade unions, at the same time bearing in mind that they are and will long remain an indispensable "school of communism" and a preparatory school that trains proletarians to exercise their dictatorship, an indispensable organisation of the workers for the gradual transfer of the management of the whole economic life of the country to the working *class* (and not to the separate trades), and later to all the working people.

In the sense mentioned above, a *certain* "reactionism" in the trade unions is *inevitable* under the dictatorship of the proletariat. Not to understand this means a complete failure to understand the fundamental conditions of the *transition* from capitalism to socialism. It would be egregious folly to fear *this* "reactionism" or to try to *evade* or leap over it, for it would mean fearing that function of the proletarian vanguard which consists in training, educating, enlightening and drawing into the new life the most backward strata and masses of the working class and the peasantry. On the other hand, it would be a still graver error to postpone the achievement of the dictatorship of the proletariat until a time when there will not be a single worker with a narrow-minded craft outlook, or with craft and craft-union prejudices. The art of politics (and the Communist's correct understanding of his tasks) consists in correctly gauging the conditions and the moment when the vanguard of the proletariat can successfully assume power, when it is able – during and after the seizure of power – to win adequate support from sufficiently broad strata of the working class and of the non-proletarian working masses, and when it is able thereafter to maintain, consolidate and extend its rule by educating, training and attracting ever broader masses of the working people.

Furthermore, in countries more advanced than Russia, a certain reactionism in the trade unions has been and was bound to be manifested in a far greater measure than in our country. Our Mensheviks found support in the trade unions (and to some extent still do so in a small number of unions), as a result of the latter's craft narrow-mindedness, craft selfishness and opportunism. The Mensheviks of the West have acquired a much firmer footing in the trade unions; there the *craft-union, narrow-minded, selfish, case-hardened, covetous, and petty-bourgeois "labour aristocracy", imperialist-minded, and imperialist-corrupted*, has developed into a much stronger section than in our country. That is incontestable. The struggle against the Gomperses, and against the Jouhaux, Hendersons, Merrheims, Legiens and Co. in Western Europe is much more difficult than the struggle against our Mensheviks, who are an *absolutely homogeneous* social and political type. This struggle must be waged ruthlessly, and it must unfailingly be brought – as we brought it – to a point when all the incorrigible leaders of opportunism and social-chauvinism are completely discredited and driven out of the trade unions. Political power cannot be captured (and the attempt to capture it should not be made) until the struggle has reached a *certain* stage. This "certain stage" will be *different* in different countries and in different circumstances; it can be correctly gauged only by thoughtful, experienced and knowledgeable political leaders of the proletariat in each particular country. (In Russia the elections to the Constituent Assembly in November 1917, a few days after the proletarian revolution of 25th October, 1917, were one of the criteria of the success of this struggle. In these elections the Mensheviks were utterly defeated; they received 700,000 votes – 1,400,000 if the vote in Transcaucasia is added – as against 9,000,000 votes polled by the Bolsheviks. See my article, "The Constituent Assembly Elections and the Dictatorship of the Proletariat"[24], in the *Communist International*[25] No. 7–8.)

We are waging a struggle against the "labour aristocracy" in the name of the masses of the workers and in order to win them over to our side; we are waging the struggle against the opportunist and social-chauvinist leaders in order to win the working class over to our side. It would be absurd to forget this most elementary and most self-evident truth. Yet it is this very absurdity that the German "Left" Communists perpetrate when, *because* of the reactionary and counter-revolutionary character of the trade union *top leadership*, they jump to the conclusion that . . . we must withdraw from the trade unions, refuse to work in them, and create new and *artificial* forms of labour organisation! This is so unpardonable a blunder that it is tantamount to the greatest service Communists could render the bourgeoisie. Like all the opportunist, social-chauvinist, and Kautskyite trade union leaders, our Mensheviks are nothing but "agents of the bourgeoisie in the working-class movement" (as we have always said the Mensheviks are), or "labour lieutenants of the capitalist class", to use the splendid and profoundly true expression of the followers of Daniel De Leon in America. To refuse to work in the reactionary trade unions means leaving the insufficiently developed or backward masses of workers under the influence of the reactionary leaders, the agents of the bourgeoisie, the labour aristocrats, or "workers who have become completely bourgeois" (cf. Engels's letter to Marx in 1858 about the British workers[26]).

This ridiculous "theory" that Communists should not work in reactionary trade unions reveals with the utmost clarity the frivolous attitude of the "Left" Communists towards the question of influencing the "masses", and their misuse of clamour about the "masses". If you want to help the "masses" and win the sympathy and support of the "masses", you should not fear difficulties, or pinpricks, chicanery, insults and persecution from the "leaders" (who, being opportunists and social-chauvinists, are in most cases directly or indirectly connected with the bourgeoisie and the police), but must absolutely *work wherever the masses are to be found*. You must be capable of any sacrifice, of overcoming the greatest obstacles, in order to carry on agitation and propaganda systematically, perseveringly, persistently and patiently in those institutions, societies and associations – even the most reactionary – in which proletarian or semi-proletarian masses are to be found. The trade unions and the workers' co-operatives (the latter sometimes, at least) are the very organisations in which the masses are to be found. According to figures quoted in the Swedish paper *Folkets Dagblad Politiken* of March 10, 1920, the trade union membership in Great Britain increased from 5,500,000 at the end of 1917 to 6,600,000 at the end of 1918, an increase of 19 per cent. Towards the close of 1919, the membership was estimated at 7,500,000. I have not got the corresponding figures for France and Germany to hand, but absolutely incontestable and generally known facts testify to a rapid rise in the trade union membership in these countries too.

These facts make crystal clear something that is confirmed by thousands of other symptoms, namely, that class-consciousness and the desire for organisation are growing among the proletarian masses, among the rank and file, among the backward elements. Millions of workers in Great Britain, France and Germany are *for the first time* passing from a complete lack of organisation to the elementary, lowest, simplest, and (to those still thoroughly imbued with bourgeois-democratic prejudices) most easily comprehensible form of organisation, namely, the trade unions; yet the revolutionary but imprudent Left Communists stand by, crying out "the masses, the masses!" but *refusing to work within the trade unions*, on the pretext that they are "reactionary", and invent a brand-new, immaculate little "Workers' Union", which is guiltless of bourgeois-democratic prejudices and innocent of craft or narrow-minded craft-union sins, a union which, they claim, will be (!) a broad organisation. "Recognition of the Soviet system and the dictatorship" will be the *only* (!) condition of membership. (See the passage quoted above.)

It would be hard to imagine any greater ineptitude or greater harm to the revolution than that caused by the "Left" revolutionaries! Why, if we in Russia today, after two and a half years of unprecedented victories over the bourgeoisie of Russia and the Entente, were to make "recognition of the dictatorship" a condition of trade union membership, we would be doing a very foolish thing, damaging our influence among the masses, and helping the Mensheviks. The task devolving on Communists is to *convince* the backward elements, to work *among* them, and not to *fence themselves off* from them with artificial and childishly "Left" slogans.

There can be no doubt that the Gomperses, the Hendersons, the Jonhaux and the Legiens are very grateful to those "Left" revolutionaries who, like the German opposition "on principle" (heaven preserve us from such "principles"!), or like some of the revolutionaries in the American Industrial Workers of the World[27] advocate quitting the reactionary trade unions and refusing to work in them. These men, the "leaders" of opportunism, will no doubt resort to every device of bourgeois diplomacy and to the aid of bourgeois governments, the clergy, the police and the courts, to keep Communists out of the trade unions, oust them by every means, make their work in the trade unions as unpleasant as possible, and insult, bait and persecute them. We must be able to stand up to all this, agree to make any sacrifice, and even – if need be – to resort to various stratagems, artifices and illegal methods, to evasions and subterfuges, as long as we get into the trade unions, remain in them, and carry on communist work within them at all costs. Under tsarism we had no "legal opportunities" whatsoever until 1905. However, when Zubatov, agent of the secret police, organised Black-Hundred workers' assemblies and workingmen's societies for the purpose of trapping revolutionaries and combating them, we sent members of our Party to these assemblies and into these societies (I personally remember one of them, Comrade Babushkin, a leading St. Petersburg factory worker, shot by order of the tsar's generals in 1906). They established contacts with the masses, were able to carry on their agitation, and succeeded in wresting workers from the influence of Zubatov's agents.[*4] Of course, in Western Europe, which is imbued with most deep-rooted legalistic, constitutionalist and bourgeois-democratic prejudices, this is more difficult to achieve. However, it can and must be carried out, and systematically at that.

The Executive Committee of the Third International must, in my opinion, positively condemn, and call upon the next congress of the Communist International to condemn both the policy of refusing to work in reactionary trade unions in general (explaining in detail why such refusal is unwise, and what extreme harm it does to the cause of the proletarian revolution) and, in particular, the line of conduct of some members of the Communist Party of Holland, who – whether directly or indirectly, overtly or covertly, wholly or partly, it does not matter – have supported this erroneous policy. The Third International must break with the tactics of the Second International, it must not evade or play down points at issue, but must pose them in a straightforward fashion. The whole truth has been put squarely to the "Independents"; the whole truth must likewise be put squarely to the "Left" Communists.

Footnotes

[22] Between the February 1917 Revolution and 1919 inclusively, the Party's membership changed as follows: by the Seventh All-Russia Conference of the R.S.D.L.P.(B.) (April 1917) the Party numbered 80,000 members, by the Sixth R.S.D.L.P.(B.) Congress in July–August 1917 – about 240,000, by the Seventh Congress of the R.C.P.(B.) in March 1918 – not less than 270,000; by the Eighth Congress of the R.C.P.(B.) in March 1919 – 313,766 members.

[23] The reference is to Party Week, which was held in accordance with the resolution of the Eighth Congress of the R.C.P.(B.) on building up the Party's membership. The Party Week was conducted in conditions of the bitter struggle waged by the Soviet state against the foreign intervention and domestic counterrevolution. Party Week was first held in the Petrograd organisation of the R.C.P.(B.), 10th-17th August, 1919 (the second Party Week was held in Petrograd in October–November 1919); between 20th and 28th September a Party Week was held in the Moscow Gubernia organisation. Summarising the experience of the first Party Weeks, the Plenum of the Central Committee of the R.C.P.(B.), held on September 26, 1919, resolved that Party Weeks should be held in cities, the countryside and the army. At the end of September, the Central Committee addressed a circular to all Party organisations pointing out that, as the re-registration and purge of the membership had been accomplished in almost all Party organisations, new members might be enrolled. The Central Committee stressed that during Party Weeks only industrial workers, peasants, and Red Army and Navy men should be admitted into the Party. As a result of Party Weeks, over 200,000 joined the Party in 38 gubernias of the European part of the R.S.F.S.R., more than a half of them being industrial workers. Over 25 per cent of the armed forces' strength joined the Party at the fronts.

[24] See *LCW, Vol. 30*, pp. 253–75.

[25] The Communist International – a journal, organ of the Executive Committee of the Communist International. It was published in Russian, German, French, English, Spanish and Chinese, the first issue appearing on 1st May, 1919.

The journal published theoretical articles and documents of the Comintern, including a number of articles by Lenin. It elucidated the fundamental questions of Marxist-Leninist theory in connection with problems confronting the international working-class and communist movement and the experience of socialist construction in the Soviet Union. It also waged a struggle against various anti-Leninist tendencies.

Publication of the journal ceased in June 1943 in connection with the resolution adopted by the Presidium of the Comintern's Executive Committee on 15th May, 1943, on the dissolution of the Communist International.

[26] See Karl Marx and Frederick Engels, *Selected Correspondence*, Moscow, 1965, p. 110.

[27] The Industrial Workers of the World (I.W.W.) – a workers' trade union organisation, founded in the U.S.A. in 1905, and in the main organising unskilled and low-paid workers of various trades. Among its founders were such working-class leaders as Daniel De Leon, Eugene Debs and William Haywood. I.W.W. organisations were also set up in Canada, Australia, Britain, Latin America and South Africa. In conditions of the mass strike movement in the U.S.A., which

developed under the influence of the Russian revolution of 1905–07, the I.W.W. organised a number of successful mass strikes, waged a struggle against the policy of class collaboration conducted by reformist leaders of the American Federation of Labor and Right-wing socialists. During the First World War of 1914–18, the organisation led a number of mass anti-war actions by the American working class. Some I.W.W. leaders, among them William Haywood, welcomed the Great October Socialist Revolution and joined the Communist Party of the U.S.A. At the same time, anarcho-syndicalist features showed up in I.W.W. activities: it did not recognise the proletariat's political struggle, denied the Party's leading role and the necessity of the proletarian dictatorship, and refused to carry on work among the membership of the American Federation of Labor. In 1920 the organisation's anarcho-syndicalist leaders took advantage of the imprisonment of many revolutionaries and against the will of the trade union masses, rejected appeal by the Comintern's Executive Committee that they join the Communist International. As a result of the leaders' opportunist policy, the I.W.W. degenerated into a sectarian organisation, which soon lost all influence on the working-class movement.

*4 The Gomperses, Hendersons, Jouhaux and Legiens are nothing but Zubatovs, differing from our Zubatov only in their European garb and polish, and the civilised, refined and democratically suave manner of conducting their despicable policy.

VII

Should We Participate in Bourgeois Parliaments?

It is with the utmost contempt – and the utmost levity – that the German "Left" Communists reply to this question in the negative. Their arguments? In the passage quoted above we read:

> ". . . All reversion to parliamentary forms of struggle, which have become historically and politically obsolete, must be emphatically rejected. . . ."

This is said with ridiculous pretentiousness, and is patently wrong. "Reversion" to parliamentarianism, forsooth! Perhaps there is already a Soviet republic in Germany? It does not look like it! How, then, can one speak of "reversion"? Is this not an empty phrase?

Parliamentarianism has become "historically obsolete". That is true in the propaganda sense. However, everybody knows that this is still a far cry from overcoming it in *practice*. Capitalism could have been declared – and with full justice – to be "historically obsolete" many decades ago, but that does not at all remove the need for a very long and very persistent struggle *on the basis* of capitalism. Parliamentarianism is "historically obsolete" from the standpoint of *world history*, i.e., the *era* of bourgeois parliamentarianism is over, and the *era* of the proletarian dictatorship has *begun*. That is incontestable. But world history is counted in decades. Ten or twenty years earlier or later makes no difference when measured with the yardstick of world history; from the standpoint of world history it is a trifle that cannot be considered even approximately. But for that very reason, it is a glaring theoretical error to apply the yardstick of world history to practical politics.

Is parliamentarianism "politically obsolete"? That is quite a different matter. If that were true, the position of the "Lefts" would be a strong one. But it has to be proved by a most searching analysis, and the "Lefts" do not even know how to approach the matter. In the "Theses on Parliamentarianism", published in the *Bulletin of the Provisional Bureau in Amsterdam of the Communist International* No. 1, February 1920, and obviously expressing the Dutch-Left or Left-Dutch strivings, the analysis, as we shall see, is also hopelessly poor.

In the first place, contrary to the opinion of such outstanding political leaders as Rosa Luxemburg and Karl Liebknecht, the German "Lefts", as we know, considered parliamentarianism "politically obsolete" even in January 1919. We know that the "Lefts" were mistaken. This fact alone utterly destroys, at a single stroke, the proposition that parliamentarianism is "politically obsolete". It is for the "Lefts" to prove why their error, indisputable at that time, is no longer an error. They do not and cannot produce even a shred of proof. A political party's attitude towards its own mistakes is one of the most important and surest ways of judging how earnest the party is and how it fulfils *in practice* its obligations towards its *class* and the *working people*. Frankly acknowledging a mistake, ascertaining the reasons for it, analysing the conditions that have led up to it, and thrashing out the means of its rectification – that is the hallmark of a serious party; that is how it should perform its duties, and how it should educate and train its *class*, and then the *masses*. By failing to fulfil this duty and give the utmost attention and consideration to the study of their patent error, the "Lefts" in Germany (and in Holland) have proved that they are not a *party of a class*, but a circle, not a *party of the masses*, but a group of intellectualists and of a few workers who ape the worst features of intellectualism.

Second, in the same pamphlet of the Frankfurt group of "Lefts", which we have already cited in detail, we read:

> "... *The millions of workers who still follow the policy of the Centre [the Catholic 'Centre' Party] are counter-revolutionary. The rural proletarians provide the legions of counter-revolutionary troops." (Page 3 of the pamphlet)*

Everything goes to show that this statement is far too sweeping and exaggerated. But the basic fact set forth here is incontrovertible, and its acknowledgment by the "Lefts" is particularly clear evidence of their mistake. How can one say that "parliamentarianism is politically obsolete", when "millions" and "legions" of *proletarians* are not only still in favour of parliamentarianism in general, but are downright "counter-revolutionary"!? It is obvious that parliamentarianism in Germany is *not yet* politically obsolete. It is obvious that the "Lefts" in Germany have mistaken *their desire*, their politico-ideological attitude, for objective reality. That is a most dangerous mistake for revolutionaries to make. In Russia – where, over a particularly long period and in particularly varied forms, the most brutal and savage yoke of tsarism produced revolutionaries of diverse shades, revolutionaries who displayed amazing devotion, enthusiasm, heroism and will power – in Russia we have observed this mistake of the revolutionaries at very close quarters; we have studied it very attentively and have a first-hand knowledge of it; that is why we can also see it especially clearly in others. Parliamentarianism is of course "politically obsolete" to the Communists in Germany; but – and that is the whole point – we must *not* regard what is obsolete *to us* as something obsolete *to a class, to the masses*. Here again we find that the "Lefts" do not know how to reason, do not know how to act as the party of a *class*, as the party of the *masses*. You must not sink to the level of the masses, to the level of the backward strata of the class. That is incontestable. You must tell them the bitter truth. You are in duty bound to call their bourgeois-democratic and parliamentary prejudices what they are – prejudices. But at the same time you must *soberly* follow the *actual* state of the class-consciousness and preparedness of the entire class (not only of its communist vanguard), and of all the *working people* (not only of their advanced elements).

Even if only a fairly large *minority* of the industrial workers, and not "millions" and "legions", follow the lead of the Catholic clergy – and a similar minority of rural workers follow the landowners and kulaks (Grossbauern) – it *undoubtedly* signifies that parliamentarianism in Germany has not *yet* politically outlived itself, that participation in parliamentary elections and in the struggle on the parliamentary rostrum is *obligatory* on the party of the revolutionary proletariat *specifically* for the purpose of educating the backward strata of *its own class*, and for the purpose of awakening and enlightening the undeveloped, downtrodden and ignorant rural *masses*. Whilst you lack the strength to do away with bourgeois parliaments and every other type of reactionary institution, you *must* work within them because *it is there* that you will still find workers who are duped by the priests and stultified by the conditions of rural life; otherwise you risk turning into nothing but windbags.

Third, the "Left" Communists have a great deal to say in praise of us Bolsheviks. One sometimes feels like telling them to praise us less and to try to get a better knowledge of the Bolsheviks' tactics. We took part in the elections to the Constituent Assembly, the Russian bourgeois parliament in September–November 1917. Were our tactics correct or not? If not, then this should be clearly stated and proved, for it is necessary in evolving the correct tactics for international communism. If they were correct, then certain conclusions must be drawn. Of course, there can be no question of placing conditions in Russia on a par with conditions in Western Europe. But as regards the particular question of the meaning of the concept that "parliamentarianism has become politically obsolete", due account should be taken of our experience, for unless concrete experience is taken into account such concepts very easily turn into empty phrases. In September–November 1917, did we, the Russian Bolsheviks, not have *more* right than any Western Communists to consider that parliamentarianism was politically obsolete in Russia? Of course we did, for the point is not whether bourgeois parliaments have existed for a long time or a short time, but how far the masses of the working people are *prepared* (ideologically, politically and practically) to accept the Soviet system and to dissolve the bourgeois-democratic parliament (or allow it to be dissolved). It is an absolutely incontestable and fully established historical fact that, in September–November 1917, the urban working class and the soldiers and peasants of Russia were, because of a number of special conditions, exceptionally well prepared to accept the Soviet system and to disband the most democratic of bourgeois parliaments. Nevertheless, the Bolsheviks did *not* boycott the Constituent Assembly, but took part in the elections both before *and after* the proletariat conquered political power. That these elections yielded exceedingly valuable (and to the proletariat, highly useful) political results has, I make bold to hope, been proved by me in the above-mentioned article, which analyses in detail the returns of the elections to the Constituent Assembly in Russia.

The conclusion which follows from this is absolutely incontrovertible: it has been proved that, far from causing harm to the revolutionary proletariat, participation in a bourgeois-democratic parliament, even a few weeks before the victory of a Soviet republic and even *after* such a victory, actually helps that proletariat to *prove* to the backward masses why such parliaments deserve to be done away with; it *facilitates* their successful dissolution, and *helps* to make bourgeois parliamentarianism "politically obsolete". To ignore this experience, while at the same time claiming affiliation to the Communist *International*, which must work out its tactics internationally (not as narrow or exclusively national tactics, but as international tactics), means committing a gross error and actually abandoning internationalism in deed, while recognising it in word.

Now let us examine the "Dutch-Left" arguments in favour of non-participation in parliaments. The following is the text of Thesis No. 4, the most important of the above-mentioned "Dutch" theses:

> *"When the capitalist system of production has broken down, and society is in a state of revolution, parliamentary action gradually loses importance as compared with the action of the masses themselves. When, in these conditions, parliament becomes the centre and organ of the counter-revolution, whilst, on the other hand, the labouring class builds up the instruments of its power in the Soviets, it may even prove necessary to abstain from all and any participation in parliamentary action."*

The first sentence is obviously wrong, since action by the masses, a big strike, for instance, is more important than parliamentary activity at *all* times, and not only during a revolution or in a revolutionary situation. This obviously untenable and historically and politically incorrect argument merely shows very clearly that the authors completely ignore both the general European experience (the French experience before the revolutions of 1848 and 1870; the German experience of 1878–90, etc.) and the Russian experience (see above) of the importance of *combining* legal and illegal struggle. This question is of immense importance both in general and in particular, because in *all* civilised and advanced countries the time is rapidly approaching when such a combination will more and more become – and has already partly become – mandatory on the party of the revolutionary proletariat, inasmuch as civil war between the proletariat and the bourgeoisie is maturing and is imminent, and because of savage persecution of the Communists by republican governments and bourgeois governments generally, which resort to any violation of legality (the example of America is edifying enough), etc. The Dutch, and the Lefts in general, have utterly failed to understand this highly important question.

The second sentence is, in the first place, historically wrong. We Bolsheviks participated in the most counterrevolutionary parliaments, and experience has shown that this participation was not only useful but indispensable to the party of the revolutionary proletariat, after the first bourgeois revolution in Russia (1905), so as to pave the way for the second bourgeois revolution (February 1917), and then for the socialist revolution (October 1917). In the second place, this sentence is amazingly illogical. If a parliament becomes an organ and a "centre" (in reality it never has been and never can be a "centre", but that is by the way) of counter-revolution, while the workers are building up the instruments of their power in the form of the Soviets, then it follows that the workers must prepare – ideologically, politically and technically – for the struggle of the Soviets against parliament, for the dispersal of parliament by the Soviets. But it does not at all follow that this dispersal is hindered, or is not facilitated, by the presence of a Soviet opposition *within* the counter-revolutionary parliament. In the course of our victorious struggle against Denikin and Kolchak, we never found that the existence of a Soviet and proletarian opposition in their camp was immaterial to our victories. We know perfectly well that the dispersal of the Constituent Assembly on 5th January, 1918 was not hampered but was actually facilitated by the fact that, within the counter-revolutionary Constituent Assembly which was about to be dispersed, there was a consistent Bolshevik, as well as an inconsistent, Left Socialist-Revolutionary Soviet opposition. The authors of the theses are engaged in muddled thinking; they have forgotten the experience of many, if not all, revolutions, which shows the great usefulness, during a revolution, of a *combination* of mass action outside a reactionary parliament with an opposition sympathetic to (or, better still, directly supporting) the revolution within it. The Dutch, and the "Lefts" in general, argue in this respect like doctrinaires of the revolution, who have never taken part in a real revolution, have never given thought to the history of revolutions, or have naïvely mistaken subjective "rejection" of a reactionary institution for its actual destruction by the combined operation of a number of objective factors. The surest way of discrediting and damaging a new political (and not only political) idea is to reduce it to absurdity on the plea of defending it. For any truth, if "overdone" (as Dietzgen Senior put it), if exaggerated, or if carried beyond the limits of its actual applicability, can be reduced to an absurdity, and is even bound to become an absurdity under these conditions. That is just the kind of disservice the Dutch and German Lefts are rendering to the new truth of the Soviet form of government being superior to bourgeois-democratic parliaments. Of course, anyone would be in error who voiced the outmoded viewpoint or in general considered it impermissible, in all and any circumstances, to reject participation in bourgeois parliaments. I cannot attempt here to formulate the conditions under which a boycott is useful, since the object of this pamphlet is far more modest, namely, to study Russian experience in connection with certain topical questions of international communist tactics. Russian experience has provided us with one successful and correct instance (1905), and another that was incorrect

(1906), of the use of a boycott by the Bolsheviks. Analysing the first case, we, see that we succeeded in *preventing* a reactionary government from *convening* a reactionary parliament in a situation in which extra-parliamentary revolutionary mass action (strikes in particular) was developing at great speed, when not a single section of the proletariat and the peasantry could support the reactionary government in any way, and when the revolutionary proletariat was gaining influence over the backward masses through the strike struggle and through the agrarian movement. It is quite obvious that *this* experience is not applicable to present-day European conditions. It is likewise quite obvious – and the foregoing arguments bear this out – that the advocacy, even if with reservations, by the Dutch and the other "Lefts" of refusal to participate in parliaments is fundamentally wrong and detrimental to the cause of the revolutionary proletariat.

In Western Europe and America, parliament has become most odious to the revolutionary vanguard of the working class. That cannot be denied. It can readily be understood, for it is difficult to imagine anything more infamous, vile or treacherous than the behaviour of the vast majority of socialist and Social-Democratic parliamentary deputies during and after the war. It would, however, be not only unreasonable but actually criminal to yield to this mood when deciding *how* this generally recognised evil should be fought. In many countries of Western Europe, the revolutionary mood, we might say, is at present a "novelty", or a "rarity", which has all too long been vainly and impatiently awaited; perhaps that is why people so easily yield to that mood. Certainly, without a revolutionary mood among the masses, and without conditions facilitating the growth of this mood, revolutionary tactics will never develop into action. In Russia, however, lengthy, painful and sanguinary experience has taught us the truth that revolutionary tactics cannot be built on a revolutionary mood alone. Tactics must be based on a sober and strictly objective appraisal of *all* the class forces in a particular state (and of the states that surround it, and of all states the world over) as well as of the experience of revolutionary movements. It is very easy to show one's "revolutionary" temper merely by hurling abuse at parliamentary opportunism, or merely by repudiating participation in parliaments; its very ease, however, cannot turn this into a solution of a difficult, a very difficult, problem. It is far more difficult to create a really revolutionary parliamentary group in a European parliament than it was in Russia. That stands to reason. But it is only a particular expression of the general truth that it was easy for Russia, in the specific and historically unique situation of 1917, to *start* the socialist revolution, but it will be more difficult for Russia than for the European countries to *continue* the revolution and bring it to its consummation. I had occasion to point this out already at the beginning of 1918, and our experience of the past two years has entirely confirmed the correctness of this view. Certain specific conditions, viz., (1) the possibility of linking up the Soviet revolution with the ending, as a consequence of this revolution, of the imperialist war, which had exhausted the workers and peasants to an incredible degree; (2) the possibility of taking temporary advantage of the mortal conflict between the world's two most powerful groups of imperialist robbers, who were unable to unite against their Soviet enemy; (3) the possibility of enduring a comparatively lengthy civil war, partly owing to the enormous size of the country and to the poor means of communication; (4) the existence of such a profound bourgeois-democratic revolutionary movement among the peasantry that the party of the proletariat was able to adopt the revolutionary demands of the peasant party (the Socialist-Revolutionary Party, the majority of whose members were definitely hostile to Bolshevism) and realise them at once, thanks to the conquest of political power by the proletariat – all these specific conditions do not at present exist in Western Europe, and a repetition of such or similar conditions will not occur so easily. Incidentally, apart from a number of other causes, that is why it is more difficult for Western Europe to *start* a socialist revolution than it was for us. To attempt to "circumvent" this difficulty by "skipping" the arduous job of utilising reactionary parliaments for revolutionary purposes is absolutely childish. You want to create a new society, yet you fear the difficulties involved in forming a good parliamentary group made up of convinced, devoted and heroic Communists, in a reactionary parliament! Is that not childish? If Karl Liebknecht in Germany and Z. Höglund in Sweden were able, even without mass support from below, to set examples of the truly revolutionary utilisation of reactionary parliaments, why should a rapidly growing revolutionary mass party, in the midst of the post-war disillusionment and embitterment of the masses, be unable to *forge* a communist group in the worst of parliaments? It is because, in Western Europe, the backward masses of the workers and – to an even greater degree – of the small peasants are much more imbued with bourgeois-democratic and parliamentary prejudices than they were in Russia because of that, it is *only* from within such institutions as bourgeois parliaments that Communists can (and must) wage a long and persistent struggle, undaunted by any difficulties, to expose, dispel and overcome these prejudices.

The German "Lefts" complain of bad "leaders" in their party, give way to despair, and even arrive at a ridiculous "negation" of "leaders". But in conditions in which it is often necessary to hide "leaders" underground, the *evolution* of good "leaders", reliable, tested and authoritative, is a very difficult matter; these difficulties *cannot* be successfully overcome without combining legal and illegal work, and *without testing the "leaders", among other ways*, in parliaments. Criticism – the most keen, ruthless and uncompromising criticism – should be directed, not against parliamentarianism or parliamentary activities, but against those leaders who are unable – and still more against those who are *unwilling* – to utilise parliamentary elections and the parliamentary rostrum in a revolutionary and communist manner. Only such criticism – combined, of course, with the dismissal of incapable leaders and their replacement by capable ones – will constitute useful and fruitful revolutionary work that will simultaneously train the "leaders" to be worthy of the working class and of all working people, and train the masses to be able properly to understand the political situation and the often very complicated and intricate tasks that spring from that situation.[*5]

Footnotes

[*5] I have had too little opportunity to acquaint myself with "Left-wing" communism in Italy. Comrade Bordiga and his faction of Abstentionist Communists (Comunista astensionista) are certainly wrong in advocating non-participation in parliament. But on one point, it seems to me, Comrade Bordiga is right – as far as can be judged from two issues of his paper, Il Soviet (Nos. 3 and 4, 18th January and 1st February, 1920), from four issues of Comrade Serrati's excellent periodical, Comunismo (Nos. 1–4, 1st October–30th November, 1919), and from separate issues of Italian bourgeois papers which I have seen. Comrade Bordiga and his group are right in attacking Turati and his partisans, who remain in a party which has recognised Soviet power and the dictatorship of the proletariat, and yet continue their former pernicious and opportunist policy as members of parliament. Of course, in tolerating this, Comrade Serrati and the entire Italian Socialist Party[28] are making a mistake which threatens to do as much harm and give rise to the same dangers as it did in Hungary, where the Hungarian Turatis sabotaged both the party and the Soviet government[29] from within. Such a mistaken, inconsistent, or spineless attitude towards the opportunist parliamentarians gives rise to "Left-wing" communism, on the one hand, and to a certain extent justifies its existence, on the other. Comrade Serrati is obviously wrong when he accuses Deputy Turati of being "inconsistent" (Comunismo No. 3), for it is the Italian Socialist Party itself that is inconsistent in tolerating such opportunist parliamentarians as Turati and Co.

[28] From its foundation in 1892, the Italian Socialist Party saw a bitter ideological struggle between the opportunist and the revolutionary trends within it. At the Reggio Emilia Congress of 1912, the most outspoken reformists who supported the war and collaboration with the government and the bourgeoisie (Ivanoe Bonomi, Leonida Bissolati and others) were expelled from the party under pressure from the Left wing. After the outbreak of the First World War and prior to Italy's

entry into it, the I.S.P. came out against the war and advanced the slogan: "Against war, for neutrality!" In December 1914, a group of renegades including Benito Mussolini, who advocated the bourgeoisie's imperialist policy and supported the war, were expelled from the party. When Italy entered the war on the Entente's side (May 1915), three distinct trends emerged in the Italian Socialist Party: 1) the Right wing, which aided the bourgeoisie in the conduct of the war; 2) the Centre, which united most of party members and came out under the slogan: "No part in the war, and no sabotage of the war" and 3) the Left wing, which took a firmer anti-war stand, but could not organise a consistent struggle against the war. The Left wing did not realise the necessity of converting the imperialist war into a civil war, and of a decisive break with the reformists.

After the October Socialist Revolution in Russia, the Left wing of the I.S.P. grew stronger, and the 16th Party Congress held on 5th-8th October, 1919, in Bologna, adopted a resolution on affiliation to the Third International. I.S.P. representatives took part in the work of the Second Congress of the Comintern. After the Congress Centrist Serrati, head of the delegation, declared against a break with the reformists. At the 17th Party Congress in Leghorn in January 1921, the Centrists, who were in the majority, refused to break with the reformists and to accept all the terms of admission into the Comintern. On 21st January, 1921, the Left-wing delegates walked out of the Congress and founded the Communist Party of Italy.

[29] Soviet rule was established in Hungary on March 21, 1919. The socialist revolution in Hungary was a peaceful one, the Hungarian bourgeoisie being unable to resist the people. Incapable of overcoming its internal and external difficulties, it decided to hand over power for a while to the Right-wing Social-Democrats so as to prevent the development of the revolution. However, the Hungarian Communist Party's prestige had grown so great, and the demands of rank-and-file Social-Democrats for unity with the Communists had become so insistent that the leaders of the Social-Democratic Party proposed to the arrested Communist leaders the formation of a joint government. The Social-Democratic leaders were obliged to accept the terms advanced by the Communists during the negotiations, i.e., the formation of a Soviet government, disarmament of the bourgeoisie, the creation of a Red Army and people's militia, confiscation of the landed estates, the nationalisation of industry, an alliance with Soviet Russia, etc.

An agreement was simultaneously signed on the merging of the two parties to form the Hungarian Socialist Party. While the two parties were being merged, errors were made which later became clear. The merger was carried out mechanically, without isolation of the reformist elements.

At its first meeting, the Revolutionary Governmental Council adopted a resolution on the formation of the Red Army. On March 26, the Soviet Government of Hungary issued decrees on the nationalisation of industrial enterprises, transport, and the banks; on 2nd April, a decree was published on the monopoly of foreign trade. Workers' wages were increased by an average of 25 per cent, and an 8-hour working day was introduced. On 3rd April, land-reform law was issued, by which all estates exceeding 57 hectares in area were confiscated. The confiscated land, however, was not distributed among the land-starved and landless peasants, but was turned over to agricultural producers' cooperatives and state farms organised after the reform. The poor peasants, who had hoped to get land, were disappointed. This prevented the establishment of a firm alliance between the proletariat and the peasantry, and weakened Soviet power in Hungary.

The Entente imperialists instituted an economic blockade of the Soviet Republic. Armed intervention against the Hungarian Soviet Republic was organised, the advance of interventionist troops stirring up the Hungarian counter-revolutionaries. The treachery of the Right-wing Social-Democrats, who entered into an alliance with international imperialism, was one of the causes of the Hungarian Soviet Republic's downfall.

The unfavourable international situation in the summer of 1919, when Soviet Russia was encircled by enemies and therefore could not help the Hungarian Soviet Republic, also played a definite role. On 1st August, 1919, as a result of joint actions by the foreign imperialist interventionists and the domestic counterrevolutionaries, Soviet power in Hungary was overthrown.

VIII

No Compromises?

In the quotation from the Frankfurt pamphlet, we have seen how emphatically the "Lefts" have advanced this slogan. It is sad to see people who no doubt consider themselves Marxists, and want to be Marxists, forget the fundamental truths of Marxism. This is what Engels – who, like Marx, was one of those rarest of authors whose every sentence in every one of their fundamental works contains a remarkably profound content – wrote in 1874, against the manifesto of the thirty-three Blanquist Communards:

> *"'We are Communists' [the Blanquist Communards wrote in their manifesto], 'because we want to attain our goal without stopping at intermediate stations, without any compromises, which only postpone the day of victory and prolong the period of slavery.'*

> "The German Communists are Communists because, through all the intermediate stations and all compromises created, not by them but by the course of historical development, they clearly perceive and constantly pursue the final aim – the abolition of classes and the creation of a society in which there will no longer be private ownership of land or of the means of production. The thirty-three Blanquists are Communists just because they imagine that, merely because they want to skip the intermediate stations and compromises, the matter is settled, and if 'it begins' in the next few days – which they take for granted – and they take over power, 'communism will be introduced' the day after tomorrow. If that is not immediately possible, they are not Communists.

> "What childish innocence it is to present one's own impatience as a theoretically convincing argument!" (Frederick Engels, "Programme of the Blanquist Communards", [30] from the German Social-Democratic newspaper Volksstaat, 1874, No. 73, given in the Russian translation of Articles, 1871–1875, Petrograd, 1919, pp. 52–53).

In the same article, Engels expresses his profound esteem for Vaillant, and speaks of the "unquestionable merit" of the latter (who, like Guesde, was one of the most prominent leaders of international socialism until their betrayal of socialism in August 1914). But Engels does not fail to give a detailed analysis of an obvious error. Of course, to very young and inexperienced revolutionaries, as well as to petty-bourgeois revolutionaries of even very respectable age and great experience, it seems extremely "dangerous", incomprehensible and wrong to "permit compromises". Many sophists (being unusually or excessively "experienced" politicians) reason exactly in the same way as the British leaders of opportunism mentioned by Comrade Lansbury: "If the Bolsheviks are permitted a certain compromise, why should we not be permitted any kind of compromise?" However, proletarians schooled in numerous strikes (to take only this manifestation of the class struggle) usually assimilate in admirable fashion the very profound truth (philosophical, historical, political and psychological) expounded by Engels. Every proletarian has been through strikes and has experienced "compromises" with the hated oppressors and exploiters, when the workers have had to return to work either without having achieved anything or else agreeing to only a partial satisfaction of their demands. Every proletarian – as a result of the conditions of the mass struggle and the acute intensification of class antagonisms he lives among – sees the difference between a compromise enforced by objective conditions (such as lack of strike funds, no outside support, starvation and exhaustion) – a compromise which in no way minimises the revolutionary devotion and readiness to carry on the struggle on the part of the workers who have agreed to such a compromise – and, on the other hand, a compromise by traitors who try to ascribe to objective causes their self-interest (strike-breakers also enter into "compromises"!), their cowardice, desire to toady to the capitalists, and readiness to yield to intimidation, sometimes to persuasion, sometimes to sops, and sometimes to flattery from the capitalists. (The history of the British labour movement provides a very large number of instances of such treacherous compromises by British trade union leaders, but, in one form or another, almost all workers in all countries have witnessed the same sort of thing.)

Naturally, there are individual cases of exceptional difficulty and complexity, when the greatest efforts are necessary for a proper assessment of the actual character of this or that "compromise", just as there are cases of homicide when it is by no means easy to establish whether the homicide was fully justified and even necessary (as, for example, legitimate self-defence), or due to unpardonable negligence, or even to a cunningly executed perfidious plan. Of course, in politics, where it is sometimes a matter of extremely complex relations – national and international – between classes and parties, very many cases will arise that will be much more difficult than the question of a legitimate "compromise" in a strike or a treacherous "compromise" by a strike-breaker, treacherous leader, etc. It would be absurd to formulate a recipe or general rule ("No compromises!") to suit all cases. One must use one's own brains and be able to find one's bearings in each particular instance. It is, in fact, one of the functions of a party organisation and of party leaders worthy of the name, to acquire, through the prolonged, persistent, variegated and comprehensive efforts of all thinking representatives of a given class,*6 the knowledge, experience and – in addition to knowledge and experience – the political flair necessary for the speedy and correct solution of complex political problems.[30]

Naïve and quite inexperienced people imagine that the permissibility of compromise *in general* is sufficient to obliterate any distinction between opportunism, against which we are waging, and must wage, an unremitting struggle, and revolutionary Marxism, or communism. But if such people do not yet know that in nature and in society *all* distinctions are fluid and up to a certain point conventional, nothing can help them but lengthy training, education, enlightenment, and political and everyday experience. In the practical questions that arise in the politics of any particular or specific historical moment, it is important to single out those which display the principal type of intolerable and treacherous compromises, such as embody an opportunism that is fatal to the revolutionary class, and to exert all efforts to explain them and combat them. During the 1914–18 imperialist war between two groups of equally predatory countries, social-chauvinism was the principal and fundamental type of opportunism, i.e., support of "defence of country", which in *such* a war was really equivalent to defence of the predatory interests of one's "own" bourgeoisie. After the war, defence of the robber League of Nations,[31] defence of direct or indirect alliances with the bourgeoisie of one's own country against the revolutionary proletariat and the "Soviet" movement, and defence of bourgeois democracy and bourgeois parliamentarianism against "Soviet power" became the principal manifestations of those intolerable and treacherous compromises, whose sum total constituted an opportunism fatal to the revolutionary proletariat and its cause.

"*. . . All compromise with other parties . . . any policy of manoeuvring and compromise must be emphatically rejected,*" the German Lefts write in the Frankfurt pamphlet.

It is surprising that, with such views, these Lefts do not emphatically condemn Bolshevism! After all, the German Lefts cannot but know that the entire history of Bolshevism, both before and after the October Revolution, is *full* of instances of changes of tack, conciliatory tactics and compromises with other parties, including bourgeois parties!

To carry on a war for the overthrow of the international bourgeoisie, a war which is a hundred times more difficult, protracted and complex than the most stubborn of ordinary wars between states, and to renounce in advance any change of tack, or any utilisation of a conflict of interests (even if temporary) among one's enemies, or any conciliation or compromise with possible allies (even if they are temporary, unstable, vacillating or conditional allies) – is that not ridiculous in the extreme? Is it not like making a difficult ascent of an unexplored and hitherto inaccessible mountain and refusing in advance ever to move in zigzags, ever to retrace one's steps, or ever to abandon a course once selected, and to try others? And yet people so immature and inexperienced (if youth were the explanation, it would not be so bad; young people are preordained to talk such nonsense for a certain period) have met with support – whether direct or indirect, open or covert, whole or partial, it does not matter – from some members of the Communist Party of Holland.

After the first socialist revolution of the proletariat, and the overthrow of the bourgeoisie in some country, the proletariat of that country remains *for a long time weaker* than the bourgeoisie, simply because of the latter's extensive international links, and also because of the spontaneous and continuous restoration and regeneration of capitalism and the bourgeoisie by the small commodity producers of the country which has overthrown the bourgeoisie. The more powerful enemy can be vanquished only by exerting the utmost effort, and by the most thorough, careful, attentive, skilful and *obligatory* use of any, even the smallest, rift between the enemies, any conflict of interests among the bourgeoisie of the various countries and among the various groups or types of bourgeoisie within the various countries, and also by taking advantage of any, even the smallest, opportunity of winning a mass ally, even though this ally is temporary, vacillating, unstable, unreliable and conditional. Those who do not understand this reveal a failure to understand even the smallest grain of Marxism, of modern scientific socialism *in general*. Those who have not proved *in practice*, over a fairly considerable period of time and in fairly varied political situations, their ability to apply this truth in practice have not yet learned to help the revolutionary class in its struggle to emancipate all toiling humanity from the exploiters. And this applies equally to the period *before* and *after* the proletariat has won political power.

Our theory is not a dogma, but a *guide to action*, said Marx and Engels.[32] The greatest blunder, the greatest crime, committed by such "out-and-out" Marxists as Karl Kautsky, Otto Bauer, etc., is that they have not understood this and have been unable to apply it at crucial moments of the proletarian revolution. "Political activity is not like the pavement of Nevsky Prospekt" (the well-kept, broad and level pavement of the perfectly straight principal thoroughfare of St. Petersburg), N. G. Chernyshevsky, the great Russian socialist of the pre-Marxist period, used to say. Since Chernyshevsky's time, disregard or forgetfulness of this truth has cost Russian revolutionaries countless sacrifices. We must strive at all costs to *prevent* the Left Communists and West-European and American revolutionaries that are devoted to the working class from paying *as dearly* as the backward Russians did to learn this truth.

Prior to the downfall of tsarism, the Russian revolutionary Social-Democrats made repeated use of the services of the bourgeois liberals, i.e., they concluded numerous practical compromises with the latter. In 1901–02, even prior to the appearance of Bolshevism, the old editorial board of *Iskra* (consisting of Plekhanov, Axelrod, Zasulich, Martov, Potresov and myself) concluded (not for long, it is true) a formal political alliance with Struve, the political leader of bourgeois liberalism, while at the same time being able to wage an unremitting and most merciless ideological and political struggle against bourgeois liberalism and against the slightest manifestation of its influence in the working-class movement. The Bolsheviks have always adhered to this policy. Since 1905 they have systematically advocated an alliance between the working class and the peasantry, against the liberal bourgeoisie and tsarism, never, however, refusing to support the bourgeoisie against tsarism (for instance, during second rounds of elections, or during second ballots) and never ceasing their relentless ideological and political struggle against the Socialist-Revolutionaries, the bourgeois-revolutionary peasant party, exposing them as petty-bourgeois democrats who have falsely described themselves as socialists. During the Duma elections of 1907, the Bolsheviks entered briefly into a formal political bloc with the Socialist-Revolutionaries. Between 1903 and 1912, there were periods of several years in which we were formally united with the Mensheviks in a single Social-Democratic Party, but we *never stopped* our ideological and political struggle against them as opportunists and vehicles of bourgeois influence on the proletariat. During the war, we concluded certain compromises with the Kautskyites, with the Left Mensheviks (Martov), and with a section of the Socialist-Revolutionaries (Chernov and Natanson); we were together with them at Zimmerwald and Kienthal,[33] and issued joint manifestos. However, we never ceased and never relaxed our ideological and political struggle against the Kautskyites, Martov and Chernov (when Natanson died in 1919, a "Revolutionary-Communist" Narodnik,[34] he was very close to and almost in agreement with us). At the very moment of the October Revolution, we entered into an informal but very important (and very successful) political bloc with the petty-bourgeois peasantry by adopting the *Socialist-Revolutionary* agrarian programme *in its entirety*, without a single alteration – i.e., we effected an undeniable compromise in order to prove to the peasants that we wanted, not to "steam-roller" them but to reach agreement with them. At the same time we proposed (and soon after effected) a formal political bloc, including participation in the government, with the Left Socialist-Revolutionaries, who dissolved this bloc after the conclusion of the Treaty of Brest-Litovsk and then, in July 1918, went to the length of armed rebellion, and subsequently of an armed struggle, against us.

It is therefore understandable why the attacks made by the German Lefts against the Central Committee of the Communist Party of Germany for entertaining the idea of a bloc with the Independents (the Independent Social-Democratic Party of Germany – the Kautskyites) are absolutely frivolous, in our opinion, and clear proof that the "Lefts" are in the *wrong*. In Russia, too, there were Right Mensheviks (participants in the Kerensky government), who corresponded to the German Scheidemanns, and Left Mensheviks (Martov), corresponding to the German Kautskyites and standing in opposition to the Right Mensheviks. A gradual shift of the worker masses from the Mensheviks over to the Bolsheviks was to be clearly seen in 1917. At the First All-Russia Congress of Soviets, held in June 1917, we had only 13 per cent of the votes; the Socialist-Revolutionaries and the Mensheviks had a majority. At the Second Congress of Soviets (25th October, 1917, old style) we had 51 per cent of the votes. Why is it that in Germany the *same* and absolutely *identical* shift of the workers from Right to Left did not immediately strengthen the Communists, but first strengthened the midway Independent Party, although the latter never had independent political ideas or an independent policy, but merely wavered between the Scheidemanns and the Communists?

One of the evident reasons was the *erroneous* tactics of the German Communists, who must fearlessly and honestly admit this error and learn to rectify it. The error consisted in their denial of the need to take part in the reactionary bourgeois parliaments and in the reactionary trade unions; the error consisted in numerous manifestations of that "Left-wing" infantile disorder which has now come to the surface and will consequently be cured the more thoroughly, the more rapidly and with greater advantage to the organism.

The German Independent Social-Democratic Party is obviously not a homogeneous body. Alongside the old opportunist leaders (Kautsky, Hilferding and apparently, to a considerable extent, Crispien, Ledebour and others) – these have revealed their inability to understand the significance of Soviet power and the dictatorship of the proletariat, and their inability to lead the proletariat's revolutionary struggle – there has emerged in this party a Left and proletarian wing, which is growing most rapidly. Hundreds of thousands of members of this party (which has, I think, a membership of some three-quarters of a million) are proletarians who are abandoning Scheidemann and are rapidly going over to communism. This proletarian wing has already proposed – at the Leipzig Congress of the Independents (1919) – immediate and unconditional affiliation to the Third International. To fear a "compromise" with this wing of the party is positively ridiculous. On the contrary, it is the *duty* of Communists to seek *and find* a suitable form of compromise with them, a compromise which, on the one hand, will facilitate and accelerate the necessary complete fusion with this wing and, on the other, will in no way hamper the Communists in their ideological and political struggle against the opportunist Right wing of the Independents. It will probably be no easy matter to devise a suitable form of compromise – but only a charlatan could promise the German workers and the German Communists an "easy" road to victory.

Capitalism would not be capitalism if the proletariat *pur sang* were not surrounded by a large number of exceedingly motley types intermediate between the proletarian and the semi-proletarian (who earns his livelihood in part by the sale of his labour-power), between the semi-proletarian and the small peasant (and petty artisan, handicraft worker and small master in general), between the small peasant and the middle peasant, and so on, and if the proletariat itself were not divided into more developed and less developed strata, if it were not divided according to territorial origin, trade, sometimes according to religion, and so on. From all this follows the necessity, the absolute necessity, for the Communist Party, the vanguard of the proletariat, its class-conscious section, to resort to changes of tack, to conciliation and compromises with the various groups of proletarians, with the various parties of the workers and small masters. It is entirely a matter of *knowing how* to apply these tactics in order to *raise* – not lower – the *general* level of proletarian class-consciousness, revolutionary spirit, and ability to fight and win. Incidentally, it should be noted that the Bolsheviks' victory over the Mensheviks called for the application of tactics of changes of tack, conciliation and compromises, not only before *but also after* the October Revolution of 1917, but the changes of tack and compromises were, of course, such as assisted, boosted and consolidated the Bolsheviks at the expense of the Mensheviks. The petty-bourgeois democrats (including the Mensheviks) inevitably vacillate between the bourgeoisie and the proletariat, between bourgeois democracy and the Soviet system, between reformism and revolutionism, between love for the workers and fear of the proletarian dictatorship, etc. The Communists' proper tactics should consist in *utilising* these vacillations, not ignoring them; utilising them calls for concessions to elements that are turning towards the proletariat – whenever and in the measure that they turn towards the proletariat – in addition to fighting those who turn towards the bourgeoisie. As a result of the application of the correct tactics, Menshevism began to disintegrate, and has been disintegrating more and more in our country; the stubbornly opportunist leaders are being isolated, and the best of the workers and the best elements among the petty-bourgeois democrats are being brought into our camp. This is a lengthy process, and the hasty "decision" – "No compromises, no manoeuvres" – can only prejudice the strengthening of the revolutionary proletariat's influence and the enlargement of its forces.

Lastly, one of the undoubted errors of the German "Lefts" lies in their downright refusal to recognise the Treaty of Versailles. The more "weightily" and "pompously", the more "emphatically" and peremptorily this viewpoint is formulated (by K. Horner, for instance), the less sense it seems to make. It is not enough, under the present conditions of the international proletarian revolution, to repudiate the preposterous absurdities of "National Bolshevism" (Laufenberg and others), which has gone to the length of advocating a bloc with the German bourgeoisie for a war against the Entente. One must realise that it is utterly false tactics to refuse to admit that a Soviet Germany (if a German Soviet republic were soon to arise) would have to recognise the Treaty of Versailles for a time, and to submit to it. From this it does not follow that the Independents – at a time when the Scheidemanns were in the government, when the Soviet government in Hungary had not yet been overthrown, and when it was still possible that a Soviet revolution in Vienna would support Soviet Hungary – were right, *under the circumstances*, in putting forward the demand that the Treaty of Versailles should be signed. At that time the Independents tacked and manoeuvred very clumsily, for they more or less accepted responsibility for the Scheidemann traitors, and more or less backslid from advocacy of a ruthless (and most calmly conducted) class war against the Scheidemanns, to advocacy of a "classless" or "above-class" standpoint.

In the present situation, however, the German Communists should obviously not deprive themselves of freedom of action by giving a positive and categorical promise to repudiate the Treaty of Versailles in the event of communism's victory. That would be absurd. They should say: the Scheidemanns and the Kautskyites have committed a number of acts of treachery hindering (and in part quite ruining) the chances of an alliance with Soviet Russia and Soviet Hungary. We Communists will do all we can to *facilitate* and *pave the way* for such an alliance. However, we are in no way obligated to repudiate the Treaty of Versailles, come what may, or to do so at once. The possibility of its successful repudiation will depend, not only on the German, but also on the international successes of the Soviet movement. The Scheidemanns and the Kautskyites have hampered this movement; we are helping it. That is the gist of the matter; therein lies the fundamental difference. And if our class enemies, the exploiters and their Scheidemann and Kautskyite lackeys, have missed many an opportunity of strengthening both the German and the international Soviet movement, of strengthening both the German and the international Soviet revolution, the blame lies with them. The Soviet revolution in Germany will strengthen the international Soviet movement, which is the strongest bulwark (and the only reliable, invincible and world-wide bulwark) against the Treaty of Versailles and against international imperialism in general. To give absolute, categorical and immediate precedence to liberation from the Treaty of Versailles and to give it *precedence over the question* of liberating *other* countries oppressed by imperialism, from the yoke of imperialism, is philistine nationalism (worthy of the Kautskys, the Hilferdings, the Otto Bauers and Co.), not revolutionary internationalism. The overthrow of the bourgeoisie in any of the large European countries, including Germany, would be such a gain for the international revolution that, for its sake, one can, and if necessary should, tolerate a *more prolonged existence of the Treaty of Versailles*. If Russia, standing alone, could endure the Treaty of Brest-Litovsk for several months, to the advantage of the revolution, there is nothing impossible in a Soviet Germany, allied with Soviet Russia, enduring the existence of the Treaty of Versailles for a longer period, to the advantage of the revolution.

The imperialists of France, Britain, etc., are trying to provoke and ensnare the German Communists: "Say that you will not sign the Treaty of Versailles!" they urge. Like babes, the Left Communists fall into the trap laid for them, instead of skilfully manoeuvring against the crafty and, *at present*, stronger enemy, and instead of telling him, "We shall sign the Treaty of Versailles now." It is folly, not revolutionism, to deprive ourselves in advance of any freedom of action, openly to inform an enemy who is at present better armed than we are whether we shall fight him, and when. To accept battle at a time when it is obviously advantageous to the enemy, but not to us, is criminal; political leaders of the revolutionary class are absolutely useless if they are incapable of "changing tack, or offering conciliation and compromise" in order to take evasive action in a patently disadvantageous battle.

Footnotes

[30] See Marx/Engels, *Werke,* Dietz Verlag, Berlin, 1962, Bd. 18, S. 533.

[31] The League of Nations was an international body which existed between the First and the Second World Wars. It was founded in 1919 at the Paris Peace Conference of the victor powers of the First World War. The Covenant of the League of Nations formed part of the Treaty of Versailles of 1919, and was signed by 44 nations. The Covenant was designed to produce the impression that this organisation's aim was to combat aggression, reduce armaments, and consolidate peace and security. In practice, however its leaders shielded the aggressors, fostered the arms race and preparations for the Second World War.

Between 1920 and 1934, the League's activities were hostile towards the Soviet Union. It was one of the centres for the organising of armed intervention against the Soviet state in 1920–21.

On September 15, 1934, on French initiative, 34 member states invited the Soviet Union to join the League of Nations, which the U.S.S.R. did, with the aim of strengthening peace. However, the Soviet Union's attempts to form a peace front met with resistance from reactionary circles in the Western powers. With the outbreak of the Second World War the League's activities came to an end, the formal dissolution taking place in April 1946, according to a decision by the specially summoned Assembly.

[32] Lenin is referring to a passage from Frederick Engels's letter to F. A. Sorge of 29th November, 1886, in which, criticising German Social-Democrat political exiles living in America, Engels wrote that for them the theory was "a credo, not a guide to action" (see Karl Marx and Frederick Engels, Selected Correspondence, Moscow, 1965, p. 395).

[33] The reference is to the international socialist conferences in Zimmerwald and Kienthal (Switzerland).

The Zimmerwald Conference, the first international socialist conference, was held on 5th-8th September, 1915. The Kienthal Conference, the second international socialist conference, was held in the small town of Kienthal on 24th-30th April, 1916.

The Zimmerwald and Kienthal conferences contributed to the ideological unity, on the basis of Marxism-Leninism, of the Left-wing elements in West-European Social-Democracy, who later played an active part in the formation of Communist parties in their countries and the establishment of the Third, Communist International.

[34] "Revolutionary Communists" – a Narodnik group which broke away from the Left Socialist-Revolutionaries after the latter's mutiny in July 1918. In September 1918, they formed the "Party of Revolutionary Communism", which favoured co-operation with the R.C.P.(B.), and pledged support for Soviet power. Their programme which remained on the platform of Narodnik utopianism was muddled and eclectic. While recognising that Soviet rule created preconditions for the establishment of a socialist system, the "revolutionary communists" denied the necessity of the proletarian dictatorship during the transitional period from capitalism to socialism. Throughout the lifetime of the "Party of Revolutionary Communism", certain of its groups broke away from it, some of them joining the R.C.P.(B.) (A. Kolegayev, A. Bitsenko, M. Dobrokhotov and others), and others, the Left Socialist-Revolutionaries. Two representatives of the "Party of Revolutionary Communism" were allowed to attend the Second Congress of the Comintern, in a deliberative capacity, but with no votes. In September 1920, following the Congress decision that there must be a single Communist Party in each country, the "Party of Revolutionary Communism" decided to join the R.C.P.(B.). In October of the same year, the R.C.P.(B.) Central Committee permitted Party organisations to enrol members of the former "Party of Revolutionary Communism" in the R.C.P.(B.).

[*6] Within every class, even in the conditions prevailing in the most enlightened countries, even within the most advanced class, and even when the circumstances of the moment have aroused all its spiritual forces to an exceptional degree, there always are – and inevitably will be as long as classes exist, as long as a classless society has not fully consolidated itself, and has not developed on its own foundations – representatives of the class who do not think, and are incapable of thinking, for themselves. Capitalism would not be the Oppressor of the masses that it actually is, if things were otherwise.

IX

"Left-Wing" Communism in Great Britain

There is no Communist Party in Great Britain as yet, but there is a fresh, broad, powerful and rapidly growing communist movement among the workers, which justifies the best hopes. There are several political parties and organisations (the British Socialist Party[35], the Socialist Labour Party, the South Wales Socialist Society, the Workers' Socialist Federation[36]), which desire to form a Communist Party and are already negotiating among themselves to this end. In its issue of 21st February, 1920, Vol. VI, No. 48, *The Workers' Dreadnought*, weekly organ of the last of the organisations mentioned, carried an article by the editor, Comrade Sylvia Pankhurst, entitled "Towards a Communist Party". The article outlines the progress of the negotiations between the four organisations mentioned, for the formation of a united Communist Party, on the basis of affiliation to the Third International, the recognition of the Soviet system instead of parliamentarianism, and the recognition of the dictatorship of the proletariat. It appears that one of the greatest obstacles to the immediate formation of a united Communist Party is presented by the disagreement on the questions of participation in Parliament and on whether the new Communist Party should affiliate to the old, trade-unionist, opportunist and social-chauvinist Labour Party, which is mostly made up of trade unions. The Workers' Socialist Federation and the Socialist Labour Party[*7] are opposed to taking part in parliamentary elections and in Parliament, and they are opposed to affiliation to the Labour Party; in this they disagree with all or with most of the members of the British Socialist Party, which they regard as the "Right wing of the Communist parties" in Great Britain. (Page 5, Sylvia Pankhurst's article.)

Thus, the main division is the same as in Germany, notwithstanding the enormous difference in the forms in which the disagreements manifest themselves (in Germany the form is far closer to the "Russian" than it is in Great Britain), and in a number of other things. Let us examine the arguments of the "Lefts".

On the question of participation in Parliament, Comrade Sylvia Pankhurst refers to an article in the same issue, by Comrade Gallacher, who writes in the name of the Scottish Workers' Council in Glasgow.

> *"The above council,"* he writes, *"is definitely anti-parliamentarian, and has behind it the Left wing of the various political bodies. We represent the revolutionary movement in Scotland, striving continually to build up a revolutionary organisation within the industries [in various branches of production], and a Communist Party, based on social committees, throughout the country. For a considerable time we have been sparring with the official parliamentarians. We have not considered it necessary to declare open warfare on them, and they are afraid to open an attack on us.*

"But this state of affairs cannot long continue. We are winning all along the line.

"The rank and file of the I.L.P. in Scotland is becoming more and more disgusted with the thought of Parliament, and the Soviets [the Russian word transliterated into English is used] or Workers' Councils are being supported by almost every branch. This is very serious, of course, for the gentlemen who look to politics for a profession, and they are using any and every means to persuade their members to come back into the parliamentary fold. Revolutionary comrades must not [all italics are the author's] give any support to this gang. Our fight here is going to be a difficult one. One of the worst features of it will be the treachery of those whose personal ambition is a more impelling force than their regard for the revolution. Any support given to parliamentarianism is simply assisting to put power into the hands of our British Scheidemanns and Noskes. Henderson, Clynes and co are hopelessly reactionary. The official I.L.P. is more and more coming under the control of middle-class Liberals, who . . . have found their 'spiritual home' in the camp of Messrs. MacDonald, Snowden and Co. The official I.L.P. is bitterly hostile to the Third International, the rank and file is for it. Any support to the parliamentary opportunists is simply playing into the hands of the former. The B.S.P. doesn't count at all here. . . . What is wanted here is a sound revolutionary industrial organisation, and a Communist Party working along clear, well-defined, scientific lines. If our comrades can assist us in building these, we will take their help gladly; if they cannot, for God's sake let them keep out altogether, lest they betray the revolution by lending their support to the reactionaries, who are so eagerly clamouring for parliamentary 'honours' (?) [the query mark is the author's] and who are so anxious to prove that they can rule as effectively as the 'boss' class politicians themselves."

In my opinion, this letter to the editor expresses excellently the temper and point of view of the young Communists, or of rank-and-file workers who are only just beginning to accept communism. This temper is highly gratifying and valuable; we must learn to appreciate and support it for, in its absence, it would be hopeless to expect the victory of the proletarian revolution in Great Britain, or in any other country for that matter. People who can give expression to this temper of the masses, and are able to evoke such a temper (which is very often dormant, unconscious and latent) among the masses, should be appreciated and given every assistance. At the same time, we must tell them openly and frankly that a state of mind is *by itself* insufficient for leadership of the masses in a great revolutionary struggle, and that the cause of the revolution may well be harmed by certain errors that people who are most devoted to the cause of the revolution are about to commit, or are committing. Comrade Gallacher's letter undoubtedly reveals the rudiments of *all* the mistakes that are being made by the German "Left" Communists and were made by the Russian "Left" Bolsheviks in 1908 and 1918.

The writer of the letter is full of a noble and working-class hatred for the bourgeois "class politicians" (a hatred understood and shared, however, not only by proletarians but by all working people, by all *Kleinen Leuten* to use the German expression). In a representative of the oppressed and exploited masses, this hatred is truly the "beginning of all wisdom", the basis of any socialist and communist movement and of its success. The writer, however, has apparently lost sight of the fact that politics is a science and an art that does not fall from the skies or come gratis, and that, if it wants to overcome the bourgeoisie, the proletariat must train its *own* proletarian "class politicians", of a kind in no way inferior to bourgeois politicians.

The writer of the letter fully realises that only workers' Soviets, not parliament, can be the instrument enabling the proletariat to achieve its aims; those who have failed to understand this are, of course, out-and-out reactionaries, even if they are most highly educated people, most experienced politicians, most sincere socialists, most erudite Marxists, and most honest citizens and fathers of families. But the writer of the letter does not even ask – it does not occur to him to ask – whether it is possible to bring about the Soviets' victory over parliament without getting pro-Soviet politicians *into* parliament, without disintegrating parliamentarianism from *within*, without working within parliament for the success of the Soviets in their forthcoming task of dispersing parliament. Yet the writer of the letter expresses the absolutely correct idea that the Communist Party in Great Britain must act on *scientific* principles. Science demands, first, that the experience of other countries be taken into account, especially if these other countries, which are also capitalist, are undergoing, or have recently undergone, a very similar experience; second, it demands that account be taken of *all* the forces, groups, parties, classes and masses operating in a given country, and also that policy should not be determined only by the desires and views, by the degree of class-consciousness and the militancy of one group or party alone.

It is true that the Hendersons, the Clyneses, the MacDonalds and the Snowdens are hopelessly reactionary. It is equally true that they want to assume power (though they would prefer a coalition with the bourgeoisie), that they want to "rule" along the old bourgeois lines, and that when they are in power they will certainly behave like the Scheidemanns and Noskes. All that is true. But it does not at all follow that to support them means treachery to the revolution; what does follow is that, in the interests of the revolution, working-class revolutionaries should give these gentlemen a certain amount of parliamentary support. To explain this idea, I shall take two contemporary British political documents: (1) the speech delivered by Prime Minister Lloyd George on 18th March, 1920 (as reported in *The Manchester Guardian* of 19th March, 1920), and (2) the arguments of a "Left" Communist, Comrade Sylvia Pankhurst, in the article mentioned above.

In his speech Lloyd George entered into a polemic with Asquith (who had been especially invited to this meeting but declined to attend) and with those Liberals who want, not a coalition with the Conservatives, but closer relations with the Labour Party. (In the above-quoted letter, Comrade Gallacher also points to the fact that Liberals are joining the Independent Labour Party.) Lloyd George argued that a coalition – and a *close* coalition at that – between the Liberals and the Conservatives was essential, otherwise there might be a victory for the Labour Party, which Lloyd George prefers to call "Socialist" and which is working for the "common ownership" of the means of production. "It is . . . known as communism in France," the leader of the British bourgeoisie said, putting it popularly for his audience, Liberal M.P.s who probably never knew it before. In Germany it was called socialism, and in Russia it is called Bolshevism, he went on to say. To Liberals this is unacceptable on principle, Lloyd George explained, because they stand in principle for private property. "Civilisation is in jeopardy," the speaker declared, and consequently Liberals and Conservatives must unite. . . .

> ". . . *If you go to the agricultural areas,*" *said Lloyd George,* "*I agree you have the old party divisions as strong as ever. They are removed from the danger. It does not walk their lanes. But when they see it they will be as strong as some of these industrial constituencies are now. Four-fifths of this country is industrial and commercial; hardly one-fifth is agricultural. It is one of the things I have constantly in my mind when I think of the dangers of the future here. In France the population is agricultural, and you have a solid body of opinion which does not move very rapidly, and which is not very easily excited by revolutionary movements. That is not the case here. This country is more top-heavy than any country in the world, and if it begins to rock, the crash here, for that reason, will be greater than in any land.*"

From this the reader will see that Mr. Lloyd George is not only a very intelligent man, but one who has also learned a great deal from the Marxists. We too have something to learn from Lloyd George.

Of definite interest is the following episode, which occurred in the course of the discussion after Lloyd George's speech:

> "*Mr. Wallace, M.P.: I should like to ask what the Prime Minister considers the effect might be in the industrial constituencies upon the industrial workers, so many of whom are Liberals at the present time and from whom we get so much support. Would not a possible result be to cause an immediate overwhelming accession of strength to the Labour Party from men who at present are our cordial supporters?*

> "The Prime Minister: I take a totally different view. The fact that Liberals are fighting among themselves undoubtedly drives a very considerable number of Liberals in despair to the Labour Party, where you get a considerable body of Liberals, very able men, whose business it is to discredit the Government. The result is undoubtedly to bring a good accession of public sentiment to the Labour Party. It does not go to the Liberals who are outside, it goes to the Labour Party, the by-elections show that."

It may be said, in passing, that this argument shows in particular how muddled even the most intelligent members of the bourgeoisie have become and how they cannot help committing irreparable blunders. That, in fact, is what will bring about the downfall of the bourgeoisie. Our people, however, may commit blunders (provided, of course, that they are not too serious and are rectified in time) and yet in the long run, will prove the victors.

The second political document is the following argument advanced by Comrade Sylvia Pankhurst, a "Left" Communist:

". . . Comrade Inkpin [the General Secretary of the British Socialist Party] refers to the Labour Party as 'the main body of the working-class movement'. Another comrade of the British Socialist Party, at the Third International, just held, put the British Socialist Party position more strongly. He said: 'We regard the Labour Party as the organised working class.'

"We do not take this view of the Labour Party. The Labour Party is very large numerically though its membership is to a great extent quiescent and apathetic, consisting of men and women who have joined the trade unions because their workmates are trade unionists, and to share the friendly benefits.

"But we recognise that the great size of the Labour Party is also due to the fact that it is the creation of a school of thought beyond which the majority of the British working class has not yet emerged, though great changes are at work in the mind of the people which will presently alter this state of affairs. . . .

"The British Labour Party, like the social-patriotic organisations of other countries, will, in the natural development of society, inevitably come into power. It is for the Communists to build up the forces that will overthrow the social patriots, and in this country we must not delay or falter in that work.

"We must not dissipate our energy in adding to the strength of the Labour Party; its rise to power is inevitable. We must concentrate on making a communist movement that will vanquish it. The Labour Party will soon be forming a government, the revolutionary opposition must make ready to attack it. . . ."

Thus the liberal bourgeoisie are abandoning the historical system of "two parties" (of exploiters), which has been hallowed by centuries of experience and has been extremely advantageous to the exploiters, and consider it necessary for these two parties to join forces against the Labour Party. A number of Liberals are deserting to the Labour Party like rats from a sinking ship. The Left Communists believe that the transfer of power to the Labour Party is inevitable and admit that it now has the backing of most workers. From this they draw the strange conclusion which Comrade Sylvia Pankhurst formulates as follows:

"The Communist Party must not compromise. . . . The Communist Party must keep its doctrine pure, and its independence of reformism inviolate, its

mission is to lead the way, without stopping or turning, by the direct road to the communist revolution."

On the contrary, the fact that most British workers still follow the lead of the British Kerenskys or Scheidemanns and have not yet had experience of a government composed of these people – an experience which was necessary in Russia and Germany so as to secure the mass transition of the workers to communism – undoubtedly indicates that the British Communists *should* participate in parliamentary action, that they should, from *within* parliament, help the masses of the workers see the results of a Henderson and Snowden government in practice, and that they should help the Hendersons and Snowdens defeat the united forces of Lloyd George and Churchill. To act otherwise would mean hampering the cause of the revolution, since revolution is impossible without a change in the views of the majority of the working class, a change brought about by the political experience of the masses, never by propaganda alone. "To lead the way without compromises, without turning" – this slogan is obviously wrong if it comes from a patently impotent minority of the workers who know (or at all events should know) that given a Henderson and Snowden victory over Lloyd George and Churchill, the majority will soon become disappointed in their leaders and will begin to support communism (or at all events will adopt an attitude of neutrality, and, in the main, of sympathetic neutrality, towards the Communists). It is as though 10,000 soldiers were to hurl themselves into battle against an enemy force of 50,000, when it would be proper to "halt", "take evasive action", or even effect a "compromise" so as to gain time until the arrival of the 100,000 reinforcements that are on their way but cannot go into action immediately. That is intellectualist childishness, not the serious tactics of a revolutionary class.

The fundamental law of revolution, which has been confirmed by all revolutions and especially by all three Russian revolutions in the twentieth century, is as follows: for a revolution to take place it is not enough for the exploited and oppressed masses to realise the impossibility of living in the old way, and demand changes; for a revolution to take place it is essential that the exploiters should not be able to live and rule in the old way. It is only when the *"lower classes" do not want* to live in the old way and the "upper classes" *cannot carry on in the old way* that the revolution can triumph. This truth can be expressed in other words: revolution is impossible without a nation-wide crisis (affecting both the exploited and the exploiters). It follows that, for a revolution to take place, it is essential, first, that a majority of the workers (or at least a majority of the class-conscious, thinking, and politically active workers) should fully realise that revolution is necessary, and that they should be prepared to die for it; second, that the ruling classes should be going through a governmental crisis, which draws even the most backward masses into politics (symptomatic of any genuine revolution is a rapid, tenfold and even hundredfold increase in the size of the working and oppressed masses – hitherto apathetic – who are capable of waging the political struggle), weakens the government, and makes it possible for the revolutionaries to rapidly overthrow it.

Incidentally, as can also be seen from Lloyd George's speech, both conditions for a successful proletarian revolution are clearly maturing in Great Britain. The errors of the Left Communists are particularly dangerous at present, because certain revolutionaries are not displaying a sufficiently thoughtful, sufficiently attentive, sufficiently intelligent and sufficiently shrewd attitude toward each of these conditions. If we are the party of the revolutionary *class*, and not merely a revolutionary group, and if we want the *masses* to follow us (and unless we achieve that, we stand the risk of remaining mere windbags), we must, first, help Henderson or Snowden to beat Lloyd George and Churchill (or, rather, compel the former to beat the latter, because the former *are afraid of their victory!*); second, we must help the majority of the working class to be convinced by their own experience that we are right, i.e., that the Hendersons and Snowdens are absolutely good for nothing, that they are petty-bourgeois and treacherous by nature, and that their bankruptcy is inevitable; third, we must bring nearer the moment when, *on the basis* of the disappointment of most of the workers in the Hendersons, it will be possible, with serious chances of success, to overthrow the government of the Hendersons at once; because if the most astute and solid Lloyd George, that big, not petty, bourgeois, is displaying consternation and is more and more weakening himself (and the bourgeoisie as a whole) by his "friction" with Churchill today and with Asquith tomorrow, how much greater will be the consternation of a Henderson government!

I will put it more concretely. In my opinion, the British Communists should unite their four parties and groups (all very weak, and some of them very, very weak) into a single Communist Party on the basis of the principles of the Third International and of *obligatory* participation in parliament. The Communist Party should propose the following "compromise" election agreement to the Hendersons and Snowdens:

let us jointly fight against the alliance between Lloyd George and the Conservatives; let us share parliamentary seats in proportion to the number of workers' votes polled for the Labour Party and for the Communist Party (not in elections, but in a special ballot), and let us retain *complete freedom* of agitation, propaganda and political activity. Of course, without this latter condition, we cannot agree to a bloc, for that would be treachery; the British Communists must demand and get complete freedom to expose the Hendersons and the Snowdens in the same way as (*for fifteen years* – 1903–17) the Russian Bolsheviks demanded and got it in respect of the Russian Hendersons and Snowdens, i.e., the Mensheviks.

If the Hendersons and the Snowdens accept a bloc on these terms, we shall be the gainers, because the number of parliamentary seats is of no importance to us; we are not out for seats. We shall yield on this point (whilst the Hendersons and especially their new friends – or new masters – the Liberals who have joined the Independent Labour Party are most eager to get seats). We shall be the gainers, because we shall carry *our* agitation among the *masses* at a time when Lloyd George *himself* has "incensed" them, and we shall not only be helping the Labour Party to establish its government sooner, but shall also be helping the masses sooner to understand the communist propaganda that we shall carry on against the Hendersons, without any reticence or omission.

If the Hendersons and the Snowdens reject a bloc with us on these terms, we shall gain still more, for we shall at once have shown the *masses* (note that, even in the purely Menshevik and completely opportunist Independent Labour Party, the *rank and file* are in favour of Soviets) that the Hendersons prefer *their* close relations with the capitalists to the unity of all the workers. We shall immediately gain in the eyes of the *masses*, who, particularly after the brilliant, highly correct and highly useful (to communism) explanations given by Lloyd George, will be sympathetic to the idea of uniting all the workers against the Lloyd George-Conservative alliance. We shall gain immediately, because we shall have demonstrated to the masses that the Hendersons and the Snowdens are afraid to beat Lloyd George, afraid to assume power alone, and are striving to secure the *secret* support of Lloyd George, who is *openly* extending a hand to the Conservatives, against the Labour Party. It should be noted that in Russia, after the revolution of 27th February, 1917 (old style), the Bolsheviks' propaganda against the Mensheviks and Socialist-Revolutionaries (i.e., the Russian Hendersons and Snowdens) derived benefit precisely from a circumstance of this kind. We said to the Mensheviks and the Socialist-Revolutionaries: assume full power without the bourgeoisie, because you have a majority in the Soviets (at the First All-Russia Congress of Soviets, in June 1917, the Bolsheviks had only 13 per cent of the votes). But the Russian Hendersons and Snowdens were afraid to assume power without the bourgeoisie, and when the bourgeoisie held up the elections to the Constituent Assembly, knowing full well that the elections would give a majority to the Socialist-Revolutionaries and the Mensheviks[*8] (who formed a close political bloc and in fact represented *only* petty-bourgeois democracy), the Socialist-Revolutionaries and the Mensheviks were unable energetically and consistently to oppose these delays.

If the Hendersons and the Snowdens reject a bloc with the Communists, the latter will immediately gain by winning the sympathy of the masses and discrediting the Hendersons and Snowdens; if, as a result, we do lose a few parliamentary seats, it is a matter of no significance to us. We would put up our candidates in a very few but absolutely safe constituencies, namely, constituencies where our candidatures would not give any seats to the Liberals at the expense of the Labour candidates. We would take part in the election campaign, distribute leaflets agitating for communism, and, in *all* constituencies where we have no candidates, we would urge the electors *to vote for the Labour candidate and against the bourgeois candidate*. Comrades Sylvia Pankhurst and Gallacher are mistaken in thinking that this is a betrayal of communism, or a renunciation of the struggle against the social-traitors. On the contrary, the cause of communist revolution would undoubtedly gain thereby.

At present, British Communists very often find it hard even to approach the masses, and even to get a hearing from them. If I come out as a Communist and call upon them to vote for Henderson and against Lloyd George, they will certainly give me a hearing. And I shall be able to explain in a popular manner, not only why the Soviets are better than a parliament and why the dictatorship of the proletariat is better than the dictatorship of Churchill (disguised with the signboard of bourgeois "democracy"), but also that, with my vote, I want to support Henderson in the same way as the rope supports a hanged man – that the impending establishment of a government of the Hendersons will prove that I am right, will bring the masses over to my side, and will hasten the political death of the Hendersons and the Snowdens just as was the case with their kindred spirits in Russia and Germany.

If the objection is raised that these tactics are too "subtle" or too complex for the masses to understand, that these tactics will split and scatter our forces, will prevent us from concentrating them on Soviet revolution, etc., I will reply to the "Left" objectors: don't ascribe your doctrinarism to the masses! The masses in Russia are no doubt no better educated than the masses in Britain; if anything, they are less so. Yet the masses understood the Bolsheviks, and the fact that, in September 1917, *on the eve* of the Soviet revolution, the Bolsheviks put up their candidates for a bourgeois parliament (the Constituent Assembly) and *on the day after* the Soviet revolution, in November 1917, took part in the elections to this Constituent Assembly, which they got rid of on 5th January, 1918 – this did not hamper the Bolsheviks, but, on the contrary, helped them.

I cannot deal here with the second point of disagreement among the British Communists – the question of affiliation or non-affiliation to the Labour Party. I have too little material at my disposal on this question, which is highly complex because of the unique character of the British Labour Party, whose very structure is so unlike that of the political parties usual on the European continent. It is beyond doubt, however, first, that in this question, too, those who try to deduce the tactics of the revolutionary proletariat from principles such as: "The Communist Party must keep its doctrine pure, and its independence of reformism inviolate; its mission is to lead the way, without stopping or turning, by the direct road to the communist revolution" – will inevitably fall into error. Such principles are merely a repetition of the mistake made by the French Blanquist Communards, who, in 1874, "repudiated" all compromises and all intermediate stages. Second, it is beyond doubt that, in this question too, as always, the task consists in learning to apply the general and basic principles of communism to the *specific relations* between classes and parties, to the *specific features* in the objective development towards communism, which are different in each country and which we must be able to discover, study, and predict.

This, however, should be discussed, not in connection with British communism alone, but in connection with the general conclusions concerning the development of communism in all capitalist countries. We shall now proceed to deal with this subject.

Footnotes

35 The British Socialist Party was founded in 1911, in Manchester, as a result of a merger of the Social-Democratic Party and other socialist groups. The B.S.P. conducted agitation in the spirit of

Marxism, it was "not opportunist and was really independent of the Liberals". However, its small membership and its poor links with the masses gave the B.S.P. a somewhat sectarian character. During the First World War, a bitter struggle developed within the British Socialist Party between the internationalists (William Gallacher, Albert Inkpin, John Maclean, Theodore Rothstein and others), and the social-chauvinists, headed by Hyndman. Within the internationalist trend were inconsistent elements that took a Centrist stand on a number of issues. In February 1916, a group of B.S.P. leaders founded the newspaper The Call, which played an important role in uniting the internationalists. The B.S.P.'s annual conference, held in Salford in April 1916, condemned the social-chauvinist stand of Hyndman and his supporters, who, after the conference, left the party.

The British Socialist Party welcomed the Great October Socialist Revolution, its members playing an important part in the "Hands Off Russia" movement. In 1919, the overwhelming majority of its organisations (98 against 4) declared for affiliation to the Communist International. The British Socialist Party, together with the Communist Unity Group formed the core of the Communist Party of Great Britain. At the First (Unity) Congress, held in 1920. the vast majority of B.S.P. local organisations entered the Communist Party.

[36] The Socialist Labour Party was organised in 1903 by a group of the Left-wing Social-Democrats who had broken away from the Social-Democratic Federation. The South Wales Socialist Society was a small group consisting mostly of Welsh coal miners. The Workers' Socialist Federation was a small organisation which emerged from the Women's Suffrage League and consisted mostly of women.

The Leftist organisations did not join the Communist Party of Great Britain when it was formed (its Inaugural Congress was held on 31st July–1st August, 1920) since the Party's programme contained a clause on the Party participation in parliamentary elections and on affiliation to the Labour Party. At the Communist Party's Congress in January 1921, the South Wales Socialist Society and the Workers' Socialist Federation, which had assumed the names of the Communist Workers' Party and the Communist Party respectively, united with the Communist Party of Great Britain under the name of the United Communist Party of Great Britain. The leaders of the Socialist Labour Party refused to join.

[*7] I believe this party is opposed to affiliation to the Labour Party but not all its members are opposed to participation in Parliament.

[*8] The results of the November 1917 elections to the Constituent Assembly in Russia, based on returns embracing over 36,000,000 voters, were as follows: the Bolsheviks obtained 25 per cent of the votes; the various parties of the landowners and the bourgeoisie obtained 13 per cent, and the petty-bourgeois-democratic parties, i.e., the Socialist-Revolutionaries, Mensheviks and a number of similar small groups obtained 62 per cent.

X

Several Conclusions

The Russian bourgeois revolution of 1905 revealed a highly original turn in world history: in one of the most backward capitalist countries, the strike movement attained a scope and power unprecedented anywhere in the world. In the *first month* of 1905 *alone*, the number of strikers was ten times the *annual* average for the previous decade (1895–1904); from January to October 1905, strikes grew all the time and reached enormous proportions. Under the influence of a number of unique historical conditions, backward Russia was the first to show the world, not only the growth, by leaps and bounds, of the independent activity of the oppressed masses in time of revolution (this had occurred in all great revolutions), but also that the significance of the proletariat is infinitely greater than its proportion in the total population; it showed a combination of the economic strike and the political strike, with the latter developing into an armed uprising, and the birth of the Soviets, a new form of mass struggle and mass organisation of the classes oppressed by capitalism.

The revolutions of February and October 1917 led to the all-round development of the Soviets on a nation-wide scale and to their victory in the proletarian socialist revolution. In less than two years, the international character of the Soviets, the spread of this form of struggle and organisation to the world working-class movement and the historical mission of the Soviets as the grave-digger, heir and successor of bourgeois parliamentarianism and of bourgeois democracy in general, all became clear.

But that is not all. The history of the working-class movement now shows that, in all countries, it is about to go through (and is already going through) a struggle waged by communism – emergent, gaining strength and advancing towards victory – against, primarily, Menshevism, i.e., opportunism and social-chauvinism (the home brand in each particular country), and then as a complement, so to say, Left-wing communism. The former struggle has developed in all countries, apparently without any exception, as a duel between the Second International (already virtually dead) and the Third International. The latter struggle is to be seen in Germany, Great Britain, Italy, America (at any rate, a certain *section* of the Industrial Workers of the World and of the anarcho-syndicalist trends uphold the errors of Left-wing communism alongside of an almost universal and almost unreserved acceptance of the Soviet system), and in France (the attitude of a section of the former syndicalists towards the political party and parliamentarianism, also alongside of the acceptance of the Soviet system); in other words, the struggle is undoubtedly being waged, not only on an international, but even on a worldwide scale.

But while the working-class movement is everywhere going through what is actually the same kind of preparatory school for victory over the bourgeoisie, it is achieving that development in its *own way* in each country. The big and advanced capitalist countries are travelling this road *far more rapidly* than did Bolshevism, to which history granted fifteen years to prepare itself for victory, as an organised political trend. In the brief space of a year, the Third International has already scored a decisive victory; it has defeated the yellow, social-chauvinist Second International, which only a few months ago was incomparably stronger than the Third International, seemed stable and powerful, and enjoyed every possible support – direct and indirect, material (Cabinet posts, passports, the press) and ideological – from the world bourgeoisie.

It is now essential that Communists of every country should quite consciously take into account both the fundamental objectives of the struggle against opportunism and "Left" doctrinarism, and the *concrete features* which this struggle assumes and must inevitably assume in each country, in conformity with the specific character of its economics, politics, culture, and national composition (Ireland, etc.), its colonies, religious divisions, and so on and so forth. Dissatisfaction with the Second International is felt everywhere and is spreading and growing, both because of its opportunism and because of its inability or incapacity to create a really centralised and really leading centre capable of directing the international tactics of the revolutionary proletariat in its struggle for a world Soviet republic. It should be clearly realised that such a leading centre can never be built up on stereotyped, mechanically equated, and identical tactical rules of struggle. As long as national and state distinctions exist among peoples and countries – and these will continue to exist for a very long time to come, even after the dictatorship of the proletariat has been established on a world-wide scale – the unity of the international tactics of the communist working-class movement in all countries demands, not the elimination of variety or the suppression of national distinctions (which is a pipe dream at present), but an application of the *fundamental* principles of communism (Soviet power and the dictatorship of the proletariat), which will *correctly modify* these principles in certain *particulars*, correctly adapt and apply them to national and national-state distinctions. To seek out, investigate, predict, and grasp that which is nationally specific and nationally distinctive, in the *concrete manner* in which each country should tackle a *single* international task: victory over opportunism and Left doctrinarism within the working-class movement; the overthrow of the bourgeoisie; the establishment of a Soviet republic and a proletarian dictatorship – such is the basic task in the historical period that all the advanced countries (and not they alone) are going through. The chief thing – though, of course, far from everything – the chief thing, has already been achieved: the vanguard of the working class has been won over, has ranged itself on the side of Soviet government and against parliamentarianism, on the side of the dictatorship of the proletariat and against bourgeois democracy. All efforts and all attention should now be concentrated on the *next* step, which may seem – and from a certain viewpoint actually is – less fundamental, but, on the other hand, is actually closer to a practical accomplishment of the task. That step is: the search after forms of the *transition* or the *approach* to the proletarian revolution.

The proletarian vanguard has been won over ideologically. That is the main thing. Without this, not even the first step towards victory can be made. But that is still quite a long way from victory. Victory cannot be won with a vanguard alone. To throw only the vanguard into the decisive battle, before the entire class, the broad masses, have taken up a position either of direct support for the vanguard, or at least of sympathetic neutrality towards it and of precluded support for the enemy, would be, not merely foolish but criminal. Propaganda and agitation alone are not enough for an entire class, the broad masses of the working people, those oppressed by capital, to take up such a stand. For that, the masses must have their own political experience. Such is the fundamental law of all great revolutions, which has been confirmed with compelling force and vividness, not only in Russia but in Germany as well. To turn resolutely towards communism, it was necessary, not only for the ignorant and often illiterate masses of Russia, but also for the literate and well-educated masses of Germany, to realise from their own bitter experience the absolute impotence and spinelessness, the absolute helplessness and servility to the bourgeoisie, and the utter vileness of the government of the paladins of the Second International; they had to realise that a dictatorship of the extreme reactionaries (Kornilov[37] in Russia; Kapp[38] and Co. in Germany) is inevitably the only alternative to a dictatorship of the proletariat.

The immediate objective of the class-conscious vanguard of the international working-class movement, i.e., the Communist parties, groups and trends, is to be able to *lead* the broad masses (who are still, for the most part, apathetic, inert, dormant and convention-ridden) to their new position, or, rather, to be able to lead, *not only* their own party but also these masses in their advance and transition to the new position. While the first historical objective (that of winning over the class-conscious vanguard of the proletariat to the side of Soviet power and the dictatorship of the working class) could not have been reached without a complete ideological and political victory over opportunism and social-chauvinism, the second and immediate objective, which consists in being able to lead the *masses* to a new position ensuring the victory of the vanguard in the revolution, cannot be reached without the liquidation of Left doctrinarism, and without a full elimination of its errors.

As long as it was (and inasmuch as it still is) a question of winning the proletariat's vanguard over to the side of communism, priority went and still goes to propaganda work; even propaganda circles, with all their parochial limitations, are useful under these conditions, and produce good results. But when it is a question of practical action by the masses, of the disposition, if one may so put it, of vast armies, of the alignment of *all* the class forces in a given society *for the final and decisive battle*, then propagandist methods alone, the mere repetition of the truths of "pure" communism, are of no avail. In these circumstances, one must not count in thousands, like the propagandist belonging to a small group that has not yet given leadership to the masses; in these circumstances one must count in millions and tens of millions. In these circumstances, we must ask ourselves, not only whether we have convinced the vanguard of the revolutionary class, but also whether the historically effective forces of *all* classes – positively of all the classes in a given society, without exception – are arrayed in such a way that the decisive battle is at hand – in such a way that: (1) all the class forces hostile to us have become sufficiently entangled, are sufficiently at loggerheads with each other, have sufficiently weakened themselves in a struggle which is beyond their strength; (2) all the vacillating and unstable, intermediate elements – the petty bourgeoisie and the petty-bourgeois democrats, as distinct from the bourgeoisie – have sufficiently exposed themselves in the eyes of the people, have sufficiently disgraced themselves through their practical bankruptcy, and (3) among the proletariat, a mass sentiment favouring the most determined, bold and dedicated revolutionary action against the bourgeoisie has emerged and begun to grow vigorously. Then revolution is indeed ripe; then, indeed, if we have correctly gauged all the conditions indicated and summarised above, and if we have chosen the right moment, our victory is assured.

The differences between the Churchills and the Lloyd Georges – with insignificant national distinctions, these political types exist in *all* countries – on the one hand, and between the Hendersons and the Lloyd Georges on the other, are quite minor and unimportant from the standpoint of pure (i.e., abstract) communism, i.e., communism that has not yet matured to the stage of practical political action by the masses. However, from the standpoint of this practical action by the masses, these differences are most important. To take due account of these differences, and to determine the moment when the inevitable conflicts between these "friends", which weaken and enfeeble *all the "friends" taken together*, will have come to a head – that is the concern, the task, of a Communist who wants to be, not merely a class-conscious and convinced propagandist of ideas, but a practical leader of the *masses* in the revolution. It is necessary to link the strictest devotion to the ideas of communism with the ability to effect all the necessary practical compromises, tacks, conciliatory manoeuvres, zigzags, retreats and so on, in order to speed up the achievement and then loss of political power by the Hendersons (the heroes of the Second International, if we are not to name individual representatives of petty-bourgeois democracy who call themselves socialists); to accelerate their inevitable bankruptcy in practice, which will enlighten the masses in the spirit of our ideas, in the direction of communism; to accelerate the inevitable friction, quarrels, conflicts and complete disintegration among the Hendersons, the Lloyd Georges and the Churchills (the Mensheviks, the Socialist-Revolutionaries, the Constitutional-Democrats, the monarchists; the Scheidemanns, the bourgeoisie and the Kappists, etc.); to select the proper moment when the discord among these "pillars of sacrosanct private property" is at its height, so that, through a decisive offensive, the proletariat will defeat them all and capture political power.

History as a whole, and the history of revolutions in particular, is always richer in content, more varied, more multiform, more lively and ingenious than is imagined by even the best parties, the most class-conscious vanguards of the most advanced classes. This can readily be understood, because even the finest of vanguards express the class-consciousness, will, passion and imagination of tens of thousands, whereas at moments of great upsurge and the exertion of all human capacities, revolutions are made by the class-consciousness, will, passion and imagination of tens of millions, spurred on by a most acute struggle of classes. Two very important practical conclusions follow from this: first, that in order to accomplish its task the revolutionary class must be able to master *all* forms or aspects of social activity without exception (completing after the capture of political power – sometimes at great risk and with very great danger – what it did not complete before the capture of power); second, that the revolutionary class must be prepared for the most rapid and brusque replacement of one form by another.

One will readily agree that any army which does not train to use all the weapons, all the means and methods of warfare that the enemy possesses, or may possess, is behaving in an unwise or even criminal manner. This applies to politics even more than it does to the art of war. In politics it is even harder to know in advance which methods of struggle will be applicable and to our advantage in certain future conditions. Unless we learn to apply all the methods of struggle, we may suffer grave and sometimes even decisive defeat, if changes beyond our control in the position of the other classes bring to the forefront a form of activity in which we are especially weak. If, however, we learn to use all the methods of struggle, victory will be certain, because we represent the interests of the really foremost and really revolutionary class, even if circumstances do not permit us to make use of weapons that are most dangerous to the enemy, weapons that deal the swiftest mortal blows. Inexperienced revolutionaries often think that legal methods of struggle are opportunist because, in this field, the bourgeoisie has most frequently deceived and duped the workers (particularly in "peaceful" and non-revolutionary times), while illegal methods of struggle are revolutionary. That, however, is wrong. The truth is that those parties and leaders are opportunists and traitors to the working class that are unable or unwilling (do not say, "I can't"; say, "I shan't") to use illegal methods of struggle in conditions such as those which prevailed, for example, during the imperialist war of 1914–18, when the bourgeoisie of the freest democratic countries most brazenly and brutally deceived the workers, and smothered the truth about the predatory character of the war. But revolutionaries who are incapable of combining illegal forms of struggle with *every* form of legal struggle are poor revolutionaries indeed. It is not difficult to be a revolutionary when revolution has already broken out and is at its height, when all people are joining the revolution just because they are carried away, because it is the vogue, and sometimes even from careerist motives. After its victory, the proletariat has to make most strenuous efforts, even the most painful, so as to "liberate" itself from such pseudo-revolutionaries. It is far more difficult – and far more precious – to be a revolutionary when the conditions for direct, open, really mass and really revolutionary struggle *do not yet exist*, to be able to champion the interests of the revolution (by propaganda, agitation and organisation) in non-revolutionary bodies, and quite often in downright reactionary bodies, in a non-revolutionary situation, among the masses who are incapable of immediately appreciating the need for revolutionary methods of action. To be able to seek, find and correctly determine the specific path or the particular turn of events that will *lead* the masses to the real, decisive and final revolutionary struggle – such is the main objective of communism in Western Europe and in America today.

Britain is an example. We cannot tell – no one can tell in advance – how soon a real proletarian revolution will flare up there, and *what immediate cause* will most serve to rouse, kindle, and impel into the struggle the very wide masses, who are still dormant. Hence, it is our duty to carry on all our preparatory work in such a way as to be "well shod on all four feet" (as the late Plekhanov, when he was a Marxist and revolutionary, was fond of saying). It is possible that the breach will be forced, the ice broken, by a parliamentary crisis, or by a crisis arising from colonial and imperialist contradictions, which are hopelessly entangled and are becoming increasingly painful and acute, or perhaps by some third cause, etc. We are not discussing the kind of struggle that will *determine* the fate of the proletarian revolution in Great Britain (no Communist has any doubt on that score; for all of us this is a foregone conclusion): what we are discussing is the *immediate cause* that will bring into motion the now dormant proletarian masses, and lead them right up to revolution. Let us not forget that in the French bourgeois republic, for example, in a situation which, from both the international and the national viewpoints, was a hundred times less revolutionary than it is today, such an "unexpected" and "petty" cause as one of the many thousands of fraudulent machinations of the reactionary military caste (the Dreyfus case)[39] was enough to bring the people to the brink of civil war!

In Great Britain the Communists should constantly, unremittingly and unswervingly utilise parliamentary elections and all the vicissitudes of the Irish, colonial and world-imperialist policy of the British Government, and all other fields, spheres and aspects of public life, and work in all of them in a new way, in a communist way, in the spirit of the Third, not the Second, International. I have neither the time nor the space here to describe the "Russian" "Bolshevik" methods of participation in parliamentary elections and in the parliamentary struggle; I can, however, assure foreign Communists that they were quite unlike the usual West-European parliamentary campaigns. From this the conclusion is often drawn: "Well, that was in Russia, in our country parliamentarianism is different." This is a false conclusion. Communists, adherents of the Third International in all countries, exist for the purpose of *changing* – all along the line, in all spheres of life – the old socialist, trade unionist, syndicalist, and parliamentary type of work into a *new* type of work, the communist. In Russia, too, there was always an abundance of opportunism, purely bourgeois sharp practices and capitalist rigging in the elections. In Western Europe and in America, the Communist must learn to create a new, uncustomary, non-opportunist, and non-careerist parliamentarianism; the Communist parties must issue their slogans; true proletarians, with the help of the unorganised and downtrodden poor, should distribute leaflets, canvass workers' houses and cottages of the rural proletarians and peasants in the remote villages (fortunately there are many times fewer remote villages in Europe than in Russia, and in Britain the number is very small); they should go into the public houses, penetrate into unions, societies and chance gatherings of the common people, and speak to the people, not in learned (or very parliamentary) language, they should not at all strive to "get seats" in parliament, but should everywhere try to get people to think, and draw the masses into the struggle, to take the bourgeoisie at its word and utilise the machinery it has set up, the elections it has appointed, and the appeals it has made to the people; they should try to explain to the people what Bolshevism is, in a way that was never possible (under bourgeois rule) outside of election times (exclusive, of course, of times of big strikes, when in Russia a *similar* apparatus for widespread popular agitation worked even more intensively). It is very difficult to do this in Western Europe and extremely difficult in America, but it can and must be done, for the objectives of communism cannot be achieved without effort. We must work to accomplish *practical* tasks, ever more varied and ever more closely connected with all branches of social life, winning branch after branch, and sphere after sphere *from the bourgeoisie*.

In Great Britain, further, the work of propaganda, agitation and organisation among the armed forces and among the oppressed and underprivileged nationalities in their "own" state (Ireland, the colonies) must also be tackled in a new fashion (one that is not socialist, but communist; not reformist, but revolutionary). That is because, in the era of imperialism in general and especially today after a war that was a sore trial to the peoples and has quickly opened their eyes to the truth (i.e., the fact that tens of millions were killed and maimed for the sole purpose of deciding whether the British or the German robbers should plunder the largest number of countries), all these spheres of social life are heavily charged with inflammable material and are creating numerous causes of conflicts, crises and an intensification of the class struggle. We do not and cannot know which spark – of the innumerable sparks that are flying about in all countries as a result of the world economic and political crisis – will kindle the conflagration, in the sense of raising up the masses; we must, therefore, with our new and communist principles, set to work to stir up all and sundry, even the oldest, mustiest and seemingly hopeless spheres, for otherwise we shall not be able to cope with our tasks, shall not be comprehensively prepared, shall not be in possession of all the weapons and shall not prepare ourselves either to gain victory over the bourgeoisie (which arranged all aspects of social life – and has now disarranged them – in its bourgeois fashion), or to bring about the impending communist reorganisation of every sphere of life, following that victory.

Since the proletarian revolution in Russia and its victories on an international scale, expected neither by the bourgeoisie nor the philistines, the entire world has become different, and the bourgeoisie everywhere has become different too. It is terrified of "Bolshevism", exasperated by it almost to the point of frenzy, and for that very reason it is, on the one hand, precipitating the progress of events and, on the other, concentrating on the forcible suppression of Bolshevism, thereby weakening its own position in a number of other fields. In their tactics the Communists in all the advanced countries must take both these circumstances into account.

When the Russian Cadets and Kerensky began furiously to hound the Bolsheviks – especially since April 1917, and more particularly in June and July 1917 – they overdid things. Millions of copies of bourgeois papers, clamouring in every key against the Bolsheviks, helped the masses to make an appraisal of Bolshevism; apart from the newspapers, all public life was full of discussions about Bolshevism, as a result of the bourgeoisie's "zeal". Today the millionaires of all countries are behaving on an international scale in a way that deserves our heartiest thanks. They are hounding Bolshevism with the same zeal as Kerensky and Co. did; they, too, are overdoing things and *helping* us just as Kerensky did. When the French bourgeoisie makes Bolshevism the central issue in the elections, and accuses the comparatively moderate or vacillating socialists of being Bolsheviks; when the American bourgeoisie, which has completely lost its head, seizes thousands and thousands of people on suspicion of Bolshevism, creates an atmosphere of panic, and broadcasts stories of Bolshevik plots; when, despite all its wisdom and experience, the British bourgeoisie – the most "solid" in the world – makes incredible blunders, founds richly endowed "anti-Bolshevik societies", creates a special literature on Bolshevism, and recruits an extra number of scientists, agitators and clergymen to combat it, we must salute and thank the capitalists. They are working for us. They are helping us to get the masses interested in the essence and significance of Bolshevism, and they cannot do otherwise, for they have *already* failed to ignore Bolshevism and stifle it.

But at the same time, the bourgeoisie sees practically only one aspect of Bolshevism – insurrection, violence, and terror; it therefore strives to prepare itself for resistance and opposition primarily in *this* field. It is possible that, in certain instances, in certain countries, and for certain brief periods, it will succeed in this. We must reckon with such an eventuality, and we have absolutely nothing to fear if it does succeed. Communism is emerging in positively every sphere of public life; its beginnings are to be seen literally on all sides. The "contagion" (to use the favourite metaphor of the bourgeoisie and the bourgeois police, the one mostly to their liking) has very thoroughly penetrated the organism and has completely permeated it. If special efforts are made to block one of the channels, the "contagion" will find another one, sometimes very unexpectedly. Life will assert itself. Let the bourgeoisie rave, work itself into a frenzy, go to extremes, commit follies, take vengeance on the Bolsheviks in advance, and endeavour to kill off (as in India, Hungary, Germany, etc.) more hundreds, thousands, and hundreds of thousands of yesterday's and tomorrow's Bolsheviks. In acting thus, the bourgeoisie is acting as all historically doomed classes have done. Communists should know that, in any case, the future belongs to them; therefore, we can (and must) combine the most intense passion in the great revolutionary struggle, with the coolest and most sober appraisal of the frenzied ravings of the bourgeoisie. The Russian revolution was cruelly defeated in 1905; the Russian Bolsheviks were defeated in July 1917; over 15,000 German Communists were killed as a result of the wily provocation and cunning manoeuvres of Scheidemann and Noske, who were working hand in glove with the bourgeoisie and the monarchist generals; White terror is raging in Finland and Hungary. But in all cases in all countries, communism is becoming steeled and is growing; its roots are so deep that persecution does not weaken or debilitate it but only strengthens it. Only one thing is lacking to enable us to march forward more confidently and firmly to victory, namely, the universal and thorough awareness of all Communists in all countries of the necessity to display the utmost *flexibility* in their tactics. The communist movement, which is developing magnificently, now lacks, especially in the advanced countries, this awareness and the ability to apply it in practice.

That which happened to such leaders of the Second International, such highly erudite Marxists devoted to socialism as Kautsky, Otto Bauer and others, could (and should) provide a useful lesson. They fully appreciated the need for flexible tactics; they themselves learned Marxist dialectic and taught it to others (and much of what they have done in this field will always remain a valuable contribution to socialist literature); however, *in the application* of this dialectic they committed such an error, or proved to be so *un*dialectical in practice, so incapable of taking into account the rapid change of forms and the rapid acquisition of new content by the old forms, that their fate is not much more enviable than that of Hyndman, Guesde and Plekhanov. The principal reason for their bankruptcy was that they were hypnotised by a definite form of growth of the working-class movement and socialism, forgot all about the one-sidedness of that form, were afraid to see the break-up which objective conditions made inevitable, and continued to repeat simple and, at first glance, incontestable axioms that had been learned by rote, like: "three is more than two". But politics is more like algebra than like arithmetic, and still more like higher than elementary mathematics. In reality, all the old forms of the socialist movement have acquired a new content, and, consequently, a new symbol, the "minus" sign, has appeared in front of all the figures; our wiseacres, however, have stubbornly continued (and still continue) to persuade themselves and others that "minus three" is more than "minus two".

We must see to it that Communists do not make a similar mistake, only in the opposite sense, or rather, we must see to it that a *similar mistake*, only made in the opposite sense by the "Left" Communists, is corrected as soon as possible and eliminated as rapidly and painlessly as possible. It is not only Right doctrinarism that is erroneous; Left doctrinarism is erroneous too. Of course, the mistake of Left doctrinarism in communism is at present a thousand times less dangerous and less significant than that of Right doctrinarism (i.e., social-chauvinism and Kautskyism); but, after all, that is only due to the fact that Left communism is a very young trend, is only just coming into being. It is only for this reason that, under certain conditions, the disease can be easily eradicated, and we must set to work with the utmost energy to eradicate it.

The old forms burst asunder, for it turned out that their new content – anti-proletarian and reactionary – had attained an inordinate development. From the standpoint of the development of international communism, our work today has such a durable and powerful content (for Soviet power and the dictatorship of the proletariat) that it can *and must* manifest itself in any form, both new and old; it can and must regenerate, conquer and subjugate all forms, not only the new, but also the old – not for the purpose of reconciling itself with the old, but for the purpose of making all and every form – new and old – a weapon for the complete and irrevocable victory of communism.

The Communists must exert every effort to direct the working-class movement and social development in general along the straightest and shortest road to the victory of Soviet power and the dictatorship of the proletariat on a world-wide scale. That is an incontestable truth. But it is enough to take one little step farther – a step that might seem to be in the same direction – and truth turns into error. We have only to say, as the German and British Left Communists do, that we recognise only one road, only the direct road, and that we will not permit tacking, conciliatory manoeuvres, or compromising – and it will be a mistake which may cause, and in part has already caused and is causing, very grave prejudices to communism. Right doctrinarism persisted in recognising only the old forms, and became utterly bankrupt, for it did not notice the new content. Left doctrinarism persists in the unconditional repudiation of certain old forms, failing to see that the new content is forcing its way through all and sundry forms, that it is our duty as Communists to master all forms, to learn how, with the maximum rapidity, to supplement one form with another, to substitute one for another, and to adapt our tactics to any such change that does not come from our class or from our efforts.

World revolution has been so powerfully stimulated and accelerated by the horrors, vileness and abominations of the world imperialist war and by the hopelessness of the situation created by it, this revolution is developing in scope and depth with such splendid rapidity, with such a wonderful variety of changing forms, with such an instructive practical refutation of all doctrinarism, that there is every reason to hope for a rapid and complete recovery of the international communist movement from the infantile disorder of "Left-wing" communism.

27th April, 1920

Footnotes

[37] This refers to the counter-revolutionary mutiny organised in August 1917 by the bourgeoisie and the landowners, under the Supreme Commander-in-Chief, the tsarist general Kornilov. The conspirators hoped to seize Petrograd, smash the Bolshevik Party, break up the Soviets, establish a military dictatorship in the country, and prepare the restoration of the monarchy.

The mutiny began on 25th August (7th September), Kornilov sending the 3rd Cavalry Corps against Petrograd, where Kornilov's counter-revolutionary organisations were ready to act. The Kornilov mutiny was crushed by the workers and peasants led by the Bolshevik Party. Under pressure from the masses, the Provisional Government was forced to order that Kornilov and his accomplices be arrested and brought to trial.

[38] The reference is to the military-monarchist coup d'état, the so-called Kapp putsch organised by the German reactionary militarists. It was headed by the monarchist landowner Kapp and Generals Ludendorff, Seeckt and Lüttwitz. The conspirators prepared the coup with the connivance of the Social-Democratic government. On 13th March, 1920, the mutinous generals moved troops against Berlin and, meeting with no resistance from the government, proclaimed a military dictatorship. The German workers replied with a general strike. Under pressure from the proletariat the Kapp government was overthrown on March 17, and the Social-Democrats again took power.

[39] The Dreyfus case – a provocative trial organised in 1894 by the reactionary-monarchist circles of the French militarists. On trial was Dreyfus, a Jewish officer of the French General Staff, falsely accused of espionage and high treason. Dreyfus's conviction – he was condemned to life imprisonment – was used by the French reactionaries to rouse anti-Semitism and to attack the republican regime and democratic liberties. When, in 1898, socialists and progressive bourgeois

democrats such as Emile Zola, Jean Jaurès, and Anatole France launched a campaign for Dreyfus's re-trial, the case became a major political issue and split the country into two camps – the republicans and democrats on the one hand, and a bloc of monarchists, clericals, anti-Semites and nationalists, on the other. Under the pressure of public opinion, Dreyfus was released in 1899, and in 1906 was acquitted by the Court of Cassation and reinstated in the Army.

Appendix

Before publishing houses in our country – which has been plundered by the imperialists of the whole world in revenge for the proletarian revolution, and which is still being plundered and blockaded by them regardless of all promises they made to their workers – were able to bring out my pamphlet, additional material arrived from abroad. Without claiming to present in my pamphlet anything more than the cursory notes of a publicist, I shall dwell briefly upon a few points.

I. The split among the German Communists

The split among the Communists in Germany is an accomplished fact. The "Lefts", or the "opposition on principle", have formed a separate Communist Workers' Party, as distinct from the Communist Party. A split also seems imminent in Italy – I say "seems", as I have only two additional issues (Nos. 7 and 8) of the Left newspaper, *Il Soviet*, in which the possibility of and necessity for a split is openly discussed, and mention is also made of a congress of the "Abstentionist" group (or the boycottists, i.e., opponents of participation in parliament), which group is still part of the Italian Socialist Party.

There is reason to fear that the split with the "Lefts", the anti-parliamentarians (in part anti-politicals too, who are opposed to any political party and to work in the trade unions), will become an international phenomenon, like the split with the "Centrists" (i.e., Kautskyites, Longuetists, Independents, etc.). Let that be so. At all events, a split is better than confusion, which hampers the ideological, theoretical and revolutionary growth and maturing of the party, and its harmonious, really organised practical work which actually paves the way for the dictatorship of the proletariat.

Let the "Lefts" put themselves to a practical test on a national and international scale. Let them try to prepare for (and then implement) the dictatorship of the proletariat, without a rigorously centralised party with iron discipline, without the ability to become masters of every sphere, every branch, and every variety of political and cultural work. Practical experience will soon teach them.

Only, every effort should be made to prevent the split with the "Lefts" from impeding – or to see that it impedes as little as possible – the necessary amalgamation into a single party, inevitable in the near future, of all participants in the working-class movement who sincerely and conscientiously stand for Soviet government and the dictatorship of the proletariat. It was the exceptional good fortune of the Bolsheviks in Russia to have had fifteen years for a systematic and consummated struggle both against the Mensheviks (i.e., the opportunists and "Centrists") and against the "Lefts", long before the masses began direct action for the dictatorship of the proletariat. In Europe and America the same work has now to be done by forced marches, so to say. Certain individuals, especially among unsuccessful aspirants to leadership, may (if they lack proletarian discipline and are not honest towards themselves) persist in their mistakes for a long time; however, when the time is ripe, the masses of the workers will themselves unite easily and rapidly and unite all sincere Communists to form a single party capable of establishing the Soviet system and the dictatorship of the proletariat.[*9]

II. The Communists and the Independents in Germany

In this pamphlet I have expressed the opinion that a compromise between the Communists and the Left wing of the Independents is necessary and useful to communism, but will not be easy to bring about. Newspapers which I have subsequently received have confirmed this opinion on both points. No. 32 of *The Red Flag*, organ of the Central Committee, the Communist Party of Germany (*Die Rote Fahne*, Zentralorgan der Kommunistischen Partei Deutschlands, Spartakusbund, of 26th March, 1920) published a "statement" by this Central Committee regarding the Kapp-Lüttwitz military *putsch* and on the "socialist government". This statement is quite correct both in its basic premise and its practical conclusions. The basic premise is that at present there is no "objective basis" for the dictatorship of the proletariat because the "majority of the urban workers" support the Independents. The conclusion is: a promise to be a "loyal opposition" (i.e., renunciation of preparations for a "forcible overthrow") to a "socialist government if it excludes bourgeois-capitalist parties".

In the main, this tactic is undoubtedly correct. Yet, even if minor inaccuracies of formulation should not be dwelt on, it is impossible to pass over in silence the fact that a government consisting of social-traitors should not (in an official statement by the Communist Party) be called "socialist"; that one should not speak of the exclusion of "bourgeois-capitalist parties", when the parties both of the Scheidemanns and of the Kautskys and Crispiens are petty-bourgeois-democratic parties; that things should never be written that are contained in §4 of the statement, which reads:

> "*. . . A state of affairs in which political freedom can be enjoyed without restriction, and bourgeois democracy cannot operate as the dictatorship of capital is, from the viewpoint of the development of the proletarian dictatorship, of the utmost importance in further winning the proletarian masses over to the side of communism.*"

Such a state of affairs is impossible. Petty-bourgeois leaders, the German Hendersons (Scheidemanns) and Snowdens (Crispiens), do not and cannot go beyond the bounds of bourgeois democracy, which, in its turn, cannot but be a dictatorship of capital. To achieve the practical results that the Central Committee of the Communist Party had been quite rightly working for, there was no need to write such things, which are wrong in principle and politically harmful. It would have been sufficient to say (if one wished to observe parliamentary amenities): "As long as the majority of the urban workers follow the Independents, we Communists must do nothing to prevent those workers from getting rid of their last philistine-democratic (i.e., 'bourgeois-capitalist') illusions by going through the experience of having a government of their 'own'." That is sufficient ground for a compromise, which is really necessary and should consist in renouncing, for a certain period, all attempts at the forcible overthrow of a government which enjoys the confidence of a majority of the urban workers. But in everyday mass agitation, in which one is not bound by official parliamentary amenities, one might, of course, add:

> "Let scoundrels like the Scheidemanns, and philistines like the Kautskys and Crispiens reveal by their deeds how they have been fooled themselves and how they are fooling the workers; their 'clean' government will itself do the 'cleanest' job of all in 'cleansing' the Augean stables of socialism, Social-Democracy and other forms of social treachery."

The real nature of the present leaders of the Independent Social-Democratic Party of Germany (about whose leaders it has been wrongly said that they have already lost all influence, whereas in reality they are even more dangerous to the proletariat than the Hungarian Social-Democrats who styled themselves Communists and promised to "support" the dictatorship of the proletariat) was once again revealed during the German equivalent of the Kornilov revolt, i.e., the Kapp-Lüttwitz *putsch*.[*10] A small but striking illustration is provided by two brief articles – one by Karl Kautsky entitled "Decisive Hours" ("Entscheidende Stunden") in *Freiheit* (*Freedom*), organ of the Independents, of 30th March, 1920, and the other by Arthur Crispien entitled "On the Political Situation" (in the same newspaper, issue of 14th April, 1920). These gentlemen are absolutely incapable of thinking and reasoning like revolutionaries. They are snivelling philistine democrats, who become a thousand times more dangerous to the proletariat when they claim to be supporters of Soviet government and of the dictatorship of the proletariat because, in fact, whenever a difficult and dangerous situation arises they are sure to commit treachery . . . while "sincerely" believing that they are helping the proletariat! Did not the Hungarian Social-Democrats, after rechristening themselves Communists, also want to "help" the proletariat when, because of their cowardice and spinelessness, they considered the position of Soviet power in Hungary hopeless and went snivelling to the agents of the Entente capitalists and the Entente hangmen?

III. Turati and co in Italy

The issues of the Italian newspaper *Il Soviet* referred to above fully confirm what I have said in the pamphlet about the Italian Socialist Party's error in tolerating such members and even such a group of parliamentarians in their ranks. It is still further confirmed by an outside observer like the Rome correspondent of *The Manchester Guardian*, organ of the British liberal bourgeoisie, whose interview with Turati is published in its issue of 12th March, 1920. The correspondent writes:

> ". . . Signor Turati's opinion is that the revolutionary peril is not such as to cause undue anxiety in Italy. The Maximalists are fanning the fire of Soviet theories only to keep the masses awake and excited. These theories are, however, merely legendary notions, unripe programmes, incapable of being put to practical use. They are likely only to maintain the working classes in a state of expectation. The very men who use them as a lure to dazzle proletarian eyes find themselves compelled to fight a daily battle for the extortion of some often trifling economic advantages so as to delay the moment when the working classes will lose their illusions and faith in their cherished myths. Hence a long string of strikes of all sizes and with all pretexts up to the very latest ones in the mail and railway

services – strikes which make the already hard conditions of the country still worse. The country is irritated owing to the difficulties connected with its Adriatic problem, is weighed down by its foreign debt and by its inflated paper circulation, and yet it is still far from realising the necessity of adopting that discipline of work which alone can restore order and prosperity."

It is clear as daylight that this British correspondent has blurted out the truth, which is probably being concealed and glossed over both by Turati himself, and his bourgeois defenders, accomplices and inspirers in Italy. That truth is that the ideas and political activities of Turati, Trèves, Modigliani, Dugoni and Co. are really and precisely of the kind that the British correspondent has described. It is downright social treachery. Just look at this advocacy of order and discipline among the workers, who are wage-slaves toiling to enrich the capitalists! And how familiar to us Russians are all these Menshevik speeches! What a valuable admission it is that the masses are *in favour of* Soviet government! How stupid and vulgarly bourgeois is the failure to understand the revolutionary role of strikes which are spreading spontaneously! Indeed, the correspondent of the British bourgeois-liberal newspaper has rendered Turati and Co. a disservice and has excellently confirmed the correctness of the demand by Comrade Bordiga and his friends on *Il Soviet*, who are insisting that the Italian Socialist Party, if it really wants to be *for* the Third International, should drum Turati and Co. out of its ranks and become a Communist Party both in name and in deed.

IV. False conclusions from correct premises

However, Comrade Bordiga and his "Left" friends draw from their correct criticism of Turati and Co. the wrong conclusion that any participation in parliament is harmful in principle. The Italian "Lefts" cannot advance even a shadow of serious argument in support of this view. They simply do not know (or try to forget) the international examples of really revolutionary and communist utilisation of bourgeois parliaments, which has been of unquestionable value in preparing for the proletarian revolution. They simply cannot conceive of any "new" ways of that utilisation, and keep on repeatedly and endlessly vociferating about the "old" non-Bolshevik way.

Herein lies their fundamental error. In *all* fields of activity, and not in the parliamentary sphere alone, communism must *introduce* (and without long and persistent effort it will be *unable* to introduce) something new in principle that will represent a radical break with the traditions of the Second International (while retaining and developing what was good in the latter).

Let us take, say, journalistic work. Newspapers, pamphlets and leaflets perform the indispensable work of propaganda, agitation and organisation. No mass movement in any country at all civilised can get along without a journalistic apparatus. No outcries against "leaders" or solemn vows to keep the masses uncontaminated by the influence of leaders will relieve us of the necessity of using, for this work, people from a bourgeois-intellectual environment or will rid us of the bourgeois-democratic, "private property" atmosphere and environment in which this work is carried out under capitalism. Even two and a half years after the overthrow of the bourgeoisie, after the conquest of political power by the proletariat, we still have this atmosphere around us, this environment of mass (peasant, artisan) bourgeois-democratic private property relations.

Parliamentarianism is one form of activity; journalism is another. The content of both can and should be communist if those engaged in these two spheres are genuine Communists, really members of a proletarian mass party. Yet, in neither sphere – and *in no other sphere of activity* under capitalism and during the period of transition from capitalism to socialism – is it possible to avoid those difficulties which the proletariat must overcome, those special problems which the proletariat must solve so as to use, for its own purposes, the services of people from the ranks of the bourgeoisie, eradicate bourgeois-intellectualist prejudices and influences, and weaken the resistance of (and, ultimately, completely transform) the petty-bourgeois environment.

Did we not, before the war of 1914–18, witness in all countries innumerable cases of extreme "Left" anarchists, syndicalists and others fulminating against parliamentarianism, deriding bourgeois-vulgarised parliamentary socialists, castigating their careerism, and so on and so forth, and yet themselves pursuing the *same kind* of bourgeois career *through* journalism and *through* work in the syndicates (trade unions)? Is not the example of Jouhaux and Merrheim, to limit oneself to France, typical in this respect?

The childishness of those who "repudiate" participation in parliament consists in their thinking it possible to "*solve*" the difficult problem of combating bourgeois-democratic influences *within* the working-class movement in such a "simple", "easy", allegedly revolutionary manner, whereas they are actually merely running away from their own shadows, only closing their eyes to difficulties and trying to shrug them off with mere words. The most shameless careerism, the bourgeois utilisation of parliamentary seats, glaringly reformist perversion of parliamentary activity, and vulgar petty-bourgeois conservatism are all unquestionably common and prevalent features engendered everywhere by capitalism, not only outside but also within the working-class movement. But the self-same capitalism and the bourgeois environment it creates (which disappears very slowly even after the overthrow of the bourgeoisie, since the peasantry constantly regenerates the bourgeoisie) give rise to what is essentially the same bourgeois careerism, national chauvinism, petty-bourgeois vulgarity, etc. – merely varying insignificantly in form – in positively every sphere of activity and life.

You think, my dear boycottists and anti-parliamentarians, that you are "terribly revolutionary", but in reality *you are frightened* by the comparatively minor difficulties of the struggle against bourgeois influences within the working-class movement, whereas your victory – i.e., the overthrow of the – bourgeoisie and the conquest of political power by the proletariat – will create *these very same* difficulties on a still larger, an infinitely larger scale. Like children, you are frightened by a minor difficulty which confronts you today, but you do not understand that tomorrow, and the day after, you will still have to learn, and learn thoroughly, to overcome the self-same difficulties, only on an immeasurably greater scale.

Under Soviet rule, your proletarian party and ours will be invaded by a still larger number of bourgeois intellectuals. They will worm their way into the Soviets, the courts, and the administration, since communism cannot be built otherwise than with the aid of the human material created by capitalism, and the bourgeois intellectuals cannot be expelled and destroyed, but must be won over, remoulded, assimilated and re-educated, just as we must – in a protracted struggle waged on the basis of the dictatorship of the proletariat – re-educate the proletarians themselves, who do not abandon their petty-bourgeois prejudices at one stroke, by a miracle, at the behest of the Virgin Mary, at the behest of a slogan, resolution or decree, but only in the course of a long and difficult mass struggle against mass petty-bourgeois influences. Under Soviet rule, these same problems, which the anti-parliamentarians now so proudly, so haughtily, so lightly and so childishly brush aside with a wave of the hand – *these self-same* problems are arising anew *within* the Soviets, within the Soviet administration among the Soviet "pleaders" (in

Russia we have abolished, and have rightly abolished, the bourgeois legal bar, but it is reviving again under the cover of the "Soviet pleaders"[40]). Among Soviet engineers, Soviet school-teachers and the privileged, i.e., the most highly skilled and best situated, *workers* at Soviet factories, we observe a constant revival of absolutely *all* the negative traits peculiar to bourgeois parliamentarianism, and we are conquering this evil – gradually – only by a tireless, prolonged and persistent struggle based on proletarian organisation and discipline.

Of course, under the rule of the bourgeoisie it is very "difficult" to eradicate bourgeois habits from our own, i.e., the workers', party; it is "difficult" to expel from the party the familiar parliamentary leaders who have been hopelessly corrupted by bourgeois prejudices; it is "difficult" to subject to proletarian discipline the absolutely essential (even if very limited) number of people coming from the ranks of the bourgeoisie; it is "difficult" to form, in a bourgeois parliament, a communist group fully worthy of the working class; it is "difficult" to ensure that the communist parliamentarians do not engage in bourgeois parliamentary inanities, but concern themselves with the very urgent work of propaganda, agitation and organisation among the masses. All this is "difficult", to be sure; it was difficult in Russia, and it is vastly more difficult in Western Europe and in America, where the bourgeoisie is far stronger, where bourgeois-democratic traditions are stronger, and so on.

Yet all these "difficulties" are mere child's play compared with the *same sort* of problems which, in any event, the proletariat will have most certainly to solve in order to achieve victory, both during the proletarian revolution and after the seizure of power by the proletariat. Compared with *these* truly gigantic problems of re-educating, under the proletarian dictatorship, millions of peasants and small proprietors, hundreds of thousands of office employees, officials and bourgeois intellectuals, of subordinating them all to the proletarian state and to proletarian leadership, of eradicating their bourgeois habits and traditions – compared with these gigantic problems it is childishly easy to create, under the rule of the bourgeoisie, and in a bourgeois parliament, a really communist group of a real proletarian party.

If our "Left" and anti-parliamentarian comrades do not learn to overcome even such a small difficulty now, we may safely assert that either they will prove incapable of achieving the dictatorship of the proletariat, and will be unable to subordinate and remould the bourgeois intellectuals and bourgeois institutions on a wide scale, or they will have to *hastily complete their education*, and, by that haste, will do a great deal of harm to the cause of the proletariat, will commit more errors than usual, will manifest more than average weakness and inefficiency, and so on and so forth.

Until the bourgeoisie has been overthrown and, after that, until small-scale economy and small commodity production have entirely disappeared, the bourgeois atmosphere, proprietary habits and petty-bourgeois traditions will hamper proletarian work both outside and within the working-class movement, not only in a single field of activity – the parliamentary – but, inevitably, in every field of social activity, in all cultural and political spheres without exception. The attempt to brush aside, to fence oneself off from *one* of the "unpleasant" problems or difficulties in some one sphere of activity is a profound mistake, which will later most certainly have to be paid for. We must learn how to master every sphere of work and activity without exception, to overcome all difficulties and eradicate all bourgeois habits, customs and traditions everywhere. Any other way of presenting the question is just trifling, mere childishness.

12ᵗʰ May, 1920

V.

In the Russian edition of this book I somewhat incorrectly described the conduct of the Communist Party of Holland as a whole, in the sphere of international revolutionary policy. I therefore avail myself of the present opportunity to publish a letter from our Dutch comrades on this question and to correct the expression "Dutch Tribunists", which I used in the Russian text, and for which I now substitute the words "certain members of the Communist Party of Holland."[41]

N. Lenin

Footnotes

[40] "Soviet pleaders" – collegiums of advocates established in February 1918, under the Soviets of Workers', Soldiers', Peasants' and Cossacks' Deputies. In October 1920, these collegiums were abolished.

[41] On the basis of this directive from Lenin the words "certain members of the Communist Party of Holland" have been substituted everywhere in this volume, in the text of "Left-Wing" Communism – an Infantile Disorder for the expression "Dutch Tribunists".

[*9] With regard to the question of future amalgamation of the "Left" Communists, the anti-parliamentarians, with the Communists in general, I would make the following additional remarks. In the measure in which I have been able to familiarise myself with the newspapers

of the "Left" Communists and the Communists in general in Germany, I find that the former have the advantage of being better able than the latter to carry on agitation among the masses. I have repeatedly observed something similar to this in the history of the Bolshevik Party, though on a smaller scale, in individual local organisations, and not on a national scale. For instance, in 1907–08 the "Left" Bolsheviks, on certain occasions and in certain places, carried on more successful agitation among the masses than we did. This may partly have been due to the fact that a revolutionary moment, or at a time when revolutionary recollections are still fresh, it is easier to approach the masses with tactics of sheer negation. This, however, is not an argument to prove the correctness of such tactics. At all events, there is not the least doubt that a Communist party that wishes to be the real vanguard, the advanced detachment, of the revolutionary class, of the proletariat – and which, in addition wishes to learn to lead the masses, not only the proletarian, but also the non-proletarian masses of working and exploited people – must know how to conduct propaganda, how to organise, and how to carry on agitation in a manner most simple and comprehensible, most clear and vivid, both to the urban, factory masses and to the rural masses.

*10 Incidentally, this has been dealt with in an exceptionally clear, concise, precise and Marxist way in the excellent organ of the Austrian Communist Party, The Red Banner, of 28th and 30th March, 1920. (Die Rote Fahne, Wien, 1920, Nos. 266 and 267; L.L.: "Ein neuer Abschnitt der deutschen Revolution" ["A New Stage of the German Revolution" – Ed.]).

Letter from Wijnkoop

Moscow, 30th June, 1920

Dear Comrade Lenin,

Thanks to your kindness, we members of the Dutch delegation to the Second Congress of the Communist International were able to read your *"Left-Wing" Communism – An Infantile Disorder* prior to its publication in the European languages. In several places in the book you emphasise your disapproval of the part played by some members of the Communist Party of Holland in international politics.

We feel, nevertheless, that we must protest against your laying the responsibility for their actions on the Communist Party. This is highly inaccurate. Moreover, it is unjust, because these members of the Communist Party of Holland take little or no part in the Party's current activities and are endeavouring, directly or indirectly, to give effect, in the Communist Party of Holland, to opposition slogans against which the Party and all its organs have waged, and continue to wage to this day, a most energetic struggle.

Fraternally yours,

D. J. Wijnkoop
(on behalf of the Dutch delegation)

In Defence
Of October

Leon Trotsky

In Defence of October

A speech delivered in Copenhagen, Denmark in November 1932.

The first time that I was in Copenhagen was at the International Socialist Congress and I took away with me the kindest recollections of your city. But that was over a quarter of a century ago. Since then, the water in the Ore-Sund and in the fjords has changed over and over again. And not the water alone. The war has broken the backbone of the old European continent. The rivers and seas of Europe have washed down not a little blood. Mankind and particularly European mankind has gone through severe trials, has become more sombre and more brutal. Every kind of conflict has become more bitter. The world has entered into the period of the great change. Its extreme expressions are war and revolution.

Before I pass on to the theme of my lecture, the Revolution, I consider it my duty to express my thanks to the organisers of this meeting, the organisation of social-democratic students. I do this as a political adversary. My lecture, it is true, pursues historic scientific and not political lines. I want to emphasise this right from the beginning. But it is impossible to speak of a revolution, out of which the Soviet Republic arose, without taking up a political position. As a lecturer I stand under the banner as I did when I participated in the events of the revolution.

Up to the war, the Bolshevik Party belonged to the Social-Democratic International[1]. On 4th August, 1914, the vote of the German social-democracy for the war credits put an end to this connection once and for all, and opened the period of uninterrupted and irreconcilable struggle of Bolshevism against social-democracy. Does this mean that the organisers of this assembly made a mistake in inviting me to lecture? On this point the audience will be able to judge only after my lecture. To justify my acceptance of the kind invitation to present a report on the Russian Revolution, permit me to point to the fact that during the thirty-five years of my political life the question of the Russian Revolution has been the practical and theoretical axis of my thought and of my actions. The four years of my stay in Turkey were principally devoted to historical elaboration of the problems of the Russian Revolution. Perhaps this fact gives me a certain right to hope that I will succeed in part at least in helping not only friends and sympathisers, but also opponents, better to understand many features of the Revolution which before had escaped their attention. At all events, the purpose of my lecture is to help to understand. I do not intend to conduct propaganda for the Revolution, nor to call upon you to join the Revolution. I intend to explain the Revolution.

Let us begin with some elementary sociological principles which are doubtless familiar to you all, but as to which we must refresh our memory in approaching so complicated a phenomenon as the Revolution.

The materialist conception of history

Human society is an historically-originated collaboration in the struggle for existence and the assurance of the maintenance of the generations. The character of a society is determined by the character of its economy. The character of its economy is determined by its means of productive labour.

For every great epoch in the development of the productive forces there is a definite corresponding social regime. Every social regime until now has secured enormous advantages to the ruling class.

It is clear, therefore, that social regimes are not eternal. They arise historically, and then become fetters on further progress. "All that arises deserves to be destroyed."

But no ruling class has ever voluntarily and peacefully abdicated. In questions of life and death, arguments based on reason have never replaced the arguments of force. This may be sad, but it is so. It is not we that have made this world. We can do nothing but take it as it is.

The meaning of revolution

Revolution means a change of the social order. It transfers the power from the hands of a class which has exhausted itself into those of another class, which is in the ascendant. Insurrection constitutes the sharpest and most critical moment in the struggle for power of two classes. The insurrection can lead to the real victory of the Revolution and to the establishment of a new order only when it is based on a progressive class, which is able to rally around it the overwhelming majority of the people.

As distinguished from the processes of nature, a revolution is made by human beings and through human beings. But in the course of revolution, too, men act under the influence of social conditions which are not freely chosen by them but are handed down from the past and imperatively point out the road which they must follow. For this reason, and only for this reason, a revolution follows certain laws.

But human consciousness does not merely passively reflect its objective conditions. It is accustomed to react actively to them. At certain times this reaction assumes a tense, passionate, mass character. The barriers of right and might are overthrown. The active intervention of the masses in historical events is in fact the most indispensable element of a revolution.

But even the stormiest activity can remain in the stage of demonstration or rebellion, without rising to the height of a revolution. The uprising of the masses must lead to the overthrow of the domination of one class and to the establishment of the domination of another. Only then have we achieved a revolution. A mass uprising is no isolated undertaking, which can be conjured up any time one pleases. It represents an objectively-conditioned element in the development of a revolution, just as a revolution represents an objectively-conditioned process in the development of society. But if the necessary conditions for the uprising exist, one must not simply wait passively, with open mouth; as Shakespeare says: "There is a tide in the affairs of men which taken at the flood, leads on to fortune."

In order to sweep away the outlived social order, the progressive class must understand that its hour has struck and set before itself the task of conquering power. Here opens the field of conscious revolutionary action, where foresight and calculation combine with will and courage. In other words: here opens the field of action of the Party.

The coup d'état

The revolutionary Party unites within itself the flower of the progressive class. Without a Party which is able to orientate itself in its environment, appreciate the progress and rhythm of events and early win the confidence of the masses, the victory of the proletarian revolution is impossible. These are the reciprocal relations between the objective and the subjective factors of insurrection and revolution.

In disputations, particularly theological ones, it is customary, as you know, for the opponents to discredit scientific truth by driving it to an absurdity. This method is called in logic Reductio ad absurdum. We shall start from an absurdity so as to approach the truth with all the greater safety. In any case, we cannot complain of lack of absurdities. Let us take one of the most recent, and crude.

The Italian writer Malaparte, who is something in the nature of a Fascist theoretician – there are such, too – not long ago, launched a book on the technique of the *coup d'état*. Naturally, the author devotes a not inconsiderable number of pages of his "investigation" to the October upheaval.

In contradistinction to the "strategy" of Lenin which was always related to the social and political conditions of Russia in 1917, "the tactics of Trotsky." in Malaparte's words, "were, on the contrary, not at all limited by the general conditions of the country." This is the main idea of the book! Malaparte compels Lenin and Trotsky in the pages of his book, to carry on numerous dialogues, in which both participants together show as much profundity of mind as Nature put at the disposal of Malaparte alone. In answer to Lenin's considerations of the social and political prerequisites of the upheaval, Malaparte has his alleged Trotsky say, literally, "Your strategy requires far too many favourable circumstances; the insurrection needs nothing, it is self-sufficing." You hear: "The insurrection needs nothing!" That is precisely the absurdity which must help us to approach the truth. The author repeats persistently, that, in the October Revolution, it was not the strategy of Lenin but the tactics of Trotsky which won the victory. These tactics, according to his words, are a menace even now to the peace of the States of Europe. "The strategy of Lenin," I quote word-for-word, "does not constitute any immediate danger for the Governments of Europe. But the tactics of Trotsky do constitute an actual and consequently a permanent danger to them." Still more concretely, "Put Poincaré[2] in the place of Kerensky[3] and the Bolshevik *coup d'état* of October, 1917 would have been just as successful." It is hard to believe that such a book has been translated into several languages and taken seriously.

We seek in vain to discover what is the necessity altogether of the historically-conditioned strategy of Lenin, if "Trotsky's tactics" can fulfil the same tasks in every situation. And why are successful revolutions so rare, if only a few technical recipes suffice for their success?

The dialogue between Lenin and Trotsky presented by the fascist author is in content, as well as in form, an insipid invention, from beginning to end. Of such inventions there are not a few floating around the world. For example, in Madrid, there has been printed a book, *La Vida del Lenin* (*The Life of Lenin*) for which I am as little responsible as for the tactical recipes of Malaparte. The Madrid weekly, *Estampa*, published in advance whole chapters of this alleged book of Trotsky's on Lenin, which contain horrible desecrations of the life of that man whom I valued and still value incomparably higher than anyone else among my contemporaries.

But let us leave the forgers to their fate. Old Wilhelm Liebknecht[4], the father of the unforgettable fighter and hero Karl Liebknecht[5], liked to say, "A revolutionary politician must provide himself with a thick skin." Doctor Stockmann even more expressively recommended that anyone who proposed to act in a manner contrary to the opinion of society should refrain from putting on new trousers. We will take note of the two good pieces of advice and proceed.

The causes of October

What questions does the October Revolution raise in the mind of a thinking man?

- Why and how did this revolution take place? More correctly, why did the proletarian revolution conquer in one of the most backward countries in Europe?

- What have been the results of the October revolution? And finally:

- Has the October Revolution stood the test?

The first question, as to the causes, can now be answered more or less exhaustively. I have attempted to do this in great detail in my *History of the Revolution*. Here I can only formulate the most important conclusions.

The law of uneven development

The fact that the proletariat reached power for the first time in such a backward country as the former Tsarist Russia seems mysterious only at a first glance; in reality it is fully in accord with historical law. It could have been predicted, and it was predicted. Still more, on the basis of the prediction of this fact the revolutionary Marxists built up their strategy long before the decisive events.

The first and most general explanation is: Russia is a backward country, but only a part of world economy, only an element of the capitalist world system. In this sense Lenin solved the enigma of the

Russian Revolution with the lapidary formula, "The chain broke at its weakest link."

A crude illustration: the Great War, the result of the contradictions of world imperialism, drew into its maelstrom countries of different stages of development, but made the same claims on all the participants. It is clear that the burdens of the war would be particularly intolerable for the most backward countries. Russia was the first to be compelled to leave the field. But to tear itself away from the war, the Russian people had to overthrow the ruling classes. In this way the chain of war broke at its weakest link.

Still, war is not a catastrophe coming from outside like an earthquake, but, as old Clausewitz[6] said, the continuation of politics by other means. In the last war, the main tendencies of the imperialistic system of "peace" time only expressed themselves more crudely. The higher the general forces of production, the tenser the competition on the world markets, the sharper the antagonisms and the madder the race for armaments, so much the more difficult it became for the weaker participants. That is precisely why the backward countries assumed the first places in the succession of collapse. The chain of world capitalism always tends to break at its weakest link.

If, as a result of exceptionally unfavourable circumstances – for example, let us say, a successful military intervention from the outside or irreparable mistakes on the part of the Soviet Government itself – capitalism should arise again on the immeasurably wide Soviet territory, its historical inadequacy would at the same time have inevitably arisen and such capitalism would in turn soon become the victim of the same contradictions which caused its explosion in 1917. No tactical recipes could have called the October Revolution into being, if Russia had not carried it within its body. The revolutionary Party in the last analysis can claim only the role of an obstetrician, who is compelled to resort to a Caesarean operation.

One might say in answer to this: "Your general considerations may adequately explain why old Russia had to suffer shipwreck, that country where backward capitalism and an impoverished peasantry were crowned by a parasitic nobility and a decaying monarchy. But in the simile of the chain and it weakest link there is still missing the key to the real enigma: How could a socialist revolution succeed in a backward country? History knows of more than a few illustrations of the decay of countries and civilisations accompanied by the collapse of the old classes for which no progressive successors had been found. The breakdown of old Russia should, at first sight have changed the country into a capitalist colony rather than into a Socialist State."

This objection is very interesting. It leads us directly to the kernel of the whole problem. And yet, this objection is erroneous; I might say, it lacks internal symmetry. On the one hand, it starts from an exaggerated conception of the phenomenon of historical backwardness in general.

Living beings, including man, of course, go through similar stages of development in accordance with their ages. In a normal five-year old child, we find a certain correspondence between the weight, size and the internal organs. But it is quite otherwise with human consciousness. In contrast with anatomy and physiology, psychology, both individual and collective, is distinguished by exceptional capacity of absorption, flexibility and elasticity; therein consists the aristocratic advantage of man over his nearest zoological relatives, the apes. The absorptive and flexible psyche confers on the so-called social "organisms", as distinguished from the real, that is biological organisms, an exceptional variability of internal structure as a necessary condition for historical progress. In the development of nations and states, particularly capitalist ones, there is neither similarity nor regularity. Different stages of civilisation, even polar opposites, approach and intermingle with one another in the life of one and the same country.

The law of combined development

Let us not forget that historical backwardness is a relative concept. There being both backward and progressive countries, there is also a reciprocal influencing of one by the other; there is the pressure of the progressive countries on the backward ones; there is the necessity for the backward countries to catch up with the progressive ones, to borrow their technology and science, etc. In this way arises the combined type of development: features of backwardness are combined with the last word in world technique and in world thought. Finally the countries historically backward, in order to escape their backwardness, are often compelled to rush ahead of the others.

The flexibility of the collective consciousness makes it possible under certain conditions to achieve the result, in the social arena, which in individual psychology is called "overcoming the consciousness of inferiority". In this sense we can say that the October Revolution was an heroic means whereby the people of Russia were able to overcome their own economic and cultural inferiority.

But let us pass over from these historico-philosophic, perhaps somewhat too abstract, generalisations, and put up the same question in concrete form, that is within the cross-section of living economic facts. The backwardness of Russia expressed itself most clearly at the beginning of the twentieth century in the fact that industry occupied a small place in that country in comparison with the peasantry. Taken as a whole, this meant a low productivity of the national labour. Suffice it to say that on the eve of the war, when Tsarist Russia had reached the peak of its well-being, the national income was eight to ten times lower than in the United States. This expresses numerically the "amplitude" of its backwardness if the word "amplitude" can be used at all in connection with backwardness.

At the same time however, the law of combined development expressed itself in the economic field at every step, in simple as well as in complex phenomena. Almost without highways, Russia was compelled to build railroads. Without having gone through the European artisan and manufacturing stages, Russia passed directly to mechanised production. To jump over intermediate stages is the way of backward countries.

While peasant agriculture often remained at the level of the seventeenth century, Russia's industry, if not in scope, at least in type, reached the level of progressive countries and in some respects rushed ahead of them. It suffices to say that gigantic enterprises, with over a thousand workers each, employed in the United States less than 18 per cent of the total number of industrial workers. In Russia it was over 41%. This fact is hard to reconcile with the conventional conception of the economic backwardness of Russia. It does not on the other hand, refute this backwardness, but dialectically complements it.

The same contradictory character was shown by the class structure of the country. The finance capital of Europe industrialised Russian economy at an accelerated tempo. The industrial bourgeoisie forthwith assumed a large scale capitalistic and anti-popular character. The foreign stock-holders moreover, lived outside of the country. The workers, on the other hand, were naturally Russians. Against a numerically weak Russian bourgeoisie, which had no national roots, there stood confronting it a relatively strong proletariat with strong roots in the depths of the people.

The revolutionary character of the proletariat was furthered by the fact that Russia in particular, as a backward country, under the compulsion of catching up with its opponents, had not been able to work out its own social or political conservatism. The most conservative country of Europe, in fact of the entire world, is considered, and correctly, to be the oldest capitalist country – England. The European country freest of conservatism would in all probability be Russia.

But the young, fresh, determined proletariat of Russia still constituted only a tiny minority of the nation. The reserves of its revolutionary power lay outside of the proletariat itself-in the peasantry, living in half-serfdom; and in the oppressed nationalities.

The peasantry

The subsoil of the revolution was the agrarian question. The old feudal monarchic system became doubly intolerable under the conditions of the new capitalist exploitation. The peasant communal areas amounted to some 140 million *dessiatines*. But 30,000 large landowners, whose average holdings were over 2,000 *dessiatines*, owned altogether 7 million *dessiatines*, that is as much as some 10 million peasant population. These statistics of land tenure constituted a ready-made programme of agrarian revolt.

The nobleman, Bokorin, wrote in 1917 to the dignitary, Rodsianko, the Chairman of the last municipal Duma[7]: "I am a landowner and I cannot get it into my head that I must lose my land, and for an unbelievable purpose to boot, for the experiment of the socialist doctrine." But it is precisely the task of revolutions to accomplish that which the ruling classes cannot get into their heads.

In Autumn, 1917, almost the whole country was the scene of peasant revolts. Of the 642 departments of old Russia, 482, that is 77%, were affected by the movements! The reflection of the burning villages lit up the arena of the insurrections in the cities.

But you may argue the war of the peasants against the landowners is one of the classic elements of bourgeois revolution, and not at all of the proletarian revolution!

Perfectly right, I reply – so it was in the past. But the inability of capitalist society to survive in an historically backward country was expressed precisely in the fact that the peasant insurrections did not drive the bourgeois classes of Russia forward but on the contrary, drove them back for good into the camp of reaction. If the peasantry did not want to be completely ruined there was nothing else left for it but to join the industrial proletariat. This revolutionary joining of the two oppressed classes was foreseen by the genius of Lenin and prepared for him long before.

Had the agrarian question been courageously solved by the bourgeoisie, the proletariat of Russia would not, obviously, have been able to arrive at the power in 1917. But the Russian, bourgeoisie, covetous and cowardly, too late on the scene, prematurely a victim of senility, dared not lift a hand against feudal property. But thereby it delivered the power to the proletariat and together with it the right to dispose of the destinies of bourgeois society.

In order for the Soviet State to come into existence, it was consequently necessary for two factors of a different historical nature to collaborate: the peasant war, that is to say, a movement which is characteristic of the dawn of bourgeois development, and the proletarian insurrection, or uprising which announces the decline of the bourgeois movement. There we have the combined character of the Russian Revolution.

Once let the Bear – the peasant – stand up on his hind feet, he becomes terrible in his wrath. But he is unable to give conscious expression to his indignation. He needs a leader. For the first time in the history of the world, the insurrectionary peasants found a faithful leader in the person of the proletariat.

Four million workers in industry and transport leading a hundred million peasants. That was the natural and inevitable reciprocal relations between proletariat and peasantry in the Revolution.

The national question

The second revolutionary reserve of the proletariat was formed by the oppressed nationalities, who moreover were also predominantly peasants. Closely allied with the historical backwardness of the country is the extensive character of the development of the State, which spread out like a grease spot from the centre at Moscow to the circumference. In the East, it subjugated the still more backward peoples, basing itself upon them, in order to stifle the more developed nationalities of the West. To the 70 million Great Russians, who constituted the main mass of the population were added gradually some 90 millions of other races.

In this way arose the empire, in whose composition the ruling nationality made up only 43 percent of the population, while the remaining 57 per cent, consisted of nationalities of varying degrees of civilisation and legal deprivation. The national pressure was incomparably cruder than in the neighbouring States, and not only than those beyond the western frontier, but beyond the eastern one too. This conferred on the national problem an enormous explosive force.

The Russian liberal bourgeoisie was not willing in either the national or the agrarian question, to go beyond certain amelioration's of the regime of oppression and violence. The "democratic" Governments of Miliukov[8] and Kerensky, which reflected the interests of the great Russian bourgeoisie and bureaucracy actually hastened to impress upon the discontented nationalities in the course of the eight months of their existence: "You will obtain what you can get by force."

The inevitability of the development of the centrifugal national movements had been early taken into consideration by Lenin. The Bolshevik Party struggled obstinately for years for the right of self-determination for nations, that is, for the right of full secession. Only through this courageous position on the national question could the Russian proletariat gradually win the confidence of the oppressed peoples. The national independence movement as well as the agrarian movement, necessarily turned against the official democracy, strengthened the proletariat, and poured into the stream of the October upheaval.

The permanent revolution

In these ways the riddle of the proletarian upheaval in an historically backward country loses its veil of mystery.

Marxist revolutionaries predicted, long before the events, the march of the Revolution and the historical role of the young Russian proletariat. I may be permitted to repeat here a passage from a work of my own in 1905.

> *"In an economically backward country the proletariat can arrive at power earlier than in a capitalistically advanced one …*

> "The Russian Revolution creates the conditions under which the power can (and in the event of a successful revolution must) be transferred to the proletariat, even before the policy of bourgeois liberalism receives the opportunity of unfolding its genius for government to its full extent.

> "The destiny of the most elementary revolutionary interest of the peasantry … is bound up with the destiny of the whole revolution, that is, with the destiny of the proletariat. The proletariat, once arrived at power, will appear before the peasantry as the liberating class.

"The proletariat enters into the Government as the revolutionary representative of the nation, as the acknowledged leader of the people in the struggle with absolutism and the barbarism of serfdom.

"The proletarian regime will have to stand from the very beginning for the solution of the agrarian question, with which the question of the destiny of tremendous masses of the population of Russia is bound up."

I have taken the liberty of quoting these passages as evidence that the theory of the October Revolution which I am presenting today is no casual improvisation and was not constructed ex-post facto under the pressure of events. No, in the form of a political prognosis it preceded the October upheaval by a long time. You will agree that a theory is in general valuable only in so far as it helps to foresee the course of development and influence it purposively. Therein, in general terms, is the invaluable importance of Marxism as a weapon of social historical orientation. I am sorry that the narrow limits of the lecture do not permit me to enlarge upon the above quotation materially. I will therefore content myself with a brief resume of the whole work which dates from 1905.

In accordance with its immediate tasks, the Russian Revolution is a bourgeois revolution. But the Russian bourgeoisie is anti-revolutionary. The victory of the Revolution is therefore possible only as a victory of the proletariat. But the victorious proletariat will not stop at the programme of bourgeois democracy: it will go on to the programme of socialism. The Russian Revolution will become the first stage of the Socialist world revolution.

This was the theory of permanent revolution formulated by me in 1905 and since then exposed to the severest criticism under the name of "Trotskyism".

To be more exact, it is only a part of this theory. The other part, which is particularly timely now, states:

The present productive forces have long outgrown their national limits. A socialist society is not feasible within national boundaries. Significant as the economic successes of an isolated workers' state may be, the programme of "Socialism in one country" is a petty-bourgeois utopia. Only a European and then a world federation of socialist republics can be the real arena for a harmonious socialist society.

Today, after the test of events, I see less reason than ever to discard this theory.

Pre-requisites for October

After all that has been said above, is it still worthwhile to recall the Fascist writer Malaparte, who ascribes to me tactics which are independent of strategy and amount to a series of technical recipes for insurrection, applicable in all latitudes and longitudes? It is a good thing that the name of the luckless theoretician of the *coup d'état* makes it easy to distinguish him from the victorious practitioner of the *coup d'état*; no one therefore runs the risk of confusing Malaparte with Bonaparte[9].

Without the armed insurrection of 7th November, 1917, the Soviet State would not be in existence. But the insurrection itself did not drop from heaven. A series of historical prerequisites were necessary for the October Revolution.

- The rotting away of the old ruling classes-the nobility, the monarchy, the bureaucracy.

- The political weakness of the bourgeoisie, which had no roots in the masses of the people.

- The revolutionary character of the agrarian question.

- The revolutionary character of the problem of the oppressed nationalities.

- The significant social burdens weighing on the proletariat.

To these organic preconditions must be added certain highly important connected conditions.

- The Revolution of 1905 was the great school or in Lenin's phrase, "the dress rehearsal" of the Revolution of 1917. The Soviet's as the irreplaceable organisational form of the proletarian united front in the Revolution were created for the first time in the year 1905.

- **The imperialist war sharpened all the contradictions, tore the backward masses out of their immobility, and thus prepared the grandiose scale of the catastrophe.**

The Bolshevik Party

But all these conditions, which fully sufficed for the outbreak of the Revolution, were insufficient to assure the victory of the proletariat in the Revolution. For this victory one condition more was necessary:

- The Bolshevik Party

When I enumerate this condition last in the series, I do it only because it follows the logical sequence, and not because I assign the last place in the order of importance to the Party.

No, I am far from such a thought. The liberal bourgeoisie can seize power and has seized it more than once as the result of struggles in which it took no part; it possesses organs of seizure which are admirably adapted to the purpose. But the working masses are in a different position; they have long been accustomed to give, and not to take. They work, are patient as long as they can be, hope, lose patience, rise up and struggle, die, bring victory to others, are betrayed, fall into despondency, bow their necks, and work again. Such is the history of the masses of the people under all regimes. To be able to take the power firmly and surely into its hands the proletariat needs a Party, which far surpasses other parties in the clarity of its thought and in its revolutionary determination.

The Bolshevik Party, which has been described more than once and with complete justification as the most revolutionary Party in the history of mankind was the living condensation of the modern history of Russia, of all that was dynamic in it. The overthrow of Tsarism had long been recognised as the necessary condition for the development of economy and culture. But for the solution of this task, the forces were insufficient. The bourgeoisie feared the Revolution. The intelligentsia tried to bring the peasant to his feet. The *muzhik*, incapable of generalising his own miseries and his aims, left this appeal unanswered. The intelligentsia armed itself with dynamite. A whole generation was wasted in this struggle.

On March 1st 1887, Alexander Ulianov carried out the last of the great terrorist plots. The attempted assassination of Alexander III failed. Ulianov and the other participants were executed. The attempt to make chemical preparation take the place of a revolutionary class, came to grief. Even the most heroic intelligentsia is nothing without the masses. Ulianov's younger brother Vladimir, the future Lenin, the greatest figure of Russian history, grew up under the immediate impression of these facts and conclusion. Even in his early youth he placed himself on the foundations of Marxism and turned his face toward the proletariat. Without losing sight of the village for a moment he sought the way of the peasantry through the workers. Inheriting from his revolutionary predecessors their capacity for self-sacrifice, and their willingness to go to the limit, Lenin, at an early age, became the teacher of the new generation of the intelligentsia and of the advanced workers. In strikes and street fights, in prisons and in exile, the workers received the necessary tempering. They needed the searchlight of Marxism to light up their historical road in the darkness of absolutism.

Among the émigrés the first Marxist group arose in 1883. In 1899 at a secret meeting, the foundation of the Russian Social-Democratic Workers Party was proclaimed (we all called ourselves Social-Democrats in those days). In 1903 occurred the split between Bolsheviks and Mensheviks[10], and in 1912 the Bolshevik faction finally became an independent Party.

It learned to recognise the class mechanics of society in its struggles during the events of twelve years (1905-1917). It educated groups equally capable of initiative and of subordination. The discipline of its revolutionary action was based on the unity of its doctrine, on the tradition of common struggles and on confidence in its tested leadership.

Such was the party in 1917. Despised by the official "public opinion" and the paper thunder of the intelligentsia Press it adapted itself to the movement of the masses. It kept firmly in hand the lever of control in the factories and regiments. More and more the peasant masses turned toward it. If we understand by "nation" not the privileged heads, but the majority of the people, that is, the workers and peasants, then the Bolsheviks became during the course of 1917 a truly national Russian Party.

In September, 1917, Lenin who was compelled to keep in hiding gave the signal, "The crisis is ripe, the hour of insurrection has approached." He was right. The ruling classes faced with the problems of the war, the land and liberation, had got into inextricable difficulties. The bourgeoisie positively lost its head. The democratic parties, the Mensheviks and Social-Revolutionaries[11], dissipated the last remaining bit of confidence of the masses in them by their support of the imperialist war, by their policy of compromise and concessions to the bourgeois and feudal property owners. The awakened army no longer wanted to fight for the alien aims of imperialism. Disregarding democratic advice, the peasantry smoked the landowners out of their estates. The oppressed nationalities of the far boundaries rose up against the bureaucracy of Petrograd. In the most important workers' and soldiers' Soviets the Bolsheviks were dominant. The ulcer was ripe. It needed a cut of the lancet.

Only under these social and political conditions was the insurrection possible. And thus it also became inevitable. But there is no playing around with insurrection. Woe to the surgeon who is careless in the use of the lancet! Insurrection is an art. It has its laws and its rules.

The party faced the realities of the October insurrection with cold calculation and with ardent resolution. Thanks to this, it conquered almost without victims. Through the victorious soviets the Bolsheviks placed themselves at the head of a country which occupies one sixth of the surface of the globe.

The majority of my present listeners, it is to be presumed, did not occupy themselves at all with politics in 1917. So much the better. Before the young generation lies much that is interesting, if not always easy. But the representatives of the old generation in this hall will certainly remember well how the seizure of power by the Bolsheviks was received: as a curiosity, as a misunderstanding, as a scandal; most often as a nightmare which was bound to disappear with the first rays of dawn. The Bolsheviks would last twenty four hours, a week, month, year. The period had to be constantly lengthened. The rulers of the whole world armed themselves up against the first workers' state: civil war was stirred up, interventions again and again, blockade. So passed year after year. Meantime, history has recorded fifteen years of existence of the Soviet power.

Can October be justified?

"Yes," some opponents will say, "the adventure of October has shown itself to be much more substantial than many of us thought. Perhaps it was not even quite an 'adventure'. Nevertheless, the question (no.8211) What was achieved at this high cost? – retains its full force. Have the dazzling promises which the Bolsheviks proclaimed on the eve of the Revolution been fulfilled?"

Before we answer the hypothetical opponent let us note that the question in and of itself is not new. On the contrary, it followed right at the heels of the October Revolution, since the day of its birth.

The French journalist, Clad Anet, who was in Petrograd during the Revolution, wrote as early as 27th October, 1917:

> "The maximalists (which was what the French called the Bolsheviks at that time) have seized power and the great day has come. At last, I say to myself, I shall behold the realisation of the socialist Eden which has been promised us for so many years ... Admirable adventure! A privileged position!"

And so on and so forth. What sincere hatred was behind the ironical salutation! The very morning after the capture of the Winter Palace, the reactionary journalist hurried to register his claim for a ticket of admission to Eden. Fifteen years have passed since the Revolution. With all the greater absence of ceremony our enemies reveal their malicious joy over the fact that the land of the Soviets, even today, bears but little resemblance to a realm of general well-being. Why then the Revolution and why the sacrifice?

Permit me to express the opinion that the contradictions, difficulties, mistakes and insufficiency of the Soviet regime are no less familiar to me than to anyone. I, personally, have never concealed them, whether in speech or in writing. I have believed and I still believe that revolutionary politics, as distinguished from conservative, cannot be built up on concealment. "To speak out that which is" must be the highest principle of the workers' State.

But in criticism, as well as in creative activity, perspective is necessary. Subjectivism is a poor adviser, particularly in great questions. Periods of time must be commensurate with the tasks, and not with individual caprices. Fifteen years! How long is that in the life of one man! Within that period not a few of our generation were borne to their graves and those who remain have added innumerable grey hairs. But these same fifteen years – what an insignificant period in the life of a people! Only a minute on the clock of history.

Capitalism required centuries to establish itself in the struggle against the Middle Ages, to raise the level of science and technique, to build railroads, to make use of electric current. And then? Then humanity was thrust by capitalism into the hell of wars and crises.

But Socialism is allowed by its enemies, that is, by the adherents of capitalism, only a decade and a half to install on earth Paradise, with all modern improvements. Such obligations were never assumed by us.

The processes of great changes must be measured by scales which are commensurate with them. I do not know if the Socialist society will resemble the biblical Paradise. I doubt it. But in the Soviet Union there is no Socialism as yet. The situation that prevails there is one of transition, full of contradictions, burdened with the heavy inheritance of the past and in addition is under the hostile pressure of the capitalistic states. The October Revolution has proclaimed the principles of the new society. The Soviet Republic has shown only the first stage of its realisation. Edison's first lamp was very bad. We must learn how to discern the future.

But the unhappiness that rains on living men! Do the results of the Revolution justify the sacrifice which it has caused? A fruitless question, rhetorical through and through; as if the processes of history admitted of a balance sheet accounting! We might just as well ask, in view of the difficulties and miseries of human existence, "Does it pay to be born altogether?" To which Heine wrote: "And the fool expects an answer" ... Such melancholy reflections haven't hindered mankind from being born and from giving birth. Even in these days of unexampled world crisis, suicides fortunately constitute an unimportant percentage. But peoples never resort to suicide. When their burdens are intolerable they seek a way out through revolution.

Besides who are they who are indignant over the victims of the social upheaval? Most often those who have paved the way for the victims of the imperialist war, and have glorified or, at least, easily accommodated themselves to it. It is now our turn to ask, "Has the war justified itself? What has it given us? What has it taught?"

The reactionary historian, Hippolyte Taine, in his eleven volume pamphlet against the great French Revolution describes, not without malicious joy, the sufferings of the French people in the years of the dictatorship of the Jacobins[12] and afterward. The worst off were the lower classes of the cities, the plebeians, who as "sansculottes" had given of their best for the Revolution. Now they or their wives stood in line throughout cold nights to return empty-handed to the extinguished family hearth. In the tenth year of the Revolution, Paris was poorer than before it began. Carefully selected, artificially pieced out facts serve Taine as Justification for his destructive verdict against the Revolution. Look, the plebeians wanted to be dictators and have precipitated themselves into misery!

It is hard to conceive of a more uninspired piece of moralising. First of all, if the Revolution precipitated the country into misery the blame lay principally on the ruling classes who drove the people to revolution. Second the great French Revolution did not exhaust itself in hungry lines before bakeries. The whole of modern France, in many respects the whole of modern civilisation, arose out of the bath of the French Revolution!

In the course of the Civil War in the United States in the '60s of the past century, 50,000 men were killed. Can these sacrifices be justified?

From the standpoint of the American slaveholder and the ruling classes of Great Britain who marched with them – no! From the standpoint of the Negro or of the British working man – absolutely. And from the standpoint of the development of humanity as a whole there can be no doubt whatever. Out of the Civil War of the '60s came the present United States with its unbounded practical initiative, its rationalised technique, its economic energy. On these achievements of Americanism, humanity will build the new society.

The October Revolution penetrated deeper than any of its predecessors into the Holy of Holies of society-into the property relations. So much the longer time is necessary to reveal the creative consequences of the Revolution in all spheres of life. But the general direction of the upheaval is already clear: the Soviet Republic has no reason whatever to bow its head before the capitalists accusers and speak the language of apology.

In order to appreciate the new regime from the stand-point of human development, one must first answer the question, "How does social progress express itself and how can it be measured?"

The balance sheet of October

The deepest, the most objective and the most indisputable criterion says: progress can be measured by the growth of the productivity of social labour. From this angle the estimate of the October Revolution is already given by experience. The principle of socialistic organisation has for the first time in history shown its ability to record results in production unheard of in a short space of time.

The curve of the industrial development of Russia expressed in crude index numbers is as follows, taking 1913, the last year before the war as 100. The year 1920, the highest point of the civil war, is also the lowest point in industry – only 25, that is to say, a quarter of the pre-war production. In 1925 it rose to 75, that is, three-quarters of the pre-war production; in 1929 about 200, in 1932: 300, that is to say, three times as much as on the eve of the war.

The picture becomes even more striking in the light of the international index. From 1925 to 1932 the industrial production of Germany has diminished one and a half times, in America twice, in the Soviet Union it has increased four-fold. These figures speak for themselves.

I have no intention of denying or concealing the seamy side of the Soviet economy. The results of the industrial index are extraordinarily influenced by the unfavourable development of agriculture, that is to say, in the domain which essentially has not yet risen to Socialist methods, but at the same time had been led on the road to collectivisation with insufficient preparation, bureaucratically rather than technically and economically. This is a great question, which however goes beyond the limits of my lecture.

The index numbers cited require another important reservation. The indisputable and, in their way, splendid results of Soviet industrialisation demand a further economic checking-up from the stand point of the mutual adaptation of the various elements of the economy, their dynamic equilibrium and consequently their productive capacity. Here great difficulties and even set backs are inevitable. Socialism does not arise in its perfected form from the five-year Plan like Minerva from the head of Jupiter, or Venus from the foam of the sea. Before it are decades of persistent work, of mistakes, corrections, and reorganisation. Moreover, let us not forget that socialist construction in accordance with its very nature can only reach perfection on the international arena. But even the most favourable economic balance sheet of the results so far obtained could reveal only the incorrectness of the preliminary calculations, the faults of planning and errors of direction. It could in no way refute the empirically firmly established fact – the possibility, with the aid of socialist methods, of raising the productivity of collective labour to an unheard of height. This conquest, of world historical importance, cannot be taken away from us by anybody or anything.

After what has been said it is scarcely worthwhile to spend time on the complaints that the October Revolution has brought Russia to the downfall of its civilisation. That is the voice of the disquieted ruling houses and salons. The feudal bourgeois "civilisation" overthrown by the proletarian upheaval was only barbarism with decorations à la Talmi. While it remained inaccessible to the Russian people, it brought little that was new to the treasury of mankind.

But even with respect to this civilisation, which is so bemoaned by the white émigrés, we must put the question more precisely – in what sense has it been destroyed? Only in one sense: the monopoly of a small minority in the treasures of civilisation has been done away with. But everything of cultural value in the old Russian civilisation has remained untouched. The "Huns" of Bolshevism have shattered neither the conquests of the mind nor the creations of art. On the contrary, they carefully collected the monuments of human creativeness and arranged them in model order. The culture of the monarchy, the nobility and the bourgeoisie has now become the culture of the historic museums.

The people visit these museums eagerly. But they do not live in them. They learn. They construct. The fact alone that the October Revolution taught the Russian people, the dozens of peoples of Tsarist Russia, to read and write stands immeasurably higher than the whole former hot-house Russian civilisation.

The October Revolution has laid the foundations for a new civilisation which is designed, not for a select few, but for all. This is felt by the masses of the whole world. Hence their sympathy for the Soviet Union which is as passionate as once was their hatred for Tsarist Russia.

Human language is an irreplaceable instrument not only for giving names to events, but also for their valuation. By filtering out that which is accidental, episodic, artificial, it absorbs into itself that which is essential, characteristic, of full weight. Notice with what sensibility the languages of civilised nations have distinguished two epochs in the developments of Russia. The culture of the nobility brought into world currency such barbarisms as Tsar, Cossack, pogrom, *nagaika*. You know these words and what they mean. The October Revolution introduced into the language of the world such words as Bolshevik, Soviet, *kolkhoz*, Gosplan, *piatileka*. Here practical linguistics holds its historical supreme court!

The most profound meaning of the Revolution, but the hardest to submit to immediate measurement, consists in the fact that it forms and tempers the character of the people. The conception of the Russian people as slow, passive, melancholy, mystical, is widely spread and not accidental. It has its roots, in the past. But in Western countries up to the present time those far reaching changes which have been introduced into the character of the people by the revolution, have not been sufficiently considered. Could it be otherwise?

Every man with experience of life can recall the picture of some youth that he has known, receptive, lyrical, all too susceptible, who later becomes suddenly under the influence of a powerful moral impetus, stronger, better balanced and hardly recognisable. In the developments of a whole nation, such moral transformations are wrought by the revolution.

The February insurrection against the autocracy, the struggle against the nobility, against the imperialist war, for peace, for land, for national equality, the October insurrection, the overthrow of the bourgeoisie and of those parties which supported it, or sought agreements with the bourgeoisie, three years of civil war on a front of 5000 miles, the years of blockade, hunger, misery, and epidemics, the years of tense economic reconstruction, of new difficulties and renunciations – these make a hard but good school. A heavy hammer smashes glass, but forges steel. The hammer of the revolution is forging the steel of the people's character.

"Who will believe," wrote a Tsarist general, Zalweski, with indignation shortly after the upheaval, "that a porter or a watchman suddenly becomes a chief justice, a hospital attendant the director of the hospital, a barber an office-holder, a corporal a commander-in-chief, a day-worker a mayor, a locksmith the director of a factory?"

"Who will believe it?" But it had to be believed. They could do nothing else but believe it, when the corporals defeated the generals, when the mayor – the former day-worker – broke the resistance of the old bureaucracy, the wagon greaser put the transportation system into order, the locksmith as director put the industrial equipment into working condition. "Who will believe it?" Let anyone only try not to believe it.

For an explanation of the extraordinary persistence which the masses of the people of the Soviet Union are showing throughout the years of the revolution, many foreign observers rely, in accord with ancient habit, on the "passivity" of the Russian character. Gross anachronism! The revolutionary masses endure privations patiently but not passively. With their own hands they are creating a better future and are determined to create it at any cost. Let the enemy class only attempt to impose his will from outside on these patient masses! No, better, he should not try!

The Revolution and its place in history

Let me now, in closing, attempt to ascertain the place of the October Revolution, not only in the history of Russia but in the history of the world. During the year of 1917, in a period of eight months, two historical curves intersect. The February upheaval – that belated echo of the great struggles which had been carried out in the past centuries on the territories of Holland, England, France, nearly all over Continental Europe – takes its place in the series of bourgeois revolutions. The October Revolution proclaimed and opened the domination of the proletariat. World capitalism suffered its first great defeat on the Russian territory. The chain broke at its weakest link. But it was the chain that broke, and not only the link.

Capitalism has outlived itself as a world system. It has ceased to fulfil its essential function: the raising of the level of human power and human wealth. Humanity cannot remain stagnant at the level which it has reached. Only a powerful increase in productive force and a sound, planned, that is, socialist organisation of production and distribution can assure humanity – all humanity – of a decent standard of life and at the same time give it the precious feeling of freedom with respect to its own economy. Freedom in two senses – first of all man will no longer be compelled to devote the greater part of his life to physical toil. Second, he will no longer be dependent on the laws of the market, that is, on the blind and obscure forces which work behind his back. He will build his economy freely, according to plan, with compass in hand. This time it is a question of subjecting the anatomy of society to the X-ray through and through, of disclosing all its secrets and subjecting all its functions to the reason and the will of collective humanity. In this sense, socialism must become a new step in the historical advance of mankind. Before our ancestor, who first armed himself with a stone axe, the whole of nature represented a conspiracy of secret and hostile forces. Since then, the natural sciences hand in hand with practical technology, have illuminated nature down to its most secret depths. By means of electrical energy, the physicist passes judgement on the nucleus of the atom. The hour is not far when science will easily solve the task of alchemists, and turn manure into gold and gold into manure. Where the demons and furies of nature once raged, now reigns ever more courageously the industrious will of man.

But while he wrestled victoriously with nature, man built up his relations to order men blindly almost like the bee or the ant. Slowly and very haltingly he approached the problems of human society.

The Reformation represented the first victory of bourgeois individualism in a domain which had been ruled by dead tradition. From the church, critical thought went on to the State. Born in the struggle with absolutism and the medieval estates, the doctrine of the sovereignty of the people and of the rights of man and the citizen grew stronger. Thus arose the system of parliamentarianism. Critical thought penetrated into the domain of government administration. The political rationalism of democracy was the highest achievement of the revolutionary bourgeoisie.

But between nature and the state stands economic life. Technical science liberated man from the tyranny of the old elements – earth,

water, fire and air – only to subject him to its own tyranny. Man ceased
to be a slave to nature to become a slave to the machine, and, still
worse, a slave to supply and demand. The present world crisis testifies in
especially tragic fashion how man, who dives to the bottom of the ocean,
who rises up to the stratosphere, who converses on invisible waves from
the Antipodes, how this proud and daring ruler of nature remains a slave
to the blind forces of his own economy. The historical task of our epoch
consists in replacing the uncontrolled play of the market by reasonable
planning, in disciplining the forces of production, compelling them to
work together in harmony and obediently serve the needs of mankind.
Only on this new social basis will man be able to stretch his weary limbs
and – every man and every woman, not only a selected few – become a
citizen with full power in the realm of thought.

The future of man

But this is not yet the end of the road. No, it is only the beginning.
Man calls himself the crown of creation. He has a certain right to that
claim. But who has asserted that present-day man is the last and highest
representative of the species Homo Sapiens? No, physically as well as
spiritually he is very far from perfection, prematurely born biologically,
with feeble thought, and has not produced any new organic equilibrium.

It is true that humanity has more than once brought forth giants of
thought and action, who tower over their contemporaries like summits
in a chain of mountains. The human race has a right to be proud of
its Aristotle, Shakespeare, Darwin, Beethoven, Goethe, Marx, Edison
and Lenin. But why are they so rare? Above all, because almost without
exception they came out of the middle and upper classes. Apart from
rare exceptions, the sparks of genius in the suppressed depths of the
people are choked before they can burst into flame. But also because
the processes of creating, developing and educating a human being
have been and remain essentially a matter of chance, not illuminated by
theory and practice, not subjected to consciousness and will.

Anthropology, biology, physiology and psychology have accumulated
mountains of material to raise up before mankind in their full scope the
tasks of perfecting and developing body and spirit. Psycho-analysis, with
the inspired hand of Sigmund Freud, has lifted the cover of the well
which is poetically called the "soul". And what has been revealed? Our
conscious thought is only a small part of the work of the dark psychic
forces. Learned divers descend to the bottom of the ocean and there

take photographs of mysterious fishes. Human thought, descending to the bottom of its own psychic sources must shed light on the most mysterious driving forces of the soul and subject them to reason and to will.

Once he has done with the anarchic forces of his own society man will set to work on himself, in the pestle and retort of the chemist. For the first time mankind will regard itself as raw material, or at best as a physical and psychic semi-finished product. Socialism will mean a leap from the realm of necessity into the realm of freedom in this sense also, that the man of today, with all his contradictions and lack of harmony, will open the road for a new and happier race.

Footnotes

[1] Social-Democratic International: Historically 'Social Democratic' was the title adopted by many workers' parties. The International collapsed in 1914 when a majority of its parties supported the imperialist war.

[2] Poincaré, Raymond (1860-1934): President of France, 1913-20, Prime Minister 1912, 1922-24, 1926-29.

[3] Kerensky, Alexander (1882-1970): Reformist Prime Minister in Russia in 1917, overthrown by the October Revolution.

[4] Liebknecht, Wilhelm (1826-1900): Alongside Bebel founder of the German Social Democracy.

[5] Liebknecht, Karl (1871-1919): Leader of the left wing of the German Social Democracy, opposed World War One, founded Spartakusbund with Rosa Luxembourg. Murdered by reactionary troops in January 1919.

[6] Clausewitz, Karl von (1780-1831): Prussian army officer, military theoretician.

[7] Duma: Parliament in Russia before 1917. Had a truncated franchise.

[8] Miliukov, Paul (1859-1943): Leader of the capitalist Cadet Party in Russia. Minister of Foreign Affairs until May 1917.

[9] Bonaparte, Napoleon I (1769-1821): Seized power in coup d'état in 1804, proclaiming the French empire and himself emperor.

[10] Mensheviks: Reformist wing of the Russian Social Democratic Workers' Party (RSDLP), until 1912 when it and the Bolsheviks became separate parties. The Mensheviks opposed the October 1917 revolution.

[11] Social-Revolutionaries (SRs): Peasant socialist party. Split in 1917, the Left SRs participated for a period in the Soviet government, the right SRs opposed the revolution.

[12] Jacobins: Popular name for members of the Society of the Friends of the Constitution, who were the radical wing of the French revolution.

Stalinism and Bolshevism

Leon Trotsky

Stalinism and Bolshevism

First published in Socialist Appeal, Vol. 1 No. 7, 25ᵗʰ September 1937 and Socialist Appeal, Vol. 1 No. 8, 2ⁿᵈ October 1937.

Reactionary epochs like ours not only disintegrate and weaken the working class and isolate its vanguard but also lower the general ideological level of the movement and throw political thinking back to stages long since passed through. In these conditions the task of the vanguard is, above all, not to let itself be carried along by the backward flow: it must swim against the current. If an unfavourable relation of forces prevents it from holding political positions it has won, it must at least retain its ideological positions, because in them is expressed the dearly paid experience of the past. Fools will consider this policy "sectarian". Actually it is the only means of preparing for a new tremendous surge forward with the coming historical tide.

The reaction against Marxism and Bolshevism

Great political defeats provoke a reconsideration of values, generally occurring in two directions. On the one hand the true vanguard, enriched by the experience of defeat, defends with tooth and nail the heritage of revolutionary thought and on this basis strives to educate new cadres for the mass struggle to come. On the other hand the routinists, centrists and dilettantes, frightened by defeat, do their best to destroy the authority of the revolutionary tradition and go backwards in their search for a "New World".

One could indicate a great many examples of ideological reaction, most often taking the form of prostration. All the literature if the Second and Third Internationals, as well as of their satellites of the London Bureau, consists essentially of such examples. Not a suggestion of Marxist analysis. Not a single serious attempt to explain the causes of defeat, About the future, not one fresh word. Nothing but clichés, conformity, lies and above all solicitude for their own bureaucratic self-preservation. It is enough to smell 10 words from some Hilferding or Otto Bauer to know this rottenness. The theoreticians of the Comintern are not even worth mentioning. The famous Dimitrov is as ignorant and commonplace as a shopkeeper over a mug of beer. The minds of these people are too lazy to renounce Marxism: they prostitute it. But it is not they that interest us now. Let us turn to the "innovators".

The former Austrian communist, Willi Schlamm, has devoted a small book to the Moscow trials, under the expressive title, *The Dictatorship of the Lie*. Schlamm is a gifted journalist, chiefly interested in current affairs. His criticism of the Moscow frame-up, and his exposure of the psychological mechanism of the "voluntary confessions", are excellent. However, he does not confine himself to this: he wants to create a new theory of socialism that would insure us against defeats and frame-ups in the future. But since Schlamm is by no means a theoretician and is apparently not well acquainted with the history of the development of socialism, he returns entirely to pre-Marxist socialism, and notably to its German, that is to its most backward, sentimental and mawkish variety. Schlamm denounces dialectics and the class struggle, not to mention the dictatorship of the proletariat. The problem of transforming society is reduced for him to the realisation of certain "eternal" moral truths with which he would imbue mankind, even under capitalism. Willi Schlamm's attempts to save socialism by the insertion of the moral gland is greeted with joy and pride in Kerensky's review, Novaya Rossia (an old provincial Russian review now published in Paris); as the editors justifiably conclude, Schlamm has arrived at the principles of true Russian socialism, which a long time ago opposed the holy precepts of faith, hope and charity to the austerity and harshness of the class struggle. The "novel" doctrine of the Russian "Social Revolutionaries" represents, in its "theoretical" premises, only a return to the pre-March (1848!) Germany. However, it would be unfair to demand a more intimate knowledge of the history of ideas from Kerensky than from Schlamm. Far more important is the fact that Kerensky, who is in solidarity with Schlamm, was, while head of the government, the instigator of persecutions against the Bolsheviks as agents of the German general staff: organised, that is, the same frame-ups against which Schlamm now mobilises his moth-eaten metaphysical absolutes.

The psychological mechanism of the ideological reaction of Schlamm and his like, is not at all complicated. For a while these people took part in a political movement that swore by the class struggle and appeared, in word if not in thought, to dialectical materialism. In both Austria and Germany the affair ended in a catastrophe. Schlamm draws the wholesale conclusion: this is the result of dialectics and the class struggle! And since the choice of revelations is limited by historical experience and ... by personal knowledge, our reformer in his search for the word falls on a bundle of old rags which he valiantly opposes not only to Bolshevism but to Marxism as well.

At first glance Schlamm's brand of ideological reaction seems too primitive (from Marx...to Kerensky!) to pause over. But actually it is very instructive: precisely in its primitiveness it represents the common denominator of all other forms of reaction, particularly of those expressed by wholesale denunciation of Bolshevism.

"Back to Marxism"?

Marxism found its highest historical expression in Bolshevism. Under the banner of Bolshevism the first victory of the proletariat was achieved and the first workers' state established. No force can now erase these facts from history. But since the October Revolution has led to the present stage of the triumph of the bureaucracy, with its system of repression, plunder and falsification – the "dictatorship of the lie", to use Schlamm's happy expression – many formalistic and superficial minds jump to a summary conclusion: one cannot struggle against Stalinism without renouncing Bolshevism. Schlamm, as we already know, goes further: Bolshevism, which degenerated into Stalinism, itself grew out of Marxism; consequently one cannot fight Stalinism while remaining on the foundation of Marxism. There are others, less consistent but more numerous, who say on the contrary: "We must return Bolshevism to Marxism." How? To *what* Marxism? Before Marxism became "bankrupt" in the form of Bolshevism it has already broken down in the form of social democracy, Does the slogan "Back to Marxism" then mean a leap over the periods of the Second and Third Internationals... to the First International? But it too broke down in its time. Thus in the last analysis it is a question of returning to the collected works of Marx and Engels. One can accomplish this historic leap without leaving one's study and even without taking off one's slippers. But how are we going to go from our classics (Marx died in 1883, Engels in 1895) to the tasks of a new epoch, omitting several decades of theoretical and political struggles, among them Bolshevism and the October revolution? None of those who propose to renounce Bolshevism as a historically bankrupt tendency has indicated any other course. So the question is reduced to the simple advice to study *Capital*. We can hardly object. But the Bolsheviks, too, studied *Capital* and not badly either. This did not however prevent the degeneration of the Soviet state and the staging of the Moscow trials. So what is to be done?

Is Bolshevism responsible for Stalinism?

Is it true that Stalinism represents the legitimate product of Bolshevism, as all reactionaries maintain, as Stalin himself avows, as the Mensheviks, the anarchists, and certain left doctrinaires considering themselves Marxist believe? "We have always predicted this" they say, "Having started with the prohibition of other socialist parties, the repression of the anarchists, and the setting up of the Bolshevik dictatorship in the Soviets, the October Revolution could only end in the dictatorship of the bureaucracy. Stalin is the continuation and also the bankruptcy of Leninism."

The flaw in this reasoning begins in the tacit identification of Bolshevism, October Revolution and Soviet Union. The historical process of the struggle of hostile forces is replaced by the evolution of Bolshevism in a vacuum. Bolshevism, however, is only a political tendency closely fused with the working class but not identical with it. And aside from the working class there exist in the Soviet Union a hundred million peasants, diverse nationalities, and a heritage of oppression, misery and ignorance. The state built up by the Bolsheviks reflects not only the thought and will of Bolshevism but also the cultural level of the country, the social composition of the population, the pressure of a barbaric past and no less barbaric world imperialism. To represent the process of degeneration of the Soviet state as the evolution of pure Bolshevism is to ignore social reality in the name of only one of its elements, isolated by pure logic. One has only to call this elementary mistake by its true name to do away with every trace of it.

Bolshevism, in any case, never identified itself either with the October Revolution or with the Soviet state that issued from it. Bolshevism considered itself as one of the factors of history, its "Conscious" factor – a very important but not decisive one. We never sinned on historical subjectivism. We saw the decisive factor – on the existing basis of productive forces – in the class struggle, not only on a national scale but on an international scale.

When the Bolsheviks made concessions to the peasant tendency, to private ownership, set up strict rules for membership of the party, purged the party of alien elements, prohibited other parties, introduced the NEP, granted enterprises as concessions, or concluded diplomatic agreements with imperialist governments, they were drawing partial conclusions from the basic fact that had been theoretically clear to them from the beginning; that the conquest of power, however important it may be in itself, by no means transforms the party into a sovereign ruler of the historical process. Having taken over the state, the party is able, certainly, to influence the development of society with a power inaccessible to it before; but in return it submits itself to a 10 times greater influence from all other elements in society. It can, by the direct attack by hostile forces, be thrown out of power. Given a more drawn out tempo of development, it can degenerate internally while holding on to power. It is precisely this dialectic of the historical process that is not understood by those sectarian logicians who try to find in the decay of the Stalinist bureaucracy a crushing argument against Bolshevism.

In essence these gentlemen say: the revolutionary party that contains in itself no guarantee against its own degeneration is bad. By such a criterion Bolshevism is naturally condemned: it has no talisman. But the criterion itself is wrong. Scientific thinking demands a concrete analysis: how and why did the party degenerate? No one but the Bolsheviks themselves have, up to the present time, given such an analysis,. To do this they had no need to break with Bolshevism. On the contrary, they found in its arsenal all they needed for the explanation of its fate. They drew this conclusion: certainly Stalinism "grew out " of Bolshevism, not logically, however, but dialectically; not as a revolutionary affirmation but as a Thermidorian negation. It is by no means the same.

Bolshevism's basic prognosis

The Bolsheviks, however, did not have to wait for the Moscow trials to explain the reasons for the disintegration of the governing party of the USSR. Long ago they foresaw and spoke of the theoretical possibility of this development. Let us remember the prognosis of the Bolsheviks, not only on the eve of the October Revolution but years before. The specific alignment of forces in the national and international field can enable the proletariat to seize power first in a backward country such as Russia. But the same alignment of forces proves beforehand that *without a more or less rapid victory of the proletariat in the advanced countries* the worker's government in Russia will not survive. Left to itself the Soviet regime must either fall or degenerate. More exactly; it will first degenerate and then fall. I myself have written about this more than once, beginning in 1905. In my *History of the Russian Revolution* (*cf. Appendix* to the last volume: *Socialism in One Country*) are collected all the statements on the question made by the Bolshevik leaders from 1917 until 1923. They all amount to the following: without a revolution in the West, Bolshevism will be liquidated either by internal counter-revolution or by external intervention, or by a combination of both. Lenin stressed again and again that the bureaucratisation of the Soviet regime was not a technical question, but the potential beginning of the degeneration of the worker's state.

At the eleventh party congress in March, 1922, Lenin spoke of the support offered to Soviet Russia at the time of the NEP by certain bourgeois politicians, particularly the liberal professor Ustrialov. "I am for the support of the Soviet power in Russia" said Ustrialov, although he was a Cadet, a bourgeois, a supporter of intervention – "because it has taken the road that will lead it back to an ordinary bourgeois state." Lenin prefers the cynical voice of the enemy to "sugary communistic nonsense". Soberly and harshly he warns the party of danger:

"We must say frankly that the things Ustrialov speaks about are possible. History knows all sorts of metamorphoses. Relying on firmness of convictions, loyalty and other splendid moral qualities is anything but a serious attitude in politics. A few people may be endowed with splendid moral qualities, but historical issues are decided by vast masses, which, if the few don't suit them, may at times, treat them none too politely."

In a word, the party is not the only factor of development and on a larger historical scale is not the decisive one.

"One nation conquers another," continued Lenin at the same congress, the last in which he participated..."This is simple and intelligible to all. But what happens to the culture of these nations? Here things are not so simple. If the conquering nation is more cultured than the vanquished nation, the former imposes its culture on the latter, but if the opposite is the case, the vanquished nation imposes its culture on the conqueror. Has not something like this happened in the capital of the RSFSR? Have the 4700 Communists (nearly a whole army division, and all of them the very best) come under the influence of an alien culture?"

This was said in 1922, and not for the first time. History is not made by a few people, even "the best"; and not only that: these "best" can degenerate in the spirit of an alien, that is, a bourgeois culture. Not only can the Soviet state abandon the way of socialism, but the Bolshevik party can, under unfavourable historic conditions, lose its Bolshevism.

From the clear understanding of this danger issued the Left Opposition, definitely formed in 1923. Recording day by day the symptoms of degeneration, it tried to oppose to the growing Thermidor the conscious will of the proletarian vanguard. However, this subjective factor proved to be insufficient. The "gigantic masses" which, according to Lenin, decide the outcome of the struggle, become tired of internal privations and of waiting too long for the world revolution. The mood of the masses declined. The bureaucracy won the upper hand. It cowed the revolutionary vanguard, trampled upon Marxism, prostituted the Bolshevik party. Stalinism conquered. In the form of the Left Opposition, Bolshevism broke with the Soviet bureaucracy and its Comintern. This was the real course of development.

To be sure, in a formal sense Stalinism did issue from Bolshevism. Even today the Moscow bureaucracy continues to call itself the Bolshevik party. It is simply using the old label of Bolshevism the better to fool the masses. So much the more pitiful are those theoreticians who take the shell for the kernel and appearance for reality. In the identification of Bolshevism and Stalinism they render the best possible service to the Thermidorians and precisely thereby play a clearly reactionary role.

In view of the elimination of all other parties from the political field the antagonistic interests and tendencies of the various strata of the population, to a greater of less degree, had to find their expression in the governing party, To the extent that the political centre of gravity has shifted form the proletarian vanguard to the bureaucracy, the party has changed its social structure as well as its ideology. Owing to the tempestuous course of development, it has suffered in the last 15 years a far more radical degeneration than did the social democracy in half a century. The present purge draws between Bolshevism and Stalinism not simply a bloody line but a whole river of blood. The annihilation of all the older generation of Bolsheviks, an important part of the middle generation which participated in the civil war, and that part of the youth that took up most seriously the Bolshevik traditions, shows not only a political but a thoroughly physical incompatibility between Bolshevism and Stalinism. How can this not be seen?

Stalinism and "State Socialism"

The anarchists, for their part, try to see in Stalinism the organic product, not only of Bolshevism and Marxism but of "state socialism" in general. They are willing to replace Bakunin's patriarchal "federation of free communes" by the modern federation of free Soviets. But, as formerly, they are against centralised state power. Indeed, one branch of "state" Marxism, social democracy, after coming to power became an open agent of capitalism. The other gave birth to a new privileged caste. It is obvious that the source of evil lies in the state. From a wide historical viewpoint, there is a grain of truth in this reasoning. The state as an apparatus of coercion is an undoubted source of political and moral infection. This also applies, as experience has shown, to the workers' state. Consequently it can be said that Stalinism is a product of a condition of society in which society was still unable to tear itself out of the strait-jacket of the state. But this position, contributing nothing to the elevation of Bolshevism and Marxism, characterises only the general level of mankind, and above all – the relation of forces between the proletariat and the bourgeoisie. Having agreed with the anarchists that the state, even the workers' state, is the offspring of class barbarism and that real human history will begin with the abolition of the state, we have still before us in full force the question: what ways and methods will lead, *ultimately*, to the abolition of the state? Recent experience bears witness that they are anyway not the methods of anarchism.

The leaders of the Spanish Federation of Labour (CNT), the only important anarchist organisation in the world, became, in the critical hour, bourgeois ministers. They explained their open betrayal of the theory of anarchism by the pressure of "exceptional circumstances". But did not the leaders of German social democracy produce, in their time, the same excuse? Naturally, civil war is not peaceful and ordinary but an "exceptional circumstance". Every serious revolutionary organisation, however, prepares precisely for "exceptional circumstances". The experience of Spain has shown once again that the state can be "denied" in booklets published in "normal circumstances" by permission of the bourgeois state, but the conditions of revolution leave no room for the denial of the state: they demand, on the contrary, the conquest of the state. We have not the slightest intention of blaming the anarchists for not having liquidated the state with the mere stroke of a pen. A revolutionary party , even having seized power (of which the anarchist leaders were incapable in spite of the heroism of the anarchist workers), is still by no means the sovereign ruler of society. But all the more severely do we blame the anarchist theory, which seemed to be wholly suitable for times of peace, but which had to be dropped rapidly as soon as the "exceptional circumstances" of the ... revolution had begun. In the old days there were certain generals – and probably are now – who considered that the most harmful thing for an army was war. Little better are those revolutionaries who complain that revolution destroys their doctrine.

Marxists are wholly in agreement with the anarchists in regard to the final goal: the liquidation of the state. Marxists are "state-ist" only to the extent that one cannot achieve the liquidation of the state simply by ignoring it. The experience of Stalinism does not refute the teaching of Marxism but confirms it by inversion. The revolutionary doctrine which teaches the proletariat to orient itself correctly in situations and to profit actively by them, contains of course no automatic guarantee of victory. But victory is possible only through the application of this doctrine. Moreover, the victory must not be thought of as a single event. It must be considered in the perspective of an historical epoch. The workers' state – on a lower economic basis and surrounded by imperialism – was transformed into the gendarmerie of Stalinism. But genuine Bolshevism launched a life and death struggle against the gendarmerie. To maintain itself Stalinism is now forced to conduct a direct *civil war* against Bolshevism under the name of "Trotskyism", not only in the USSR but also in Spain. The old Bolshevik party is dead but Bolshevism is raising its head everywhere.

To deduce Stalinism form Bolshevism or from Marxism is the same as to deduce, in a larger sense, counter-revolution from revolution. Liberal-conservative and later reformist thinking has always been characterised by this cliche. Due to the class structure of society, revolutions have always produced counter-revolutions. Does not this indicate, asks the logician, that there is some inner flaw in the revolutionary method? However, neither the liberals nor reformists have succeeded, as yet, in inventing a more "economical" method. But if it is not easy to rationalise the living historic process, it is not at all difficult to give a rational interpretation of the alternation of its waves, and thus by pure logic to deduce Stalinism from "state socialism", fascism from Marxism, reaction from revolution, in a word, the antithesis from the thesis. In this domain as in many others anarchist thought is the prisoner of liberal rationalism. Real revolutionary thinking is not possible without dialectics.

The political "sins" of Bolshevism as the source of Stalinism

The arguments of the rationalists assume at times, at least in their outer form, a more concrete character. They do not deduce Stalinism from Bolshevism as a whole but from its political sins. the Bolsheviks – according to Gorter, Pannekoek, certain German "Spartacists" and others – replaced the dictatorship of the proletariat with the dictatorship of the party; Stalin replaced the dictatorship of the party with the dictatorship of the bureaucracy, the Bolsheviks destroyed all parties except their own; Stalin strangled the Bolshevik party in the interests of a Bonapartist clique. The Bolsheviks compromised with the bourgeoisie; Stalin became its ally and support. The Bolsheviks recognised the necessity of participation in the old trade unions and in the bourgeois parliament; Stalin made friends with the trade union bureaucracy and bourgeois democracy. One can make such comparisons at will. For all their apparent effectiveness they are entirely empty.

The proletariat can take power only through its vanguard. In itself the necessity for state power arises from the insufficient cultural level of the masses and their heterogeneity. In the revolutionary vanguard, organised in a party, is crystallised the aspiration of the masses to obtain their freedom. Without the confidence of the class in the vanguard, without support of the vanguard by the class, there can be no talk of the conquest of power. In this sense the proletarian revolution and dictatorship are the work of the whole class, but only under the leadership of the vanguard. The Soviets are the only organised form of the tie between the vanguard and the class. A revolutionary content can be given this form only by the party. This is proved by the positive experience of the October Revolution and by the negative experience of other countries (Germany, Austria, finally, Spain). No one has either shown in practice or tried to explain articulately on paper how the proletariat can seize power without the political leadership of a party that knows what it wants. the fact that this party subordinates the Soviets politically to its leaders has, in itself, abolished the Soviet system no more than the domination of the conservative majority has abolished the British parliamentary system.

As far as the *prohibition* of other Soviet parties is concerned, it did not flow from any "theory" of Bolshevism but was a measure of defence of the dictatorship on a backward and devastated country, surrounded by enemies on all sides. For the Bolsheviks it was clear from the beginning that this measure, later completed by the prohibition of factions inside the governing party itself, signalised a tremendous danger. However, the root of the danger lay not in the doctrine or the tactics but in the material weakness of the dictatorship, in the difficulties of its internal and international situation. If the revolution had triumphed, even if only in Germany, the need of prohibiting the other Soviet parties would have immediately fallen away. It is absolutely indisputable that the domination of a single party served as the juridical point of departure for the Stalinist totalitarian regime. The reason for this development lies neither in Bolshevism nor in the prohibition of other parties as a temporary war measure, but in the number of defeats of the proletariat in Europe and Asia.

The same applies to the struggle with anarchism. In the heroic epoch of the revolution the Bolsheviks went hand in hand with genuinely revolutionary anarchists. Many of them were drawn into the ranks of the party. The author of these lines discussed with Lenin more than once the possibility of allotting the anarchists certain territories where, with the consent of the local population, they would carry out their stateless experiment. But civil war, blockade and hunger left no room for such plans. The Kronstadt insurrection? But the revolutionary government could naturally not "present" to the insurrectionary sailors the fortress which protected the capital only because the reactionary peasant-soldier rebellion was joined by a few doubtful anarchists. The concrete historical analysis of the events leaves not the slightest room for legends, built up on ignorance and sentimentality, concerning Kronstadt, Makhno and other episodes of the revolution.

There remains only the fact that the Bolsheviks from the beginning applied not only conviction but also compulsion, often to a most severe degree. It is also indisputable that later the bureaucracy which grew out of the revolution monopolised the system of compulsions in its own hands. Every stage of development, even such catastrophic stages as revolution and counter-revolution, flows from the preceding stage, is rooted in it and carries over some of its features. Liberals, including the Webbs, have always maintained that the Bolshevik dictatorship represented only a new edition of Tsarism. They close their eyes to such "details" as the abolition of the monarchy and the nobility, the handing over of the land to the peasants, the expropriation of capital, the introduction of the planned economy, atheist education, and so on. In exactly the same way liberal- anarchist thought closes its eyes to the fact that the Bolshevik revolution, with all its repressions, meant an upheaval of social relations in the interests of the masses, whereas Stalin's Thermidorian upheaval accompanies the reconstruction of Soviet society in the interest of a privileged minority. It is clear that in the identification of Stalinism with Bolshevism there is not a trace of socialist criteria.

Questions of theory

One of the most outstanding features of Bolshevism has been its severe, exacting, even quarrelsome attitude towards the question of doctrine. The 26 volumes of Lenin's works will remain forever a model of the highest theoretical conscientiousness. Without this fundamental quality Bolshevism would never have fulfilled its historic role. In this regard Stalinism, coarse, ignorant and thoroughly empirical, is its complete opposite.

The Opposition declared more than 10 years ago in its programme:

"Since Lenin's death a whole set of new theories has been created, whose only purpose is to justify the Stalin group's sliding off the path of the international proletarian revolution."

Only a few days ago an American writer, Liston M. Oak, who has participated in the Spanish revolution, wrote:

"The Stalinists are in fact today the foremost revisionists of Marx and Lenin – Bernstein did not dare go half as far as Stalin in revising Marx."

This is absolutely true. One must add only that Bernstein actually felt certain theoretical needs: he tried conscientiously to establish a correspondence between the reformist practices of social democracy and its programme. The Stalinist bureaucracy, however, not only had nothing in common with Marxism but is in general foreign to any doctrine or system whatsoever. Its "ideology" is thoroughly permeated with police subjectivism, its practice is the empiricism of crude violence. In keeping with its essential interests the caste of usurpers is hostile to any theory: it can give an account of its social role neither to itself nor to anyone else. Stalin revises Marx and Lenin not with the theoretician's pen but with the heel of the GPU.

Questions of morals

Complaints of the "immorality" of Bolshevism come particularly from those boastful nonentities whose cheap masks were torn away by Bolshevism. In petit-bourgeois, intellectual, democratic, "socialist", literary, parliamentary and other circles, conventional values prevail, or a conventional language to cover their lack of values. This large and motley society for mutual protection – "live and let live" – cannot bear the touch of the Marxist lancet on its sensitive skin. The theoreticians, writers and moralists, hesitating between different camps, thought and continue to think that the Bolsheviks maliciously exaggerate differences, are incapable of "loyal" collaboration and by their "intrigues" disrupt the unity of the workers' movement. Moreover, the sensitive and touchy centrist has always thought that the Bolsheviks were "calumniating" him – simply because they carried through to the end for him his half-developed thoughts: he himself was never able to. But the fact remains that only that precious quality, an uncompromising attitude towards all quibbling and evasion, can educate a revolutionary party which will not be taken unawares by "exceptional circumstances".

The moral qualities of every party flow, in the last analysis, from the historical interests that it represents. The moral qualities of Bolshevism, self-renunciation, disinterestedness, audacity and contempt for every kind of tinsel and falsehood – the highest qualities of human nature! – flow from revolutionary intransigence in the service of the oppressed. The Stalinist bureaucracy imitates also in this domain the words and gestures of Bolshevism. But when "intransigence" and "flexibility" are applied by a police apparatus in the service of a privileged minority they become a force of demoralisation and gangsterism. One can feel only contempt for these gentlemen who identify the revolutionary heroism of the Bolsheviks with the bureaucratic cynicism of the Thermidorians.

Even now, in spite of the dramatic events in the recent period, the average philistine prefers to believe that the struggle between Bolshevism ("Trotskyism") and Stalinism concerns a clash of personal ambitions, or, at best, a conflict between two "shades" of Bolshevism. The crudest expression of this opinion is given by Norman Thomas, leader of the American Socialist Party: "There is little reason to believe," he writes (*Socialist Review*, September 1937, p. 6), "that if Trotsky had won (!) instead of Stalin, there would be an end of intrigue, plots, and a reign of fear in Russia." And this man considers himself ... a Marxist. One would have the same right to say: "There is little reason to believe that if instead of Pius XI, the Holy See were occupied by Norman I, the Catholic Church would have been transformed into a bulwark of socialism". Thomas fails to understand that it is not a question of antagonism between Stalin and Trotsky, but of an antagonism between the bureaucracy and the proletariat. To be sure, the governing stratum of the USSR is forced even now to adapt itself to the still not wholly liquidated heritage of revolution, while preparing at the same time through direct civil war (bloody "purge" – mass annihilation of the discontented) a change of the social regime. But in Spain the Stalinist clique is already acting openly as a bulwark of the bourgeois order against socialism. The struggle against the Bonapartist bureaucracy is turning before our eyes into class struggle: two worlds, two programmes, two moralities. If Thomas thinks that the victory of the socialist proletariat over the infamous caste of oppressors would not politically and morally regenerate the Soviet regime, he proves only that for all his reservations, shufflings and pious sighs he is far nearer to the Stalinist bureaucracy than to the workers. Like other exposers of Bolshevik "immorality", Thomas has simply not grown to the level of revolutionary morality.

The traditions of Bolshevism and the Fourth International

The "lefts" who tried to skip Bolshevism in their return to Marxism generally confined themselves to isolated panaceas: boycott of parliament, creation of "genuine" Soviets. All this could still seem extremely profound in the heat of the first days after the war. But now, in the light of most recent experience, such "infantile diseases" have no longer even the interest of a curiosity. The Dutchmen Gorter and Pannekoek, the German "Spartakists", the Italian Bordigists, showed their independence from Bolshevism only by artificially inflating one of its features and opposing it to the rest. But nothing has remained either in practice or in theory of these "left" tendencies: an indirect but important proof that Bolshevism is the *only* possible form of Marxism for this epoch.

The Bolshevik party has shown in action a combination of the highest revolutionary audacity and political realism. It established for the first time the correspondence between the vanguard and the class which alone is capable of securing victory. It has p roved by experience that the alliance between the proletariat and the oppressed masses of the rural and urban petit bourgeoisie is possible only through the political overthrow of the traditional petit-bourgeois parties. The Bolshevik party has shown the entire world how to carry out armed insurrection and the seizure of power. Those who propose the abstraction of the Soviets from the party dictatorship should understand that only thanks to the party dictatorship were the Soviets able to lift themselves out of the mud of reformism and attain the state form of the proletariat. The Bolshevik party achieved in the civil war the correct combination of military art and Marxist politics. Even if the Stalinist bureaucracy should succeed in destroying the economic foundations of the new society, the experience of planned economy under the leadership of the Bolshevik party will have entered history for all time as one of the greatest teachings of mankind. This can be ignored only by sectarians who, offended by the bruises they have received, turn their backs on the process of history.

But this is not all. The Bolshevik party was able to carry on its magnificent "practical" work only because it illuminated all its steps with theory. Bolshevism did not create this theory: it was furnished by Marxism. But Marxism is a theory of movement, not of stagnation. Only events on such a tremendous historical scale could enrich the theory itself. Bolshevism brought an invaluable contribution to Marxism in its analysis of the imperialist epoch as an epoch of wars and revolutions; of bourgeois democracy in the era of decaying capitalism; of the correlation between the general strike and the insurrection; of the role of the party, Soviets and trade unions in the period of proletarian revolution; in its theory of the Soviet state, of the economy of transition, of fascism and Bonapartism in the epoch of capitalist decline; finally in its analysis of the degeneration of the Bolshevik party itself and of the Soviet state. Let any other tendency be named that has added anything essential to the conclusions and generalisations of Bolshevism. Theoretically and politically Vandervilde, De Brouckere, Hilferding, Otto Bauer, Leon Blum, Zyromski, not to mention Major Attlee and Norman Thomas, live on the tattered leftovers of the past. The degeneration of the Comintern is most crudely expressed by the fact that it has dropped to the theoretical level of the Second International. All the varieties of intermediary groups (Independent Labour Party of Great Britain, POUM and their like) adapt every week new haphazard fragments of Marx and Lenin to their current needs. Workers can learn nothing from these people.

Only the founders of the Fourth International, who have made their own the whole tradition of Marx and Lenin, take a serious attitude towards theory. Philistines may jeer that 20 years after the October victory the revolutionaries are again thrown back to modest propagandist preparation. The big capitalists are, in this question as in many others, far more penetrating than the petit bourgeois who imagine themselves "socialists" or "communists". It is no accident that the subject of the Fourth International does not leave the columns of the world press. The burning historical need for revolutionary leadership promises to the Fourth International an exceptionally rapid tempo of growth. The greatest guarantee of its further success lies in the fact that it has not arisen away from the great historical road, but has organically grown out of Bolshevism.

28th August 1937

Introductary Titles from Wellred Books

THE CLASSICS OF MARXISM
VOLUME ONE
Marx, Engels, Lenin and Trotsky

Published 2013
Paperback
225 Pages
ISBN: 978 1 900 007 49 8

Now for the first time, *The Communist Manifesto*, *Socialism: Utopian and Scientific*, *The State and Revolution*, and *The Transitional Programare* available in a single, compact volume.

WHAT IS MARXISM?
Rob Sewell and Alan Woods

Publication Date: 2015 Paperback
238 Pages
ISBN: 978 1 900 007 57 3

This book is aimed specifically at newcomers to Marxism. A bestseller in its second edition, it comprises introductory pieces on the three component parts of Marxist theory: dialectical materialism, historical materialism and Marxist economics.

LENIN AND TROTSKY: WHAT THEY REALLY STOOD FOR
Alan Woods and Ted Grant

Published 2000
Paperback
224 Pages
ISBN: 978 8 492 183 26 5

The ideas of Lenin and Trotsky are among the most slandered and distorted in history. Originally written as a reply to Monty Johnstone, a leading theoretician of the British Communist Party, this book uncovers their real legacy.

Order online at www.wellredbooks.net
or send orders to PO Box 50525, London E14 6WG,
United Kingdom.

Latest Titles from Wellred Books

THE REVOLUTION BETRAYED
Leon Trotsky

Publication Date: 2015
Paperback
252 Pages
ISBN: 978 1 900 007 54 2

The Revolution Betrayed is one of the most important Marxist texts of all time. It is the only serious Marxist analysis of what happened to the Russian Revolution after the death of Lenin. In this book, Trotsky provided a brilliant and profound analysis of Stalinism, which has never been improved upon, let alone superseded. With a delay of 60 years, it was completely vindicated by history.

MARXISM AND ANARCHISM
Engels, Lenin, Plekhanov and others

Publication Date: 2015
Paperback
372 Pages
ISBN: 978 1 900 007 53 5

This collection of classic and contemporary writings helps to clarify the Marxist perspective on Anarchist theory and practice, and the need for a revolutionary party.

GERMANY: FROM REVOLUTION TO COUNTER-REVOLUTION
Rob Sewell

Published 2014
Paperback
142 Pages
ISBN: 978 1 900 007 51 1

From 1918 to 1933 revolution and counter-revolution followed hot on each others' heels. The barbarity of the Nazis is well-documented. Rob Sewell gives a picture of the less well-known, tumultuous events that preceded Hitler's rise to power.

More Titles

Bolshevism: The Road to Revolution

by Alan Woods

Ted Grant Writings: Volumes 1-2

by Ted Grant

Reason in Revolt

by Alan Woods and Ted Grant

Reformism and Revolution

by Alan Woods

Kashmir's Ordeal

by Lal Khan

Dialectics of Nature

by Frederick Engels

Coming Soon

China: From Permanent Revolution to Counter-Revolution

by John Peter Roberts

Ireland: Republicanism and Revolution

by Alan Woods

The Selected Works of James Connolly

by James Connolly

Stalin: An Appraisal of the Man and His Influence

by Leon Trotsky

Ted Grant Writings: Volume Three

by Ted Grant

Lightning Source UK Ltd.
Milton Keynes UK
UKHW022017040121
376415UK00007B/1207